Mark Crispin Miller is a Professor of Media Ecology at New York University, where he also directs the Project on Media Ownership (PROMO). His writings on various aspects of the media – propaganda, advertising, television, cinema, rock music and the news – are well known in the United States. He is also an influential activist and speaker on the need for a more diverse and democratic media system in the US and other nations. His books include *Boxed In: The Culture of TV*, *Seeing Through Movies* and *Mad Scientists*, a forthcoming study of war propaganda. Miller lives in New York City with his wife, Amy Smiley, their two sons and special cat.

Also by Mark Crispin Miller

Boxed In: The Culture of TV
Seeing Through Movies

THE BUSH DYSLEXICON

THE SAYINGS OF PRESIDENT DUBYA

MARK CRISPIN MILLER

BANTAM BOOKS

LONDON · NEW YORK · TORONTO · SYDNEY · AUCKLAND

THE BUSH DYSLEXICON
A BANTAM BOOK: 0 553 81422 2

First publication in Great Britain
Also published in the United States of America by W. W. Norton

PRINTING HISTORY
Bantam Books edition published 2001

3 5 7 9 10 8 6 4 2

Set in Sabon and Optima by
Phoenix Typesetting, Ilkley, West Yorkshire.

Bantam Books are published by Transworld Publishers,
61–63 Uxbridge Road, London W5 5SA,
a division of The Random House Group Ltd,
in Australia by Random House Australia (Pty) Ltd,
20 Alfred Steet, Milsons Point, Sydney, NSW 2061, Australia,
in New Zealand by Random House New Zealand Ltd,
18 Poland Road, Glenfield, Auckland 10, New Zealand
and in South Africa by Random House (Pty) Ltd,
Endulini, 5a Jubilee Road, Parktown 2193, South Africa.

Printed and bound in Great Britain by
Clays Ltd, St Ives plc.

For my parents

ACKNOWLEDGEMENTS

This book was written quickly. It would have been impossible without considerable help.

I would like first of all to thank the people at Transworld: Larry Finlay, for agreeing to this project; the able and intrepid Sadie Mayne; and Fiona Nelson, without whose work you might not know this book exists. I am very grateful to my US editor, Star Lawrence, and Drake Bennett, his assistant, both at W. W. Norton. I also thank my agent, Emma Parry, for getting everything in order quickly and efficiently, and always with good cheer. I was also very fortunate to be assisted by Carrie McLaren, who took time out from editing her excellent magazine, *Stayfree!*, to help me put this book together. Aside from managing a colossal research task, Carrie was an indispensable collaborator, offering many trenchant insights and editorial suggestions. Her own assistant, Ryan Creed, was kind enough to pitch in, too.

Several people read the manuscript with care, and gave me counsel: Ross Posnock and Marilyn Young, close friends and colleagues here at New York University; my buddy Robert W. McChesney, who has taught me more than I can say, and who greatly added to this book; my dear old friend, Linda DeLibero;

the wise and clever Inger Forland; independent scholar Rochelle Gurstein, a kindred spirit; and the generous Josh Ozersky. I would like especially to thank Ronald Walters of the History Department at Johns Hopkins University. Ron responded graciously, and brilliantly, to an abrupt request for guidance in the middle of what was for him a very busy time.

Many other people came through with answers to specific questions and requests: Bruce J. Miller, J. H. Hatfield, Bill Minutaglio, Garry Mauro, Sander Hicks, Katrina van den Heuvel, Richard Lingeman, Hersch Fischler, Petra Lent McCarron, Angie Nosari, John Nichols, Todd Gitlin, Susan Greene, Jeff Cohen, Arvind Rajagopal, Tracy Chin, Vivek Chibber, Ted Magder, Peter Beinart, Eli Kintisch, Frank Bruni, Jerry Politex of Bushwatch, Jim Naureckas of Fairness and Accuracy in Reporting (FAIR), Billy Beaune and Fritz von Spüchen. I was given more extensive help by Karla Hale and Andrew Elmore.

Close to home, I was extraordinarily blessed. My parents, Jordan and Anita Miller, gave me the benefit not only of their opposition research (both are hardened Democrats), but of their long experience as publishers. As Dan Quayle might say, I wouldn't be here if it weren't for them, and so I thank them from the bottom of my heart. My son, Louie Miller, was in part the inspiration for the writing of this book, which I hope heartens him, and others of his generation, to do the right thing for democracy. Louie's decency and sense of humor are a great encouragement to me in these dark times, and I would be delighted to return the favor.

Finally, I must try to find the words to thank my wife, Amy Smiley, whose rare warmth, keen intelligence and common sense have been an inspiration to me from the day we met. She is the love of my life, and my dearest friend. I hope that her sweet influence shines through in everything I do, including even this.

CONTENTS

The firmness with which the people have withstood the late abuses of the press, the discernment they have manifested between truth and falsehood, show that they may safely be trusted to hear everything true and false, and to form a correct judgment between them. As little is it necessary to impose on their senses, or dazzle their minds by pomp, splendor, or forms. Instead of this artificial, how much surer is that real respect, which results from the use of their reason, and the habit of bringing everything to the test of common sense.

Thomas Jefferson to Judge James Tyler, 28 June 1804

See, I believe in the power of the people. I truly do. I do.

George W. Bush, 6 March 2001

LOOK WHO'S TALKING

On picking up *The Bush Dyslexicon*, you may think you've seen this sort of thing a hundred times before; and not only in bookstores, but on TV. This book, you figure, must be just another snickering *ad hominem* attack on yet another US president – a blast of easy satire, meanly motivated. On the one hand, it might be a piece of laughing propaganda by, or for, the party out of power, the Democrats in this case now doing to George W. Bush what, say, the Republicans, and/or the Christian Coalition did to Bill Clinton, or what the Democrats had done to Richard Nixon, or what the right had done to FDR: putting out a mocking version of 'the record', full of campaign lies and comic gaffes and damning statements taken out of context. Or this book might be a mere commercial venture, with no partisan affiliation – a light anthology of famous bloopers, offering a bound equivalent of an evening's worth of campaign-season stand-up, TV's sharpest wiseguys taking on the latest round of flubs and pratfalls. Thus this *Dyslexicon* would fall into the rich and often lucrative tradition of David Frye (doing Nixon), Chevy Chase (doing Gerald Ford), countless mimics doing Jimmy Carter, and so on, right up through the last campaign, when everyone was doing the 'robotic' Gore and Bush the Bumbler. And so – whether you regard it as a partisan assault or an attempt at cashing in – this book may strike you either as a cheap shot or a guilty pleasure, depending on which man you voted for, assuming you could vote, or even wanted to.

First impressions often tell the truth (as I will argue here). Your first impression of this book may be off the mark, however. For one thing, the *Dyslexicon* is not a piece of party propaganda. Its aim is not to work the masses up to take some simple action, nor is it part of any broader effort by the Democrats. (As a New Yorker, I voted for Ralph Nader, the Green Party's presidential candidate, and I did so with a certain wary pride.) Nor does this book play any propaganda tricks. It includes no items altered or abbreviated, nor is it cunningly selective, but reprints passages at length, and places entries in their proper context – at times even debunking certain unfair raps against this Bush or his father. Most important, this book does not promote the dangerous simplicity that marks *all* propaganda, good or bad, backward or enlightened. ('All propaganda is a lie, even when it is telling the truth,' as George Orwell put it.) While it is clearly 'anti-Bush', it is not a tacit advertisement for some simple Other Way. Indeed, its tacit purpose is to warn *against* the sort of war-like either/or that is destroying our democracy, through both the Grand Old Party (or GOP, as the Republicans are often known) and the major media. On the contrary, this book admits complexity, honoring paradox and ambiguity – a flexible approach that doesn't make for propaganda, which tightly answers every question, so as to leave you grinning in assent.

While it promotes no party line, moreover, neither is this book a mere pastiche of funny bits. Amusing as it often is, *The Bush Dyslexicon* has not been crafted just for laughs, although

that would have been an easy job. For one thing, such manipulation would have been dishonest – and irrelevant, because the
situation that we're in today is really not so funny. Even if our
President were the cheery cretin that such satire makes him out
to be, it wouldn't make our plight a comic one; for he has a
highly seasoned, wholly ruthless and, for that matter, deeply
humorless cabal of rightist operatives around him – and that's
no joke. In any case, our President is not an imbecile, but an
operator just as canny as he is hard-hearted, which is to say that
he's extraordinarily shrewd. To smirk at his alleged stupidity is,
therefore, not just to miss the point, but to do this unelected
President a giant favor, since, as Shakespeare's Prince Hal
reminds us – and as Bush himself has often said – it suits a politician to have everybody underestimate him, especially if he
wants to do things his way. The satire that sells him short, therefore, can only work to his advantage, by blinding us to his
team's big-time plans, and causing us to overlook his own
prodigious skill at propaganda.

Far from merely goofing on this President, then, this book is
meant to shed some light on propaganda in our time. The
Dyslexicon attempts to give the lie to that enormous wave of
propaganda – a joint production of the GOP and major media
– whereby George W. Bush was forced on us as President,
then, after his inauguration, hailed near-universally for his
amazing charm, his democratic ease, his rare ability to be all
things to all Americans, and so on. Our experience of this
transparent coup has been disorienting from the start. On the
one hand, TV has clearly shown the truth about him – with his
own inadvertent help, since Bush is strangely frank about
himself. His body language bellows his uninterest, his distraction, his uneasiness, his callousness; and he tends to blurt out
all or part of what he's really thinking, even as he's trying to

lie about it – a linguistic struggle that intensifies his incoherence. Meanwhile, his handlers and the mainstream media all keep trying to play down such revelations, forever countering the obvious with lots of upbeat spin and tactful silence. Thus TV keeps sending us an eerie double message, by showing us one thing and telling us another. Those who want to buy the pitch prefer the latter, naturally, while those who just can't buy it feel as if they must be going crazy, what with all those smooth authoritative voices claiming that this man *should* be our President – when we can see, and have seen all along, that that is simply not the case.

Thus we are the victims of a strange new national disorder. It is as if the US body politic were itself afflicted with a corporate version of dyslexia. The individual dyslexic cannot learn to read because he is unable, for whatever reasons, to translate letters into sounds. Because he can't decode those printed symbols for their phonic content, the writing on the page can make no sense to him. Today our body politic is comparably disabled, although it isn't written language that's the problem. The head that drives that body forward is, of course, the media machine – the busy neural network of producers, editors, reporters, anchors, pundits (all subtly guided by the propagandists of the right). While it has no trouble scanning press releases, or providing copy for the cameras, that swift collective mind is fatally dyslexic when it comes to reading the very spectacle it presents to us. Unable to perceive the glaring daily evidence of absolute hypocrisy and cynical manipulation, it cannot read the writing on the wall – which, meanwhile, is crystal-clear to many of the rest of us. The dyslexics at the top may be extremely savvy, yet they lack (to quote Orwell again) that all-important knowledge 'in the bones' whereby we try, down here, to make our way. Seeing that it's all gone wrong, yet always hearing, from on high, that everything is perfectly all right, we each feel – whether we can read or not – as helpless and perplexed as any undiagnosed dyslexic faced with street signs, menus, newspapers and exams.

Against all that, *The Bush Dyslexicon* is meant to set the record straight: to remind us of the truth that TV shows us, even as it keeps on lying about it – much like the President, who, unless he knows his script by heart, often tells the truth despite himself, and does it most transparently when he is lying. (In this he is much like his dad, as we shall see.) By thus corroborating what TV so viscerally conveys, the book may also help dispel the great myth of 'the liberal media' – a preposterous notion, or Big Lie, that Rush Limbaugh and his screaming brethren have long since sold to millions of Americans. And, more subtly, by pointing out the truths that television has revealed to us, this book may also shed some light on the bizarre postmodern form that propaganda often takes today, here in the culture of TV, wherein the falseness of the spectacle before us is a sort of open secret, obvious to any viewer who wants to see it, and, strangely, all the more deceptive for that fact.

FIRST IN HIS CLASS

Of all his flaws, the President's illiteracy is – or was – the one most noted by the media. Governor Bush's way with words (and logic, and books) was prominently covered in the months before Election Day (although the journalists eased off as time went on). His bite-sized gaffes were perfect for TV, which duly replayed some of them, while Frank Bruni of the *New York Times* tracked the candidate's most ludicrous misstatements. (Meanwhile, long lists of Bushisms – carefully compiled for

Slate by Jacob Weisberg – criss-crossed the country via e-mail, so that the Democratic precincts of all cyber-space were finally saturated by 7 November.) More influentially, the televisual concentration on Son of Bushspeak, George H. W. Bush having had a similar problem, extended quickly to the realm of late-night comedy, which is the surest way to the nation's consciousness. (Of course, the schtick on Bush was more glee-ful, and far more insulting, than the tittering journalistic bits.) Such reportage-cum-stand-up did the trick, to some extent. Soon everybody knew that Bush could not pronounce 'sublim-inal' (while few had heard – or ever would – of his neglected military service, his many shady business dealings, or his close ties to the likes of Representative Tom DeLay, to name a few of his more substantive and complicated failings).

The Governor was not the first American presidential candi-date to stand accused of gross illiteracy. In the fierce campaign of 1828, the genteel supporters of incumbent John Quincy Adams – that dour, stand-offish veteran of the Harvard faculty – tried to beat back the advance of Andrew Jackson, much-loved hero of the war of 1812, by casting him as far too rough-edged and unthinking to 'discharge the complicated and arduous duties of President', as one Whig politician put it. To make their case that Jackson was a man 'who cannot spell *more than about one word in four*' (to quote one piece of Adams propaganda), the Whigs circulated letters that included stark examples of Old Hickory's faulty English, proof that he was too coarse, too 'savage', to be entrusted with the nation's leader-ship. The general was 'a barbarian who could not write a sentence of grammar', Adams later hotly reminisced, 'and hardly could spell his own name'.[1]

There are, however, some big differences between the anti-Jackson campaign and the recent coverage of the Governor's defective English. First of all, the Whigs themselves invented those 'examples' of the general's illiteracy – as they were forced to do, since Jackson was in fact an eloquent haranguer, whether at the podium or at his desk, even if his syntax wasn't always perfect. The Governor's linguistic record, on the other hand, is all preserved on video and/or audio. It is therefore as authentic as the secret tapes of Richard Nixon, or as any flub or pratfall broadcast on *America's Funniest Home Videos*.

As the *Dyslexicon* makes clear, this President would seem to be the most illiterate in US history. His is not the merely technical illiteracy of most Americans who, irrespective of their class or education, routinely make grammatical mistakes so slight that only pedants mind them: George W. Bush is so illiterate as to turn completely incoherent when he speaks without a script, or unless he thinks his every statement through so carefully beforehand that the effort empties out his face. His eyes go blank, as he consults the TelePrompTer in his head, and he chews uneasily at the corner of his mouth, as if to keep his lips in motion for the coming job, much as a batter swings before the pitch. Thus prepared, he then meticulously sounds out *every . . . single . . . word*, as if asking for assistance in a foreign language. Without such hasty mental planning, Bush is liable to make statements that either don't mean anything ('I will have a foreign-handed foreign policy'), or that require unscrambling ('Families is where our nation finds hope, where wings take dream'), or that say the opposite of what he means ('Well, I think if you say you're going to do something and don't do it, that's trustworthiness'), or that are just dead wrong ('The legislature's job is to write law. It's the executive branch's job to interpret law'), and so on.

Indeed, our President's illiteracy is something of a miracle – as rich in its own way as the expository genius of the Founding

Fathers. His incapacity does not reflect one problem in particular, but several kinds of verbal defect. As Gail Sheehy has argued, the President may actually suffer from dyslexia. Surely that condition may explain his tendency to transpose words and to blurt out the opposite of what he means. It may also explain his frequent malapropisms ('hostile' for 'hostage,' 'arbitrary' for 'arbitration,' 'preserve' for 'persevere,' 'cufflink' for 'handcuff,' etc.). However, dyslexia would not account for his incessant violation of the fundamental rules of grammar ('The question is, how many hands have I shaked?'), his syntactic accidents ('It's not the way America is all about'), or his utter prepositional confusion. Nor – far more important – would dyslexia explain the President's thorough unacquaintance with the system that he now purports to lead, or his unawareness of the world beyond our borders (except for northern Mexico). To believe that Social Security is somehow not a federal program, and that the word 'insurance' is mere Washington bureaucratese, and to think that Kosovars are 'Kosovarians' (and the Greeks 'Grecians', and the East Timorese 'East Timorians'), and to confuse Slovenia with Slovakia, and the judicial branch of our own government with the executive, is to suffer from no disability but ignorance.*

Clearly, we have come a long way from the discursive model of the Founders, those broadly educated and 'profoundly reasonable people' whose language was exemplary for its 'everyday businesslike sanity', as Bernard Bailyn has observed. Of course it is unfair to measure Bush against the likes of

---

* Here it should be noted that dyslexia bears no relation to acuteness, eloquence, or the capacity for knowledge. The dyslexic population has included brilliant figures boasting high intelligence of every kind – Albert Einstein, George S. Patton, Winston Churchill, and Thomas Edison among them.

Madison, Monroe and Jefferson, since, as expositors, they surely have *no* peer among the modern tenants of the White House. Perhaps, then, we should compare Bush not with the very greatest of his literate predecessors, but with those who tend to be placed *last* in historians' rankings of American presidents. Yet even in comparison with most of them as users of the language, this Bush does not compete. The one likely peer who comes to mind is Zachary Taylor, an arrogant patrician dunce renowned for his contempt of learning. Otherwise, the least of our pre-modern presidents are daunting in their eloquence and erudition, since all of them were well instructed in the art of rhetoric (which, back then, meant far more than 'baloney', which is all that word means in the street today). The well-read James Buchanan could make thorny legalisms understandable to common folk; Franklin Pierce – a distant forebear of our President on Mother's side – was fluent in Greek and Latin, like so many of his peers, and an adept of Locke's philosophy; John Tyler also was a cultivated lawyer; and the autodidact Millard Fillmore was assiduous in compensating for the rudimentary education of his early years. (Throughout his unimpressive stint as President, Fillmore was never 'heard [to] utter a foolish or unmeaning word', claimed his Attorney General.) The disastrous Andrew Johnson was a first-rate speaker, while his bibulous successor, Ulysses Grant, could boast some literary genius, as readers of his *Memoirs* know. In the last century, the dim and genial Warren Harding – although a stunning windbag – at least had what it took to edit several newspapers, and the hapless Herbert Hoover was a copious and able author.[2]

For all their faults as chief executives, none of those men could ever have said anything like, 'A leadership is someone who brings people together,' or the celebrated 'Is our children learning?' Yet here again, it may be unreasonable to hold Bush

– a child of television, and a product of modern education – to the vanished standards of nineteenth-century schooling. Against them, such precise and ready talkers as Bill Clinton also fail, and so do nearly all the rest of us. ('If we wish to become great and useful in the world, we must improve our time in school,' wrote Grover Cleveland, aged nine, in 1846.) Perhaps, then, we should measure Bush against those post-war presidents who also took flak, in their time, for verbal failure. Eisenhower was often ridiculed for the syntactic murk of his ad-libbed remarks – but such obfuscatory rambling was deliberate, a canny way to dodge the question without seeming to. Despite his folksy aspect, Eisenhower was a subtle and exacting rhetorician (as John Emmett Hughes, his top political adviser, points out in *The Ordeal of Power*), and at his best a vivid writer, as *Crusade in Europe* demonstrates. Obsessively prolific, the mad Nixon was, throughout his public life, often faulted – rightly – for the deep dishonesty and egocentric bias of his output, both written and spoken; yet even his most violent memos were drafted in sound English, and, in his lucid intervals, he could indeed be 'perfectly clear', as we can see from his debates with Kennedy. And even Ronald Reagan, although much-mocked for his simplicity, was in fact an avid reader (albeit one with a hearty appetite for anti-Soviet propaganda), and, when he knew his lines, an excellent speaker, a talent that depended on the vast archive of quips and anecdotes stored in his head. 'His mental cassettes,' Lou Cannon writes, 'were crammed with odd scraps of information and obscure insights that he had acquired from his reading [and, of course, his viewing] and committed to memory.' Thus Reagan did have an absorptive and inquiring mind of sorts (even if he did think that the singular of 'indices' was 'indice').[3]

And yet without a script, of course, the Great Communicator

tended either to fall mute or to make no sense at all; nor was he capable of writing books or full-length speeches by himself. However, Ronald Reagan was another Winston Churchill by comparison with George W. Bush – whose only competition for the anti-crown of presidential barbarism would appear to be the gentleman who sired him. In his day, the frenetic and uneasy George I was just as tongue-tied as the laid-back W. Throughout the 1988 campaign, in fact, his penchant for 'Bushspeak' was a subject of much tittering coverage, which pushed the contrast between his awkwardness and Reagan's way with (scripted) words. Just like his son, that Bush was ridiculed for meaningless assertions worthy of Sam Goldwyn ('It's no exaggeration to say the undecideds could go one way or another'), for mangled syntax (he claimed to oversee the writing of his speeches, 'inarticulate as though I may be'), for using the wrong word (the Democrats had 'cramped down on any discussion of individual initiatives'), and for non sequiturs, mixed metaphors, and wild allusions ('You cannot be President of the United States if you don't have faith. Remember Lincoln, going to his knees in times of trial and the Civil War and all that stuff. You can't be. And we are blessed. So don't feel sorry for – don't cry for me, Argentina'). The elder Bush was also given to bizarre remarks whose psychic roots are best left unexplored: 'We have made mistakes, we have had sex,' he once claimed in a public testimonial to Ronald Reagan. (For his part, the son once told a crowd of Iowans, 'The most important job is not to be governor, or first lady in my case.')[4]

Despite their similarity, however, Bush *père et fils* are not coequals at the mangling of the mother tongue. If Bush the Elder spoke 'like a 16-year-old from Andover,' as one political consultant sneered in 1988, the son sounds often like an even younger child, and one who hasn't been to any school at all, so much more basic are his errors. ('Will the highways on the Internet become more few?') In the annals of executive un-learnedness, in fact, the only figure near-identical to Bush the Younger is, of course, his dad's unfortunate Vice-President (whose choicest flubs are frequently confused with W's). Like past blatherers beyond number – his running-mate included – Quayle excelled at grave assertions of the wholly obvious. 'This election is about who's going to be the next President of the United States!' he once exulted on the stump. ('More and more of our imports come from overseas,' the Governor of Texas once observed.) Quayle was also an impressive malapropist, remarking, for example, that 'We [Republicans] understand the importance of having the bondage between the parent and the child.' ('We cannot let terrorists or rogue nations hold this nation hostile or hold our allies hostile,' warned the Governor.) And yet Quayle's English was, like W's, a brew so rich and strange that no specific types of defect can explain its dizzying effect. As every gaffe-collector knows, Quayle's richest bits are idiotic gems, each one as exquisitely perplexing as a Zen koan or line of Hegel. 'Bobby Knight told me this: "There is nothing that a good defense cannot beat a better offense." In other words, a good offense wins.' ('This is a world that is much more uncertain than the past. In the past we were certain, we were certain it was us versus the Russians in the past. We were certain, and therefore we had huge nuclear arsenals aimed at each other to keep the peace . . . You see, even though it's an uncertain world, we're certain of some things,' Bush the Younger once explained.)[5]

Even in this contest our President stands out, however. He has outdone his dad's clueless second-in-command in part because his goofs are so much more abundant even than the much-derided Quayle's, and also because his bloopers often are so much more primitive grammatically than those of Quayle – who, even if he couldn't spell 'potato', never seems to have said anything quite like this: 'Laura and I really don't realize how bright our children is until we get an objective analysis.'

And yet the true distinction of our President lies not in his illiteracy *per se* but in the fact that he could not care less about it. He shows a perfect grinning unconcern that is unprecedented in the history of American leadership. There was no such princely callowness about Bush/Quayle, those other rich kids at the top. After his terrific hazing at the outset of the '88 campaign, the Indianan knuckled down and made a manful effort to improve his mind, or at least his standing, by plowing through a lot of heavyweight biographies and publicly regretting having goofed off at DePauw: 'Looking back, I should have pursued philosophy and history and economics and things of that sort in college more, but I didn't.' Marilyn Quayle had also tried to help, by telling journalists out on the stump that Dan 'really is the studious sort', a guy who 'tries to read Plato's Republic every year'. ('He isn't an egghead intellectual, which I find very refreshing,' she added hastily.) Although George Bush also was a lightweight, he came across like Lincoln next to his frenetic little running-mate, so there was no need for him to play the scholar once elected.[6]

Yet even he took pains to seem as if he cared about the precincts of the mind. He claimed to want to be 'the education President', and Barbara Bush pitched in by making 'literacy' her major issue as First Lady. In a pinch, Bush could even shoot the breeze about his reading, which included Tom Clancy (a Reagan favorite), non-fiction about flyers in World War II (Bush having been one), business sagas like *Barbarians at the Gate* and *Liar's Poker*, prophetic works like *Megatrends 2000*, the fishing magazine *Bassmaster*, and, for laughs, Dave Barry. Bush was frankly put off by anything too challenging (*War and Peace*, an Andover assignment, had flummoxed him, but then so did the movie *Field of Dreams*) or just 'too fat'. Although his reading wasn't highbrow, it was a miracle that he could read at all, considering his wild hyperactivity and minuscule attention span. 'He jogged and drove his boat *Fidelity* and played tennis and pitched horseshoes with the restlessness of a teenager,' writes Dan Quayle, capturing a speedy adolescent spirit that just wasn't made for reading books, or any text much longer than a thank-you note. Bush was even tired out by his own speeches, if they weren't bite-sized. 'He usually got bored in the middle, even if it was only two pages long,' writes John Podhoretz.* And yet the father still was far more literarily inclined than his impatient eldest son. Our President stands out not merely for his lifelong inability to sit and read (a feature of dyslexia, after all), but for his proud uninterest in the pleasures, and rewards, of reading.[7]

Such deep indifference was apparent in Bush the Younger's own half-hearted efforts to persuade the audience that it was otherwise. On the one hand, he, or his communications capo Karen Hughes, was always ready to assert his Barbara Bush-like dedication to the world of letters: 'Our capacity for discovery is never lost as long as we continue to read,' he (or someone) told the *American Spectator*. He would also rattle on about his 'love' of 'history', as he did on C-SPAN, and insist that he did 'read books all the time', and yet was seldom able

---

* 'Clark Judge, who had written for him when he was vice-president, would deliver a speech to Bush and the first thing he would do was weigh it in his hands; if it was more than a five-minute peroration, he would say, "I don't know, this looks pretty heavy to me."' John Podhoretz, *Hell of a Ride: Backstage at the White House Follies, 1989–1993* (New York, 1993), p.82.

to come up with any titles. That unconvincing pose of his would break apart repeatedly when someone asked him – sometimes meanly, sometimes innocently – for details. In December 1999, Bush took up a disarming prop: a nice new copy of James Chace's *Acheson*, which he schlepped everywhere he went, and which he cited ostentatiously at the Republican debate in Manchester, New Hampshire. Asked just what the book had taught him, he came up with a windy C+ answer (and then John McCain upstaged him with a pointed reference to an anecdote in Chace's book). As a constant reader, Bush fared no better in the world of children. 'I can't remember any specific books,' he 'fessed up in South Carolina, to a schoolchild who asked him what he'd liked to read when he was small. (When he was small, the only thing he read was baseball cards.)*[8]

Bush was not only unembarrassed by such revelations, but was clearly miffed that anyone would care, since he was 'a guy who's been an accomplished governor of the second-biggest state in the union', as he put it to the *Washington Post*.[9]

---

* That gaffe only worsened Bush's credibility problem over children's literature. A few weeks earlier, responding to a Pizza Hut survey of the nation's governors, the candidate claimed that his very favorite children's book had been Eric Carle's *The Very Hungry Caterpillar* – which came out in 1969, when Bush was almost twenty-three. And of the seven titles Bush (or someone) had sent in to Pizza Hut, another three – *James and the Giant Peach* (1961), *Tuck Everlasting* (1975) and *Sarah's Flag for Texas* (1993) – were published some years after Bush left grade school. That snafu clearly was not Bush's fault. The titles on his list were books that had been read to his own daughters. Several other governors (that is, their staffs) had made the same mistake, which suggests an ambiguity in the questionnaire from Pizza Hut. Nevertheless, what counted was the mass perception of the error – a mass perception that, as in Bush Sr's case, was basically correct, since Governor Bush, as it turned out, could not remember any books from his own childhood. Nor, off the cuff, could he recall his daughters' favorite childhood books, since Laura clearly was the one who had always read the girls to sleep.

25

Furthermore, although he didn't say it outright, he was, after all, George Bush. (On Bush's reading, see 'Curious George'.) Such brazenness reflected badly, and not just on the candidate. That Bush could be so cavalier about his ignorance, whereas the brainless Quayle had felt obliged to mime profundity, suggests a certain decadence within the culture of TV – a serious decline in 'standards', as Bush himself would say.

THE PLOWMAN

Such frank boobery would seem to represent a culmination of the long, strange history of anti-intellectualism in America. Certainly George W. Bush has always postured as a good ole boy, who don't go in fer usin' them five-dollar words, like 'snippy' and 'insurance'. That pose recalls, again, the case of Andrew Jackson, whose campaign was the first to deploy the Jeffersonian distinction between 'the plowman and the professor', casting Adams as a European sort of fancy-pants, book-smart and effete, while praising General Jackson as a man of mighty deeds and lightning intuitions. 'Behold, then, the unlettered man of the West, the nursling of the wilds, the farmer of the Hermitage, little versed in books, unconnected by science with the tradition of the past, raised by the will of the people to the highest pinnacle of honor, to the central post in the civilization of republican freedom,' gushed one Jackson propagandist. 'What wisdom will he bring with him from the forest?' Although such ripe encomia were based less on the candidate's biography than on the writings of Rousseau, they did the trick; and they helped set up a hardy paradigm that's still persuasive after all these years, at least in certain circles. Because of it, the shiftless W could seem, to some, a viable alternative to the far more seasoned and intelligent Al Gore, whose very strengths could be perceived, or spun, as weaknesses by contrast with the Texan's 'naturalness' and 'likeability' (as TV's punditocracy kept asserting).[10]

However, the comparison with Andrew Jackson is, to put it mildly, problematic. That military hero was, of course, a fiery democrat, whose unaffected style bespoke an ardent dedication to the common people over all.* He thought it was his aim to serve them, and he said as much, and said it clearly. (Indeed, such 'calculated bluntness' was quite typical of nineteenth-century democratic oratory, as Kenneth Cmiel observes.) When 'the laws' are used 'to make the rich richer and the potent more powerful,' Jackson wrote in 1832, 'the humble members of society – the farmers, mechanics, and laborers – who have neither the time nor the means of securing like favors to themselves, have a right to complain of the injustice to their Government.' Our President, on the other hand, is at the service only of the haves – as any cursory study of his record will make clear, and as even he himself acknowledged often, inadvertently, out on the stump: 'I'm trying to protect my invest – my contributors from unscrupulous practices,' he said, in one interesting slip of the tongue. And as he put it, famously, in New Hampshire: 'I know how hard it is for you to put food on your family' – which, if what he'd meant to say were true, he probably would not have said. 'This campaign,' he said in Iowa, 'not only hears the voices of the entrepreneurs and the farmers and the entrepreneurs, we hear the voices of those struggling to get ahead.' That 'the farmers', in his view, belong among 'the

---

* Naturally, that group did not include the slaves – or the Indians, whom Jackson slaughtered with a gusto quite extraordinary even by contemporary standards.

entrepreneurs' (a subgroup so important to him that he named them twice) tells us where this 'unlettered man of the West' is really coming from, despite the twang and cowboy boots. (For more on his oblique class consciousness, see 'It's the Economy, Your Excellency'.)[11]

Although the GOP machine has spun his elementary goofs as signs of kinship with the Common Man, they are, in fact, an insult to the people. Every bit of broken English, every flash of comfy ignorance, reminds us of a privilege blithely squandered: Bush attended Phillips Andover Academy, then Yale – Olympian institutions that would never have admitted him if he were not a Bush (both schools are heavily shadowed by the family), and surely rigorous enough to have taught him English and a little history, if he had been receptive to the benefits of such a gift. However, he was both too limited and too secure to take full advantage of an opportunity that count-less brighter, poorer folks have worked for, prayed for, and then been denied. Bush did the minimum at Yale, mainly party-ing and making good connections.* 'He was intellectually lazy, not particularly interested in anything serious, rather arrogant, contemptuous of studying, and purposeless,' recalls Dick Hermann, a classmate who knew him well. (Bush himself has chucklingly conceded that he was 'never a great intellec-tual' at Yale.) Thus, in the matter of his education, this President, despite his folksy pretense, is something of an anti-Lincoln: one who did not learn prodigiously in humble circumstances, but who learned almost nothing at the finest institutions in the land. When he comments on how many

---

* Whereas Bush's Yale transcript was published in the *New Yorker*, his grades at Andover are in protective custody, kept in a safe in the registrar's office.

hands he's shaked, or frets that quotas 'vulcanize' society, or claims that he has been 'miscalculated,' he is flaunting not, of course, his costly education, but his disdain for it – much as some feckless prince, a crowd of beggars watching from the street, might take a few bites from the feast laid out before him, then let the servants throw away the rest.

The insult is compounded by the myriad successes that Bush met with after graduation, following a stint at Harvard Business School. Having been admitted first to Phillips, then to Yale, then Harvard, all despite a mediocre record, he now succeeded brilliantly despite a mediocre record at those schools, performing just as if he'd studied like a monk and graduated with full honors.

Like his dad before him, Bush did well because the Family always went to bat for him, pulled strings for him, shelled out for him, and let him freely trade on his relations – getting him that plum assignment to the Texas Air National Guard, so that he wouldn't have to go to Vietnam; pumping capital into his failing company Arbusto Energy, which never made a dime – although it did enable giant write-offs; letting him exploit the family name to merge his way to wealth, despite a downturn in the oil business; helping him to exit that same business at a hefty profit, even though his corporation was about to tank; letting him exploit the family name to set up the consortium that bought the Texas Rangers, and to rebuild the stadium at Arlington, which feat of networking enabled his political career; helping him to get elected, and then re-elected, Chief Executive of Texas, in part by working their connections to provide him with the largest gubernatorial war-chests in American history; and so on. Indeed, it was such lofty patronage that, despite a glitch or two, would soon convey the lucky W into the White House, the election having been decided for him by those jurists whom his dad and Ronald Reagan had conveniently appointed to the Supreme Court. Again the case of Andrew Jackson comes to mind, for its absolute *dis*similarity to what we have today. 'Little versed in books', this President of ours was *not* 'raised by the will of the people to the highest pinnacle of honor', but ended up there thanks to an enormous effort (managed by his brother, Governor of Florida, his brother's comrade, Katherine Harris, and by his dad's old friends Jim Baker and Dick Cheney) to *suppress* – through widespread fraud, selective force and unrelenting propaganda – the people's will; for although that race was close (too close), a bare majority of voters still could see, apparently, that this man is not one of them, and hasn't got the wherewithal to serve them as their Chief Executive (or 'Chief Executive Officer', as he has put it tellingly). Many of them could perceive, in other words, that his sloppy speech was not a way of saying, 'I am one of you,' but, rather, of asserting, 'The rules just don't apply to me.'

Indeed, the candidate's transparency was sometimes overwhelming, so unapologetically did he present himself; and President Bush has been extraordinarily self-revealing, his natural indolence and unabashable complacency up front for all to see. ('I'll answer some questions, and I'm going to head home and take a nap,' he told a group of Democrats soon after his inauguration.)[12] Although this President's transparency is often wonderful, however, it is not unprecedented. Certain prior chief executives have also stood before us naked on TV, while others have been magically ennobled by the medium. The history of this post-war phenomenon is worth recounting, for the light it sheds on TV's sometime veracity. That history may also help illuminate the true ancestry of our see-through leader who is, as we shall see, the child not only of George Herbert Walker Bush, but also of Richard Nixon.

FIRST IMPRESSIONS

They say the camera doesn't lie. Of course, that axiom requires elaboration in the culture of TV, wherein 'the camera', while it may not 'lie' outright, routinely stretches the truth. This is not just a matter of transforming people's looks, as TV tends to do (like all photography), making them seem heavier/taller/older/younger than they appear when you run into them. More pervasively, the medium is an acute and unrelenting caricaturist – the Mother of all late-night stand-up. Whomever it presents to us, it instantaneously magnifies some tic or feature that we might not even notice in that person face-to-face, but which – therefore – is *all* we'll see in the persona jabbering and blinking on the screen (especially once we've seen that tic or feature worked into the repertoire of TV's wiseguys). Often the outstanding trait – like Katherine Harris's face-lift, Al Gore's lisp, Ted Koppel's hair, the wizened elfishness (i.e., big ears) of Ross Perot – is a material particularity, authentic or cosmetic, that marks the person whether he or she is on TV or not, even if it's not so ostentatious off the air. Such televisual tags are, in themselves, not necessarily revealing. When parties are at war, however, such accidental details take on an acute significance for the livid fighters on the other side, who see that superficial oddity as a profound reflection not just of the person through and through, but of an evil ideology that threatens all the world. Thus did Madame Harris's thick rouge and rigid smile (and flirty eagerness to do the boss's dirty work) appear, to half of us, symbolic of a Southern-style coquettishness that might set feminism back to the days of the Missouri Compromise, while Parson Gore's censorious lisp and schoolmasterish demeanor seemed, to the other half, expressive of a haughty top-down liberalism that would tax every breath you take and padlock all the righteous churches. That such ostensible dead giveaways might be mere televisual accidents, quite without significance – and, indeed, irrelevant – is a possibility that cannot come to many minds in time of war. In any case, there is no doubt that TV urges us to overestimate the fine points of appearance, a bias that now rules out a career in national politics for anyone who doesn't look as though he (or she) could be an anchor on CNBC. What with those eyebrows and the funky clothes, Honest Abe would never be allowed into Dick Cheney's GOP, and not just because its honor roll includes Trent Lott, Bob Barr and other white supremacists.

While the candid camera does exaggerate, it also makes some big mistakes, for some gifted actors can fool it just as easily as certain hardened types can fool the lie detector. There are among us (and above us) charismatics who can project a high or deep or comfortable 'humanity' that's sheer illusion – a sort of magic trick played by nice looks and subtle acting on an audience eager to be scammed. (The trickster might be perfectly, or partially, sincere.) Such magnetic personalities have been with us forever – Socrates and Jesus each discuss the type – but they have come to thrive especially through the electronic media, radio and TV each having radically empowered them, keeping them as inaccessible as gods while vastly spreading, and unaccountably enhancing, their seductive influence. Conversely, such ingratiating players have exactly what it takes to break through in the culture of TV, their narcissistic drive and inexhaustible appeal enabling them to make it to the top, and, usually, to stay there.

Our most successful post-war presidents have been such ultra-smooth performers – as Machiavelli would agree.* In each of them the camera could discover nothing of the inner man (if any), except for glimpses now and then in times of crisis. Eisenhower was just such a marvel, with his unassuming ways and plainsman's grin. Those telegenic properties helped the Man from Abilene to wrest his party's nomination from the large and frosty Robert Taft, who looked like the heartless banker in a Frank Capra classic, while Ike – although not really warm at all – came off like everybody's grandpa. His air of folksy affability allowed the GOP to wear a human face throughout the years of Joe McCarthy, the House Un-American Activities Committee (HUAC), nuclear proliferation and the rise of Allen Dulles' CIA; the global threat of Foster Dulles' 'brinksmanship', in other words, was softened somewhat by the President's 'aw-shucksmanship'. ('He was a far more complex and devious man than most people realized,' wrote Nixon later, with the usual hint of rancor.) As an impregnable persona, Ike was followed, and surpassed, by John F. Kennedy – who was, in fact, the smoothest of them all. With his wry wit and kingly gaze, that young bronzed god, the golden glow a sign of Addison's disease, offered not a hint of his distracting appetite; nor could any viewer of his urbane TV performances have guessed how risk-averse he really was (as on race relations), or how vengeful (as toward Cuba). Cut down prematurely (and with his lustre posthumously burnished to a blinding sheen by the authors of the Camelot mythology), JFK went out with his

---

* Such players are ubiquitous not only in politics, however, but also in the movies, TV, advertising and the music business, on Wall Street, and in the nation's jails.

mystique intact, which all those tawdry revelations haven't quite dispelled.

The next Chief Executive to put on the impenetrable mantle was Ronald Reagan, our Teflon President, who never once appeared to peek out from behind his happy mask. The camera failed to glorify him only at those moments when it mercilessly showed that there was *no one there* (because of Alzheimer's, perhaps), his ruddy and anachronistic visage standing empty, like an old brick high school soon to be converted into loft apartments. (This happened at his first debate with Walter Mondale – 'I'm all confused now' – and once again when, having been asked, out at his ranch, what was being done to free the hostages in Lebanon, he just stood there, beaming vacantly, with Nancy tensed up next to him: 'We're doing everything we can,' she muttered at the ground, through gritted teeth, and he, uncomprehendingly, repeated it, still smiling.)

And there was Bill Clinton, whose epic durability owed so much to his iron self-possession on TV. (He was also greatly aided by the toxic hatefulness of his attackers.) Whether belting out a State of the Union speech, riffing on some policy detail, or working a crowd Oprah-style, the Comeback Kid always maintained his air of genial equanimity, never showing so much as a flash of weakness, and little of his famous temper. The camera hurt him only by recording Clinton's trivial (and yet epoch-making) lie about 'that woman, Miss Lewinsky', a flagrant whopper that would haunt him, and the rest of us, for years to come. Tellingly, it was only after he was safely out of sight that his enemies could finally dim his lustre (by harping on those 'stolen' gifts, and the sleazy pardon of Marc Rich).

Those winning presidents each had something of the regal mien of FDR, whom all four honored, despite their differences (and although two of them did plenty to dismantle Roosevelt's achievement). Of course, FDR's heroic air of dauntless optimism was, to some extent, a product of reportorial discretion, the members of the press, back then, remaining silent on such proofs of frailty as the president's paralysis and his relationship with Lucy Page Mercer. A like tactfulness marked JFK's press coverage, despite his thin achievement, serious illnesses and raging satyriasis; and the Gipper, too, although completely out of it, was treated reverently by a press corps that let Michael Deaver and his propaganda elves run rings around them. And yet such forbearance by the press does not itself explain those politicians' rare ability to stand tall in the camera's eye; Clinton, after all, received no such indulgence. The fact is that the TV cameras loved him, much as they had loved Eisenhower, Kennedy and Reagan, and as the newsreel cameras (and radio transmitters) had loved FDR for years; and love, as we all know, is blind.*

Most politicians aren't so blessed. Lacking the invisible armor that protects the special few from televisual embarrassment, those mortals run the risk – if they appear more often than the average pol – of being *seen*. It is, in short, about such

---

* Of course, not everyone succumbs to such televisual charm, whose sway requires a mass predisposition that is merely general, not universal. Only those inclined already to adore that face and voice will do so, while those who, for whatever reason, just can't see it, never will. Here it is pertinent to note Oliver Sacks's memorable account of how an audience of aphasic mental patients reacted to a speech of Ronald Reagan's: 'There he was, the old Charmer, the Actor, with his practiced rhetoric, his histrionisms, his emotional appeal – and all the patients were convulsed with laughter'. Deaf to his words, but acutely sensitive to all his 'extraverbal cues', those viewers saw him only as a comic charlatan.

'Here then was the paradox of the President's speech. We normals aided, doubtless, by our wish to be fooled, were indeed well and truly fooled. And so cunningly was deceptive word-use combined with deceptive tone, that only the brain-damaged remained intact, undeceived.' *The Man Who Mistook His Wife for a Hat* (New York, 1985), pp. 80–84.

lesser players that the camera never lies. Whereas each gifted heir of FDR was clearly 'comfortable in his own skin', as the cliché has it, the common strugglers often suffer deep and fatal insecurities that, somehow, come across on television, as a hidden tumor shows up on the X-ray.

Such flaws have shone most glaringly in those post-Camelot pretenders who have strained to mimic JFK. The harder Lyndon Johnson worked at aping Kennedy, the less like Kennedy he seemed – and the more ape-like, the earthy Texan only looking clownish and constrained in so Hyannisport a guise, like an orang-utan in a tuxedo. For all his genius as a politician – and his great accomplishments on the domestic front – LBJ just couldn't hack it with the national audience, through *any* medium.* But it was Kennedy's main forum that obsessed him: 'TV is still to him a sort of *bête noire*,' Lady Bird noted in her diary in early 1964; and after the election it was downhill all the way. He tried to wow the journalists as JFK had done at *his* press conferences (which LBJ referred to, with envious contempt, as 'vaudeville'), and postured as a modern Medici, *à la* Jack and Jackie, by throwing fêtes for intellectuals and artists, but such efforts never worked.[13] (In the élite consensus there was, of course, an element of northern snobbery, which was encouraged, among the pundits, by the Kennedy machine.) And Johnson also had another, larger TV problem: the 'credibility gap', which grew still wider as he kept on sending more and

---

* As the war blitzed his ratings, LBJ took to posing wildly out of character for magazines like *GQ* and *Life* – lounging on his front porch in a nicely tailored suit (like Jack), frisking heavily 'among the young people' (one aide having urged him thus to replicate 'the Kennedy image'), and even going boating in a bathing suit (like Jack and Bobby). 'Reviews were poor,' notes Jeff Shesol. See his *Mutual Contempt: Lyndon Johnson, Robert Kennedy, and the Feud that Defined a Decade* (New York, 1997), pp. 310–13.

more Americans to Vietnam – and as ever more of them were coming home in body bags, while LBJ gabbed on about how bright the outlook was. Surely no-one could talk away that national agony, but Johnson was especially bad at trying. His back-room style of politics was literally hands-on, a domineering one-on-one approach that TV obviated, although the urge to twist your arm was visible. As we now know, his attempts to sell the war were strained by his own secret qualms about it – an ambivalence that TV also showed the viewers, more and more of whom could see that he was lying. In short, as he sat facing us, bespectacled and huge, and drawling out his pious homilies, you sensed the same dishonest bully who, on the one hand, was grimly raping Vietnam* and, on the other, so deftly forced the Congress into realizing all of those heroic domestic feats that Kennedy had only talked about. Like the body count mounting inexorably on the nightly news, Johnson's evident bad faith was a major televisual strike against him.

And yet, compared to *his* successor, LBJ was as inscrutable as Mona Lisa; for we have had no president as naked to the camera's X-ray eye as Richard Nixon. 'I'm not a bit thin-skinned,' he once asserted (privately), and although the claim was ludicrous it told an accidental truth, since Nixon really had no skin at all.[14] Thus TV was finally one of his great enemies – along with the eastern WASP élite, the Kennedys, the Democrats, 'the Jews', 'the intellectuals', the 'bastards' in the press, 'the bums on the campuses', and the 'vipers' in the federal bureaucracy. On TV, the man of cover-ups was so transparent

---

* 'During a private conversation with some reporters who pressed him to explain why we were in Vietnam, Johnson lost his patience. According to Arthur Goldberg, "LBJ unzipped his fly, drew out his substantial organ, and declared, 'This is why'!"' Robert Dallek, *Flawed Giant: Lyndon Johnson and His Times, 1961–1973* (New York, 1998), p. 491.

that the nation could see everything he was laboring to conceal: his bone-deep awkwardness, his festering resentment, and the hot joy he took in sticking it to 'them'.

Until 1960, Nixon had no TV problem. As Eisenhower's top agitator, he managed to defame the 'pinks' and flay the non-existent reds with a certain tidy zeal that played well with many viewers (unlike the jeering, slovenly McCarthy, whose gross judicial manners finally did him in, once people got a look at them). In full control of his resentments, Nixon could, back then, perform them brilliantly – as in the 'Checkers speech', that little masterpiece of petit-bourgeois grievance (and Nixon's *only* televisual triumph).* But things changed, changed utterly when Kennedy went national, with his amazing looks and money, and that ineluctable aplomb. Thus equipped, the Kennedy machine turned televisual politics into a whole new game, one that the man from Whittier could never play. This was apparent at their first debate, where CBS's cameras did a job on Nixon that, in fact, destroyed him. As most viewers know by now, that night 'the Fighting Anti-Communist' – although he sounded fine on radio – looked like a neglected mental patient next to Kennedy, who seemed as hale and masterful as his opponent looked awestruck and underfed.

Several factors had contributed to that effect, as Nixon later wrote. He wore no makeup, pulled his punches, had lost weight, had banged his knee, while Jack was tanned and fit and fought unfairly. Moreover, he did better in the second two debates. And yet that glaring contrast was not just a televisual construction. The spectral bumpkin glimpsed on CBS that

---

* His famous TV speech of 3 November 1969, to 'the great Silent Majority of my fellow Americans', received tens of thousands of supportive calls and letters, most of them secretly arranged by the White House.

night *was* Richard Nixon, at his most abject – the shabby, furtive Nixon facing his worst nightmare in the form of the resplendent Kennedy, who now towered over him, a glowing incarnation of the caste he had always hated more than anything. (That Jack, for years, had been his friend and comrade only made his plight more galling.) The exclusive network of great Yankee dynasties – Lodges, Mellons, Rockefellers, Roosevelts et al – had always been the sharpest thorn in Nixon's mind. 'I don't think you can possibly overestimate the importance of all that,' Robert Odle Jr has observed. 'It's at the core of understanding Nixon.'[15] The Kennedys, of course, had also long resented those imperious WASPs. Nevertheless, that family – and Jack especially – now became the focus of Nixon's grand resentment, which thenceforth grew beyond his power to control, or conceal it.

Traumatized by Jack's hypnotic savoir faire, the haunted President kept on trying, impossibly, to be as smooth a player as his departed nemesis.* Deeply humorless, he labored to be effortlessly funny, just like Jack – a mission he could carry out, he thought, with just a few good hires. 'One weakness in our research shop is on the humor side,' he wrote to Haldeman, urging that they siphon some new blood into the operation. Until then, it would help 'If I could get a few suggestions from time to time for either humor or just warm color which might trigger an extemporaneous comment or two'.[16] And yet not even Mark Twain could have helped the uptight Nixon with his humor problem, which was apparent every time he lobbed a

---

* Nixon's emulation was, however, tellingly selective. His mimicry of JFK included none of the familial touches – at play with Caroline, John-John under Daddy's desk: Nixon wanted to project not warmth but an imperial augustness, and therefore kept the wife and girls off-camera.

jest, deadpanning broadly in a stiff impersonation of Bob Hope. He was very funny, on the other hand, when he tried to be majestic, like Jack. For example, there was a picture of him standing pensive at the seashore, the image strongly reminiscent of those famous shots of JFK out resting at Hyannisport – except that Jack was dressed for a vacation in the sun, while Nixon wore a suit and tie, and dress shoes, as he stood there grimly eyeing the horizon. Thus he looked not like a lonely visionary dreaming of a better world, but like a federal agent out to bust a boatload of illegal immigrants. The clueless President was again attempting glamor when he had the White House police dressed up in double-breasted tunics with gold braids and buttons, and topped with high-crowned military caps festooned with plumes. Nixon thought it was the sort of thing that Kennedy would do, but those costumes smacked less of Camelot than of *The Merry Widow*. (They were used just once, and then retired to gales of laughter.)

And yet such propaganda slip-ups weren't just funny. They were the chronic errors of a mind inflexible and grandiose, and fatally inclined to *force* the issue. Although he deemed himself a whiz at 'public relations', he was built only for attack.* He had a peerless instinct for the jugular, rare stamina, and a fanatic's single-mindedness – the very gifts he admired in other 'sons-of-bitches', American and Soviet alike. And yet he lacked

---

* His approach was poundingly aggressive whether the campaign was positive or negative. Sherman Adams describes a telling moment during the Eisenhower cabinet's 'post-mortem discussion' of the 1954 midterm elections. 'He pulled out of his pocket a toy figure of a drummer, released its mechanism and placed it on the Cabinet table. While the President and the Secretaries stared at it in surprise and amusement, the toy drummer marched briskly across the table, banging on its drum. "We've got to keep beating the drum about our achievements," Nixon said.' It was, Adams writes, 'a scene unique in the annals of the Eisenhower cabinet'. *First-Hand Report: The Story of the Eisenhower Administration* (New York, 1961), p. 168.

those subtler qualities that propaganda warriors require as well. He had no detachment. He could shrug off nothing as 'just politics', or let bygones be bygones, or agree to disagree, but took every counter-thrust as a vicious swipe at *him*, and so bore countless grudges through the years. He was also militantly unadaptable, a lifelong total square whose unsophistication was a sign not, as he thought, of innocence but of a sharp provincial bent that made him always the divider, never a uniter (despite his early vow to 'bring us together'). And Nixon, finally, was a man without ideals, although he did some twilight maundering about 'a higher purpose'. His only program was the imposition of his will, a goal that he pursued on every front with equal brutal clumsiness. Thus was his flat-footed drive to shine like JFK continuous with his attempts to flatten Southeast Asia, strangle Chile, wipe out all dissent at home and sweep himself to re-election, by whatever means.

All those defects we could see: the nastiness, the morbid sensitivity, the deep unhipness and the will to win at any cost would all flash forth on TV now and then, his slogans notwithstanding. It was therefore not all that surprising when his dark TV persona was authenticated by the documentary outpouring after Watergate – the secret tapes, internal memos, frank memoirs and diaries all starkly certifying that what we saw was what we got. The man behind that gloomy scowl, it now turned out, was just as furious *in camera* as he often looked on camera, the rancor flowing out of him in a fetid torrent of hateful epithets, sadistic threats and scatological eruptions. Likewise, the obviously tricky Dick turned out to be a propaganda micro-manager psychotically intent on absolute dictation of his image, the President devoting nearly all his time – before *and* after Watergate – to crafting cover stories, rehearsing spin, conceiving and stage-managing 'big plays' and otherwise conniving at his exaltation in the viewers' eyes, and in the eyes of 'history'.* What *was* a bit surprising was the fact that Nixon was already livid, and already scheming, long before the big leaks and the Plumbers. As early as July 1969, the President – fired up by NASA's landing on the moon – launched into a proleptic three-hour monologue on what his men now had to do to make him awesome. 'Need now to establish the mystique of the presidency,' scribbled Haldeman, as Nixon ranted that 'we haven't used the power of the White House, to reward and punish', that US authority 'must be used more effectively, at home and abroad or we go down the drain as a great power', and that the time had come for systematic ' "dirty tricks"'.[17]

And the revelations keep on coming, each new batch reconfirming that the cameras never lied about him, and so refuting, again, the stubborn efforts of his epigones to prettify the picture. It is his tragicomic fate that all such posthumous PR is swiftly wrecked by further nauseous evidence of his true nature. In 1998, for example, Monica Crowley published *Nixon in Winter*, the second of two glowing memoirs of the four years that she spent ingenuously taking down his spin. The best part of that vicarious self-advertisement is its long account of Nixon's putative adventures in political philosophy. 'When I walked into his study, he had Aristotle's *Politics* marked and open in his hands,' writes Crowley, an acolyte as credulous as the ex-President was calculating. He had his views on all the greats from Machiavelli ('Boy, there's the truth!') to Hegel ('It's

---

* No detail was too trivial for his concern: 'the George Washington painting over the fireplace' ('It should either be moved up or the clock should be moved out'), 'the horrible modern art in some of our embassies' (should be 'cleaned out' ASAP), 'the portions of meat' served at official dinners ('too large'), and so on. See Bruce Oudes, ed., *The President: Richard Nixon's Secret Files* (New York, 1989), pp. 32, 86, 156 *et passim*.

so complex, so German!'), but it was 'the ancient Greeks' he most revered: 'No wonder the Greeks are timeless! They were asking the timeless questions!' Such theatrics would be slightly more convincing if we didn't know what Nixon really thought about the Greeks, and how he'd talked about them back when Monica was not around. In 1999, the National Archives released 445 hours of White House tapes, including one in which the President, having vented on the subject of 'these little Negro bastards on the welfare rolls', turns to the subject of 'All in the Family', which he complains is 'glorifying homosexuality' – a giant leap toward national decline and fall. 'You know what happened to the Greeks!' he yells at Haldeman and Ehrlichman. 'Homosexuality destroyed them. Sure, Aristotle was a homo. We all know that. So was Socrates.' And, he goes on, 'the Catholic Church' was also 'homosexual, and it had to be cleaned out', and so's 'the upper class in San Francisco' ('I can't shake hands with anybody from San Francisco'), and so are all the 'decorators,' and 'the goddamned designers,' who 'hate women' (which is why they keep designing all those 'sexy things'). The release of that moronic tirade, coming, as it did, soon after Crowley's whitewash, confirms the truth of JFK's own terse appraisal of his ever-flailing adversary – a judgment just as apt since Nixon's death as it had been in 1962: 'He went out like he came in. No class.'[18]

Although LBJ and Nixon were both daunted by the Kennedys' big money, the sort of presidential 'class' that plays well on TV is not an economic but a temperamental factor. This is clear not only from the televisual successes of Ike Eisenhower, Dutch Reagan and Bill Clinton, all men of humble origin, but also from the televisual disasters of George Herbert Walker Bush, a scion just as privileged as Jack Kennedy, yet nowhere near as smooth. Indeed, Bush's posh class background *was* his major TV problem, the cameras mercilessly outing the big sissy within. Thus that stilted princeling also suffered by comparison with Kennedy, who had the common touch – a contrast that has galled the noble House of Bush almost as much as it enraged the shabby Nixon.

This is not to say that Bush was too 'aristocratic' for the medium, and/or for postmodern times, a frequent claim by journalists, who make (too) much of the famous reticence that Dorothy Walker Bush drummed into her patrician son. In fact, the Bush clan, although fabulously wealthy, is not aristocratic *enough* to do well on TV, if by that modifier we mean 'elegant' and 'polished'. First of all, the Bushes often have let fly in the most boorish way – as when Barbara Bush hinted coyly that Geraldine Ferraro was a 'bitch', or when the President, losing it completely in the late campaign of 1992, called Clinton/Gore 'two bozos', and dubbed Gore 'Ozone Man' (or when the younger Bush addressed obstructive staff and uncooperative journalists as 'assholes', which he did routinely when co-managing his dad's campaign in 1988).* Such crudity is, obviously, not 'aristocratic' (even if aristocrats are often crude) – nor, more importantly, is it 'aristocratic' to make everyone around you conscious of your plummy background: on the contrary. As one who could not help but wear his class advantage like a letter sweater, the elder Bush was no aristocrat. Such was the fatal flaw that TV kept exposing (with his help), although it was a problem that pre-dated his encounters with the medium. There was an exemplary moment back in 1950, when young 'Poppy' Bush, who had lately moved to Midland,

---

* The elder Bush also betrayed a certain impropriety when, as Vice President, he boasted, after his debate with Representative Ferraro, 'We kicked a little ass tonight.'

Texas (where he sold oil drilling rigs), stepped out one day to run an errand, then ran back in and quickly changed his clothes. 'He had on Bermuda shorts, and the truck drivers were whistling at him,' writes Barbara. 'I don't believe he wore shorts ever again, except to play tennis.'[19]

And yet those shorts were almost always in your face, whatever he might do to cover them. Throughout the 1988 campaign, his top imagineers – Roger Ailes and Lee Atwater, the latter heatedly abetted by George W – worked manfully to keep him, as it were, dressed up in overalls and cowboy boots, but on TV those prissy knee-length jobs kept glowing through the denim. The ambivalent Nixon (Bush had been his protégé) said as much to Monica: 'It's not that he doesn't like people; it's just that he's not very comfortable out there on the stump trying to connect with them. He tries too hard to be one of them, eating pork rinds and the rest, but he is not one of them, and it comes across. He's better off just being himself.' That advice would not have helped, since Bush's true self only raised guffaws whenever it skipped into view. When asked if, as US envoy to China, he had gotten close to any of the natives, he replied: 'Oh, yes. They gave us a boy to play tennis with.' He had made that lordly statement in a private conversation in the seventies, but he sounded that way on the stump a decade later. His hoity-toity slips were justly famous – as when he asked for 'just a splash' of coffee at Cuzzin' Ritchie's Truck Stop in New Hampshire, or thus explained why he had lost the straw poll in Ames, Iowa: 'A lot of people who support me were at an air show, they were off at their daughter's coming-out party, they were teeing up at the golf course,' he speculated philosophically, apparently mistaking Iowa for Greenwich.[20]

By Election Day of 1988, Bush and his propaganda team had finally managed to democratize his image just enough to get him into office. (He feigned a hearty appetite for pork rinds and country music, while his spinmasters played up the chilly, technocratic vibe of Governor Dukakis.) His shorts were also hidden well in times of war, which he therefore brought about as often as he could. In general, however, the cameras tended to expose his inner twit, even when they misconstrued him. This had been true all along – as, for example, when Vice President Bush threw out the first pitch at the Houston Astrodome, to open the National League Championship Series in 1986, and did a really half-assed job (caught brilliantly by Richard Ben Cramer in *What It Takes*). Watching that slow spastic dance on ABC, you had no way of knowing that Bush had been a champion baseball player at Yale, or that he was still quite an athlete. That early flub was just embarrassing, however. At the end, his major gaffes helped do him in – although, strictly speaking, they were not his fault. At a convention of the National Grocers Association in Orlando, Bush took a tour of the exhibits, and paused to marvel courteously at a state-of-the-art supermarket scanner: 'This is for checking out?' It was that gizmo's new ability to read torn labels, and not the thing itself, that Bush was lauding; but the *New York Times* front-paged him as 'amazed' by the very notion of a scanner, as if he'd never been inside a supermarket; and the videotape appeared to bear that out. The White House protested, but the damage had been done – because George Herbert Walker Bush was, let's face it, not a supermarket kind of guy.* Similarly, the President lost points when, in his second debate with Clinton and Perot, he made a big deal of looking at his watch, an impatient gesture to suggest

---

* Shortly after moving back to Houston after Clinton's swearing-in, George and Barbara 'made an amazing discovery: You can call out for pizza!' Barbara Bush, *Barbara Bush: A Memoir* (New York, 1994), p. 517.

that Clinton had run on too long: 'Time's up,' Bush meant to say, but it looked like he was saying, 'I have better things to do,' and that apparent display of haughty boredom turned off many viewers. And yet, while they were wrong, those viewers were also right; for Bush *did* think himself above such lowly rituals (especially after having worn the laurels of Desert Storm).[21]

As with Nixon, so with Bush, the quirks accentuated on TV were not just funny. That sense of high entitlement was dangerously aggravated by a need to show the world – to show his sons – that he was not a softie, but a guy as hard as Dorothy and Prescott Bush had raised their kids to be. Such upper-class machismo was, of course, a common feature of the monied East; it had marked the Kennedys, and all those buccaneering Ivy Leaguers who had made the CIA (which Bush ran under Gerald Ford, and whose headquarters is now named after him). And yet Bush seems to have felt especially bedevilled by his insecurity. It drove him, strangely, into Nixon's arms, as if he craved the fatherly approval of that bitter, low-born character. Bush was a Nixon man by 1968, sharing Nixon's hard-line anti-Communism and taking his political advice. (Both players used the same ad-man to help them win elections in the sixties.)*
After losing his first senatorial bid in Texas – a bad idea proposed by Nixon – Bush went on to front wholeheartedly for the beleaguered President throughout Watergate, that crafty

---

* This was Harry Treleaven, who had handled the accounts of Ford, Singer and PanAm for J. Walter Thompson. He approached the tasks of selling Bush (as a congressman in 1966) and Nixon (as presidential timber two years later) with the same expert disregard for anything of 'substance'. For Treleaven's views on pitching Nixon, see his memos in Joe McGinniss, *The Selling of the President, 1969* (New York, 1969), esp. pp. 171–80 *et seq*. Elizabeth Mitchell quotes Treleaven's plan for pitching Bush in W: *Revenge of the Bush Dynasty* (New York, 2000), pp. 90–92.

operator having asked him to direct the Republican National Committee, so that Bush's pedigree and moderate ties might help defuse the crisis. Bush put his straight persona wholly at the service of the crooked White House ('He takes our line beautifully,' Charles Colson noted), and otherwise sought Nixon's manly reassurance that he was no Yalie faggot but a serviceable thug. 'I am convinced that deep in his heart he feels I'm soft, not tough enough, not willing to do the "gut job" that his political instincts have taught him must be done,' Bush wrote ruefully to his boys.

The charge that he was sissified – a creature of 'privilege and softness in a tea-sipping, martini-drinking, tennis-playing sense' – was one that he could not shrug off, whether he inferred it from the guarded Nixon or, years later, read it in *Newsweek*'s cover story on 'the wimp factor', a piece that drove him (and his eldest) permanently up the wall. Indeed, his presidency was distinguished *only* by his violent serial efforts to disprove the charge, from his Nixonian run against Dukakis ('card-carrying member of the ACLU [American Civil Liberties Union]'), to his unnecessary, ruinous invasion of Panama ('a political jackpot', Lee Atwater called it), to the over-hyped, atrocious and half-finished war against Iraq ('Saddam is going to get his ass kicked'), to the propaganda drive to smear Anita Hill and salvage Clarence Thomas ('the best man for the job'). And yet not even all those victories could ease his sense of impotence. Even after Desert Storm, which had boosted his approval ratings to a stratospheric 89 percent, the President was still grousing about *Newsweek*'s cover story. Nor did those wins exalt him in the camera's eye. After all the countless handsome photo ops, the TV image that defined Bush in the end came from that unlucky moment when he tossed his cookies on Japan's Prime Minister, and then collapsed.[22]

A VERY GENEROUS ALLOWANCE

As a TV performer, President George W. Bush is in the same camp with his father and his father's mentor. He does not have their superficial flaws, however. While both Bushes speak much the same amusing lingo, this President is, of course, infinitely better at the grip-and-grin of retail politics, having been reared not back East but in West Texas. (He is also made of sterner stuff, his character reflecting less of the compliant George I than of Queen Barbara, a blunt, ferocious partisan, despite the pearls and silver crown.)*

Whereas his father, like Nixon, just could not get down, this George doesn't have to fake the sort of pseudo-populist rough-housing that it takes to charm a lot of voters in the Sun Belt, the farm states, the Rocky Mountain states and other strongholds of far-right Republican emotion. A jolly veteran of the DKE frat-house and the Austin statehouse, and a seasoned traveller of the dusty roads between them, Bush the Younger has no trouble givin' strangers jokey nicknames, or grabbin' fellas by the neck, or squeezin' folks in big bear-hugs, or – more important – talkin' the draconian talk of hard-right ideology, which always sounded just a little funny on his father's famous lips.

Thus Bush can easily play the game that stumped his dad. What places him among the televisual losers is the obvious fact that that's his *only* talent – and it's one that doesn't count for much, unless he finds the time, these next four years, to go out

---

* Bush inherited one political talent from his father: a prodigious knack for remembering people's names. Once, when he and other pledges at Yale's DKE house were ordered to recite as many names as possible of that year's fifty new initiates, 'George got up and named all fifty,' recalls a classmate. 'He just has such an interest in people that he remembers their names, which is his medium, like writing numbers are [*sic*] for somebody else.' George Sr has throughout his life displayed the same ability.

and fondle every voter in the USA. Beyond the campaign trail, or certain sections of it, Bush's chummy manner cannot hide the fact that he's an amateur in way over his head, as the political cartoonists and late-night comics have all merrily observed. TV is their authority, this President's unfitness coming through as clearly as the logo in a thirty-second spot, whenever he attempts to handle an unforeseen question, or free-associates a bit too long. Of course, his spinmasters and partisans, and most members of the mainstream press, say otherwise, attempting endlessly to hitch his little wagon to the presidential stars of yesteryear. 'He connects with people like a Jack Kennedy,' said one Bush propagandist early on, and we also heard repeatedly that this Bush represents the Second Coming of the Gipper, who was also written off as inexperienced and slow, a cipher, 'just an actor'.[23] And yet it is precisely Reagan's histrionic talent that this President lacks.* He is unable to feign 'presidentiality,' or put on *gravitas*, or even to project much confidence – despite his famous smirk (which only reconfirms the sense that this is all a terrible mistake). In short, such incapacity is the defining feature of W's TV persona. As LBJ was *insincere*, as Richard Nixon was *vindictive*, and as George Bush was *effete*, this President is *undeserving*.

Of course, that impression was burned for ever into the record by the sedentary putschists of the Supreme Court, on that Day of Infamy, 12 December 2000. And yet the Governor

---

* While it exaggerates our President's charisma, that comparison also belittles Reagan's pre-presidential record. By 1980, Reagan was, as a leader, far more experienced than Bush was by 2000, having served two full terms as governor of California, where that post is constitutionally stronger than in Texas; and he oversaw a number of reforms – both liberal and conservative – much more impressive than the legislative feats of Gov. Bush, whose six years in office paid off largely for his friends.

seemed undeserving long before he got the ultimate in un-deserved rewards. From the outset of the presidential race in 1998 (if not before), TV ruthlessly played up the candidate's peculiar air of groundless egotism. His propagandists therefore had their work cut out for them, because Americans, however they may vote, don't like rich slackers, or anybody else who gets by without paying for it. And so, under the command of Karl Rove (who started out doing dirty tricks for Nixon), the Governor's spinmasters got to work denying the obvious, trying to talk away his bratty aura with loud paeans to his 'likeability', and carefully suppressing, or dismissing, all the evidence of the numerous special favors that had finally put him where he was.

The latter task was easy, since, throughout the race, 'the liberal media' laid off the lucky candidate.[24] While there was much solid work done by print journalists, it never took – i.e., it wasn't picked up by the networks. Those giant players walked politely around the gaping potholes in the Governor's record – a marked departure from the telejournalistic *modus operandi* of the not-so-distant past. On Bush's easy entry into the Texas Air National Guard, and then his lax observance of that outfit's rules, reporters were discreet (as they had not been with Dan Quayle, or with Bill Clinton, *vis-à-vis* their draft-dodging). And unless you searched, you might know nothing about Bush's shady self-enrichment down in Texas, both in business and in politics – a fortune based entirely on his link to Dad. (The contrast with Whitewater, that epoch-making non-story, is instructive.) The only news that threatened to confirm the obvious about the over-privileged sprout came from an independent author – and W's men fixed him but good. The darkest aspect of the Governor's career was its Texas-sized hypocrisy, the rich kid keenly punishing the poor for crimes that he himself had once (or twice) committed with impunity. That sin stands out in J. H. Hatfield's *Fortunate Son*, a sound biography whose afterword alleges, via three unnamed sources, that the 26-year-old was busted down in Texas for cocaine possession in 1972, and that his father had the crime expunged by an obliging judge. The boom dropped fast and hard. Just before the book was published by St Martin's Press, the Bush team hit the mattresses, hollering indignantly ('Mindless garbage,' Dad exploded), and leaking word that Hatfield had done time for attempted murder. Although that item was, albeit true, beside the point, its propagation – and whatever other pressures *la famiglia* brought to bear – induced St Martin's not just to withdraw the book, but to promise publicly to *burn* it.* Thus the campaign ruined Hatfield, to kill that inconvenient story (which, despite the uproar, may not go away).

There was usually no need for such rough stuff, however, since Bush was good at shrugging off his priors – brawling, drunk driving and whatever else – as mere youthful friskiness, which seemed to satisfy the press (although it did clash somewhat with his motto of 'accountability', and also failed to square with his big crackdown on juvenile crime in Texas). That what-the-hell-now-let's-move-on approach to his own checkered past helped also to enhance the Governor's 'likeability', the campaign's main objective, since it was necessary to promote the fiction that this lazy child of wealth was really 'just like you and me', Odessa-style. This was, of course, the same stylistic strategy that had elected George H. W. Bush in 1988; and, like Dad back then, this George was also blessed with an opponent tight-assed and

---

* Despite that archaic pledge – which roused little protest from the punditocracy – St Martin's actually did not turn the unsold copies into 'furnace fodder'. They sold them off, so that the remaindered copies ended up competing with the new edition, published by the independent Soft Skull Press.

mechanical (and linked with Harvard), traits that, by contrast, enhanced the grand illusion that George Walker Bush is just a good ole boy. Formerly, both Bushes got their candy asses whupped when they made runs at Texans who were more convincing than themselves: Senator Ralph Yarborough in the elder Bush's case, Representative Kent Hance in W's. Skilled at populist derision, and gifted with the drawls and faces for it, such men played the Bushes' Yalie heritage for laughs, whereas the Massachusetts bureaucrat Dukakis, and Al Gore, the over-eager Beltway Bandit, made it all too easy for the Bush machine to play it low and rural, notwithstanding the estates in Greenwich, Kennebunkport and on Jupiter Island, an exclusive Florida enclave near Hobe Sound. George Bush took especial pleasure in out-shufflin' the fastidious Gore, and was surely better at that posture than his father; but his success at it owed less to his own acting talent than to *Gore*'s exposure by the camera. An over-sharp perfectionist who could not play it cool to save his life (or the Republic), the inner man as televised was far too glaringly intent on making just the right impression on the audience – a major propaganda no-no, since we must never be reminded that the actor has designs on us. Gore's deportmental zigzag was too obvious, the air of strain sometimes embarrassing.* By contrast, the addled one-note Bush appeared – that is, could be depicted – as a reg'lar sorta guy (although his family fortune puts Gore's in the shade).

In its effort to conceal the Governor's gilt-edged bonds,

---

* This ceased to be the case after Election Day. Although he made some major tactical mistakes, Gore weathered the five-week post-election crisis with extraordinary dignity, behaving just as graciously and tactfully as the stalwarts of the GOP were bellicose, intransigent and snide. Perhaps it will be said one day of Gore that nothing so became his public life like the leaving of it.

the Bush campaign went well beyond playing up his affability. In order to affirm the boy's egalitarian credentials (and thereby turn his celebrated weaknesses into a strength), the Bush/Cheney operation supervised a grand revival of the anti-intellectual diatribe that flourished in the heyday of McCarthy/Nixon, and then reblossomed with the national careers of Spiro Agnew and George Wallace. (The diatribe recurred a bit when Bush's dad – despite his Yale degree – joined Danny Quayle in taking childish shots at 'Harvard Yard'.) The Bush/Cheney drive was easily the biggest, and the slickest, in our history, however, since it used such smart technologies to spread the word, and had the help of *all* the propaganda armies of the right – 'free-market' and neo-conservative as well as Christian fundamentalist. Guided by the campaign's daily talking points, all those loud Judaeo-Christian soldiers were unanimous in arguing that George Bush was a second Andrew Jackson, braving the élitist smart-pants 'Prince Albert'. They cast the Governor's thick tongue as a sign of unpretentiousness, his ignorance as strength – as if he'd come to talk that way from working long hours at the docks and in the fields, and not from drinking heavily (at least) and blowing off his studies, notwithstanding the sky-high tuition.

In its divisiveness, the tactic was pure Nixon. Cunningly – and absurdly – it identified the much-mocked W with those Midwestern elders who had also been derided by the snooty Pharisees of Washington, New York and Hollywood, the infernal 'they' so damningly invoked by countless all-American rabble-rousers (and certain demagogues elsewhere).* 'I

---

* Dan Quayle depended heavily on the same quasi-Nixonian tactic in his last quest for the Republican nomination – as he had in 1988 and 1992. ('I wear their scorn as a badge of honor!' he had railed against 'them' during the 'Murphy Brown'

remember what *they* did to Ronald Reagan. *They* belittled him, and *they* said, "Oh, he can't possibly be smart enough to be President of the United States,"' the Governor told Larry King (emphasis added). Predictably, the propaganda also placed this Bush alongside Eisenhower, whom 'they' had likewise taken for a 'dumbie' (*sic*), but who 'twice mopped the floor with . . . Adlai Stevenson, the darling of the smart-set [*sic*],' wrote Dennis Byrne in the *Chicago Sun-Times*. 'The intelligentsia said the bovine electorate had been beguiled by Eisenhower's smile,' wrote George Will, without naming names. The Nixonian subtext of such seething discourse was that 'they' are fewer by far than 'we', and therefore lord it over 'us' not democratically but through Satanic guile. Intelligence itself, in this equation, is a sign of wickedness, as in the Great Awakening some years before our Revolution. Thus Bush's plain unbookishness was taken to evince his godliness, while Gore was just too goddamn smart for our own good – his complex clauses a temptation and a snare, like the devil Clinton's.** 'The country can afford a 40-watt president. It cannot allow the Clinton-Gores, corroded

---

affair.) As the *Wall Street Journal* reported in May 1999, time had not dimmed the mass perception of Quayle's thickness, which was still getting easy laughs on TV and elsewhere: 'But fresh derision serves the Quayle strategy perfectly. "When the establishment laughs at Dan Quayle," says spokesman Jonathan Baron, "they're laughing at people who are pro-life, who go to church, who believe in core conservative values." The campaign's strategic challenge, says campaign manager Kyle McSlarrow, is "to channel what's happened to Quayle into an emotional response" among GOP voters.' Since Quayle had no appeal beyond the rightist 'core', that masochistic 'strategy' could not succeed.

** That quaint formulation was by no means new. The conception of intelligence itself as somehow un-American – an ancient notion in our history – found especially loud expression in the presidential race of 1952, in which, for example, Senator Richard Nixon charged that Adlai Stevenson 'got his PhD from Dean Acheson's College of Cowardly Communist Containment'. On the anti-intellectual subtext of that campaign, see Richard Hofstadter, *Anti-Intellectualism in American Life* (New York, 1963), pp. 3–51.

to the core, to further define corrosion down,' warned Michael Kelly tartly (and unclearly). For George Will, the Governor's 'modesty' was preferable by far to all those 'clever people' in the Democratic Party, which has *no* popular support, unlike the GOP, a party deeply rooted in our richest soil. 'A Gore administration would have the mentality of Washington's Northwest quadrant; a Bush administration would have a West Texas attitude,' wrote the boyish, bow-tied buckaroo, whose burst of prairie populism ought to give us pause.[25]

For there was a vast self-contradiction in the rightist snowjob on behalf of the unlettered Governor – a contradiction that explodes the right's conservative pretensions. All at once, those nativists and highbrows – Rush Limbaugh, William Bennett, Robert Bork, *et al* – who had long bemoaned the colored masses' inability to speak 'grammatical English' (to quote Limbaugh) were now saying nothing (publicly) about the Governor's West Texas version of Ebonics ('Is our children learning?'), or about his weird vocabulary or syntactic haplessness.[26] Likewise, the Governor's supporters adamantly looked away from his bald ignorance of US and world history, US government, world geography and literature in general, as well as his peculiar way with 'fuzzy math'. Such forbearance is surprising, given the reactionary zest with which those partisans – Lynne Cheney, for example – have long deplored the ignorance of our young about the glories of Our History in particular, and Western Culture generally. Toward the privileged Governor, in short, the tribunes of the right have happily extended just the sort of condescending tolerance that they attack in anyone who would make the same allowances for poor black children. Thus Bush himself is a big-time beneficiary of what he likes to call 'the bigotry of soft expectations' – an indulgence his champions never grant to any politician who would speak up for the under-privileged.

George Will, for example, was among the staunchest of the Governor's post-debate spinmasters. Although the Bush performance was, by any reasonable gauge, not good, the rootin'-tootin' Will adeptly skirted the reality by making up quaint allegories based on his fanatic's view of how the candidates appeared: 'Bush's ambling on the stage and his low-voltage delivery exhibited a kind of behavioral modesty, analogous to and expressive of conservatism's modest expectations for the uses of government,' while Gore 'strode and gesticulated and generally overflowed with the sort of confidence with which liberalism would wield government for grant purposes,' etc.[27] Even before he made that sort of case in many columns and TV appearances, however, Will had already been quite generous with the befuddled candidate. On a broadcast of ABC's *This Week* in January 2000, Bush told Will that he was 'not sure' whether Congress should naturalize Elian Gonzalez: 'I really haven't thought through the, a – a – a law that would make him a citizen.' Then, moments later, Bush told Cokie Roberts that he would advise the senators to pass the law. 'So you've n— so you now think citizenship is a good—?' Roberts wondered, and the Governor said this:

> 'Well, I think – I – It – listen, I don't understand the full ramifications of what they're going to do. But I – I – I think it'd be a – a – a wonderful gesture. I guess the man c– the boy could still go back to Cuba as a citizen of the United States. I'm concerned about, you kn– you know, family relations, and I think the dad ought to come here. And I think the dad ought to be given time to understand the greatness of America. I don't think – I – I would suspect he's not – he's not able to make a rational decision in Cuba. I'm sure the pressure's enormous on

this man, an– t– t– t– to toe the Castro line. But I– as I said to George, I hadn't really thought about the citizenship issue. It's an interesting idea, but if I were in the Senate, I'd vote aye.'

Although both illogical and ill-considered (if Elian were made 'a citizen of the United States,' his Miami relatives could then *prevent* his going 'back to Cuba'), that dim reply earned no rebuke from his bespectacled inquisitor, who had taken an entirely different tack with Jesse Jackson. On ABC's *This Week* in 1988, during the contest for the presidential nominations, George Will did everything but try to rope and brand that uppity contender, hitting him with questions of a sort that would have knocked the Governor unconscious. 'As President, would you support measures such as the G-7 measures in the Louvre accords?' he asked sharply, then looked well pleased that Jackson didn't understand the question (which referred to the ongoing GATT negotiations). Will also homed in on some of Jackson's leftist economic claims, with a pedantic ruthless-ness entirely absent from his later puff-pieces on Bush – although the latter could not even clarify the fuzzy math in his own plans. (Jackson's economic answers made some sense, despite the interviewer's jeering.) The set-to caused a stir, with Jackson charging racism, whereupon Will wrote a column boasting of how gutsy he had been to blow the whistle on that candidate, which Jackson's fellow-Democrats, he claimed, were all afraid to do: 'Because he is black, his white rivals sit silently beside him, leaving his foolishness unremarked.'[28] Faced with a peerless 'foolishness' some twelve years later, the smitten pundit did not just leave it 'unremarked' but praised it as the highest wisdom. Thus George Will showed himself to be a stalwart double-standard-bearer for the GOP – one of many who were willing to say anything to represent the rich kid as a populist, the novice as experienced, the ignoramus as a proper heir to Thomas Jefferson.

NIXON'S REVENGE

The anti-intellectual appeal goes way back in American history, and is still a potent one; and the Bush team made it with enormous skill, alleging W's rusticity and hyping Gore's aggressive braininess with all due unanimity and vehemence. It is therefore remarkable (and cause for optimism) that that drive ultimately failed, although it surely did a lot for Bush in those states where he won. Despite Gore's inability to warm the cockles of the national heart (and, more importantly, despite the media's gigantic bias against him), the majority of voters did *not* find W so 'likeable' or, if they did, were not convinced that he was any deeper or more able than he seemed. TV's daily revelation of his absolute unfitness was, or should have been, a killer. Just as Nixon's men could never make him seem like fun, Bush's propagandists couldn't make that party animal seem capable of running the United States; it finally took five members of the nation's highest court, and the journalists' blind eye to what went down in Florida, to place him in the nation's highest office.

And yet TV's exposure of the Governor's unfitness was itself misleading, for it allowed the quick construction of a caricature that has served to *idealize* the candidate, however cruelly it's been rendered. The dim bulb played by Will Ferrell on *Saturday Night Live*, and roasted nightly by Leno, Letterman, O'Brien and the rest, and satirized by countless political cartoonists, is, on the one hand, an appalling figure, the sort of idiot prince who might slouch in the throne of some exhausted monarchy, perhaps, but who should never sit in charge of our democracy. While shockingly out of his depth, however, that plain half-wit is himself benign, a danger only insofar as evil others might manipulate him (as in *Saturday Night Live*'s mock-soap *Palm Beach*). For all his faults, that butt *is* kind of 'likeable', a simpleton as genial, blithe and innocent as Alfred E. Neuman (with whom our President has often been compared). In short, that cheerful moron is a figure not much different from the smirking anti-Gore extolled by the Republicans throughout the recent contest. ('You don't have to be smart to be President!' yelled Representative J.C. Watts, in introducing W at a rally in South Carolina.)[29] He may be dumb, in other words, but he's not ambitious, and he's a real nice fella, wouldn't hurt a fly.

The overall good-naturedness of that cartoonish image has been subtly amplified by Bush's own public response to such derision. Like all postmodern politicians from Ronald Reagan on, this Bush has understood that, in the culture of TV, there is no balm like Self-Effacing Humor. However much the satire galls him (and it's obvious it does), he has managed somewhat, and so far, to rise above it – and ensure its harmlessness – by seeming to take part in it himself. Thus he started, early on, to use that weary little joke about his tendency to 'stress the wrong syl-*lab*-ble,' and told Letterman that he 'would make sure the White House library has lots of books with big print and big pictures'. Likewise, just before Election Day, he and Al Gore co-starred in the opening bit on *Saturday Night Live*, he riffing broadly on his own dyslexia (he said he was 'ambilavent' about appearing on the show, which he at times had found 'offensible'), while Gore sat stiffly sighing. That defensive comic *pas de deux* brought down the house, which made it clear, if further proof were needed, that such self-parody has no subversive edge at all. Indeed, such frank cooperation often works to power's advantage, since it appears to demonstrate a kingly magnanimity, by showing the world that such burlesque is really licensed by the sovereign. Thus Ronald Reagan had Rich Little doing Ronald Reagan at his big inaugural bash in 1984, the Gipper laughing richly through it all; and the elder Bush was just delighted to have Dana Carvey come and do him at the White House, no hard feelings – and not very funny, either. Real satire always draws a little blood, or else it's just court entertainment: Harry Shearer would never have been asked to play the Reagan White House, nor would Governor Bush have visited *The Daily Show*; and the Clintons got a bit more than they bargained for – as did all the other attendees that night – from Don Imus, when he gave his raucous keynote at the annual dinner of the Radio/TV Correspondents Association in 1996. The comedy that's politician-friendly, on the other hand, is always trivial, even if it's sort of funny – as are the politician's self-inflicted jabs. Far from being self-critical, in fact, the politician who cracks wise about himself (it seems to be a male thing, by and large)* is actually thereby betraying a certain shamelessness, both in himself and in the culture that sits

---

* Of course, there are exceptions. Concerning Katherine Harris's 'mischievous sense of humor', Katherine G. Seelye tells this story: 'In a recent television interview with Diane Sawyer, Ms Harris told a story about Christmas shopping at Target one night when she could not sleep. "The woman looked at my credit card and looked at me and she goes, 'Katherine Harris.' And like, she didn't, she said, 'Are you Katherine Harris?' And I said, 'Yeah. I only have on one layer of makeup. I'm incognito.'"' 'Katherine Harris Redux: No Longer Larger Than Life,' *New York Times*, 5 February 2001.

laughing with him. (For examples, see 'The Wit and Humor of George W. Bush'.)

And so to snicker at this President for his stupidity is not productive; for his unfitness isn't really funny – and in any case he isn't stupid. True, he is the most uneducated president in US history, and probably the most illiterate, and easily among the least concerned about the contents of his mind. Moreover, his off-the-cuff remarks betray what is apparently an inability to reason, an intellectual handicap much worse than, say, a lack of interest in the sort of wonkish fare that he himself has always gleefully dismissed. ('Sitting down and reading a 500-page book on public policy or philosophy or something' is just not his thing, he told Tucker Carlson.) At issue here is not the President's distaste for slogging through tough prose, but the incessant hints of a profound confusion that ought not to cloud the mind of anyone who has his finger on the trigger: a penchant for non sequiturs, a hard time making elementary distinctions, a tendency to merge cause and effect. Tautologies abound in Bush's speech: 'In terms of being a President that says there is no place in [i.e., for] racism, it starts with saying there's no place for racism in America.' 'If you don't stand for anything you don't stand for anything.' And when asked about the prospect of there not being sufficient unity at his Republican convention, he replied: 'I am confident there will be. I'm confident people are coming together. And the reason I believe this is because our party is united.' (For more on Bush's illogic, see 'Let Me Make One Thing Perfectly Clear'.)

We can cite such examples till the cows come home, but it won't change the fact that George W. Bush *is* our President, despite his obvious lack of interest in, or preparation for, the job (and despite the further fact that the American people didn't vote him into office) – a momentous sign that he is by no means the cheery imbecile that many people would prefer to think he is. That he performs as front-man for Dick Cheney's shadow government does not mean that he's a figurehead, like Henry Pu Yi, the last emperor of China, or Reich President von Hindenburg. Although he is as overwhelmed as he appears, this President is neither as dim-witted nor as easy-going as TV made him out to be. That first impression now requires a clear corrective; for, as he might say, we misunderestimate him at our peril. For just beneath that 'What, Me Worry?' grin, there burns the adamant, ill-shaven glare of Richard Nixon. Uncannily, the vengeful spirit of that most *un*likeable of presidents is back upon us once again – reincarnate in our hyper-chummy Chief Executive, who, TV keeps telling us, is *marvellously* 'likeable'.

By his own description 'a political animal' – or, in Mary Matalin's admiring phrase, a 'political campaign terrorist'* – Bush, like Nixon, has exactly what it takes to win elections at their dirtiest: a taste for blood, and a sharp sense of how to agitate his base (the right). He is also driven by ferocious tribal loyalty – a trait entirely missing from the loner Nixon, who had 'the soul of an alley cat', as William Rusher put it once. The feudal urge to glorify his clan, exalt his vassals and reward his friends has taken Bush a long, long way. Although bored stiff by governance, moreover, he is capable of SWAT-like focus in the war room. As Hatfield (alone among biographers) has pointed out, the first son exerted a great influence on the Bush/Quayle campaign in 1988, giving it his terroristic all. He

---

* 'He is not as ham-handed as the typical terrorist,' Matalin told Bill Minutaglio. 'He's much more of a stiletto as opposed to an ax murderer. He comes into a room, you know he's there.' Bill Minutaglio, *First Son: George W. Bush and the Bush Family Dynasty* (New York, 1999), p. 260.

joined the team to keep an eye on Lee Atwater, whose lowbrow antics – he appeared on the cover of *Esquire* with his pants down – had offended Mother Bush. Soon, however, young George was collaborating closely with the dirty trickster, working hard to give offense on a far grander scale. The two of them devised the tactics, then George would urge the necessary measures on his then-reluctant dad. 'He'll do positive things, but that's all,' Nixon had noted of the loyal George H. W. fifteen years before. The first son helped the candidate get past such inhibitions. It was he who got the elder Bush to go ballistic on Dan Rather in a live exchange on CBS, to stifle any further talk of Iran/contra, and to show off the candidate's king-sized *cojones* for the media-hating right (a gambit that restored the campaign's faltering momentum). Thus W aggressively exploited the old anti-telejournalistic animus of which Nixon was the first to take advantage through the medium of Spiro Agnew. It was also W who persuaded Dad to go along with the strategic smear of Jimmy Swaggart just two weeks before the South Carolina primary, where Swaggart's man Pat Robertson was threatening Bush's chances; Bush/Atwater leaked word of Swaggart's motel assignations to the local press (a covert op that saved the state for Bush Sr). And, crucially, it was W who ensured that the notorious – and effective – Willie Horton ads could be blamed plausibly on mavericks unaffiliated with the Bush campaign. The first son raised the money for those ads, and devised the cover operation that could then be said to have produced them on its own (a ruse that, to paraphrase our President, allowed Bush/Quayle to claim the high horse while taking the low road).[30]

While he has the sort of smarts required for work of that clandestine sort, our President has also long been sharp enough to keep his disparate warriors inside the GOP's big tent. This, too, is a Nixonian ability – although our President is actually much better at it, since the necessary schmoozing comes much easier to him than to his dad's uneasy mentor. It was the younger Bush who, in the eighties, made the peace between the Christian far-right and his Episcopalian father – no mean feat, since, as far as those believers were concerned, George Bush, with his membership in Skull and Bones and the Trilateral Commission, was about as worthy a Republican as Che Guevara.* As the man responsible for outreach to the Pentecostalists, the Southern Baptists and their brethren, W forged many bonds secure enough to see him through the last election, his victory throughout the largely rural states owing everything to that connection; and yet, even as he always talked the talk of Christian rectitude, Bush has also walked the walk of Wall Street, and in him the twain do meet. Thus he has shown the sort of coalition-building savvy that defined his idol, Ronald Reagan. As long as all the players are on the right, W can talk to 'em – as in Texas, where, as Governor, Bush *did* work with some Democrats, but where he did *not* work with any Democrats who weren't essentially Republicans. (There are quite a few such players in Texas politics.) Whoever can pull off such diplomatic coups cannot be half retarded, however comical his grammar.

Bush's link to Nixon is not merely temperamental, for his team has long included operatives who made their bones in Nixon's service. Lee Atwater was a Nixon acolyte (and devotee of both the Gipper and veteran segregationist Strom Thurmond) who transferred to the Bush machine in 1988, after having used Jew-baiting tactics to get Carroll Campbell

---

* That W. was able to stay tight with the Christian Coalition even after having worked to sink Pat Robertson (by smearing Jimmy Swaggart) is an indication of his rare adroitness.

into Congress. Likewise, there was Roger Ailes, who got his start in 1968 producing *Ask Richard Nixon!*, a series of canned TV forums that placed the candidate 'in the arena' with a hand-picked audience of grinning milquetoasts, and ended up coordinating Bush/Quayle's media drive, while coaching Bush on how to come off manly at the podium. (Ailes now runs Rupert Murdoch's Fox TV in the United States.) For his part, W was mentored by Atwater, whose early cohort, Karl Rove, has been with Bush the Younger from the start. Known to the inner circle as 'Turd Blossom' (the nickname came from Bush), the war-addicted Rove is just the sort of 'mean, tough son-of-a-bitch' whose dedication Nixon always craved: 'If you're not with Karl 100 percent, you're an enemy,' as Texas GOP chair Tom Pauken has marveled. From his early days as a dirty trickster for the College Republican National Committee in 1973 – stealing stationery, forging invitations to fictitious parties, sifting garbage for discarded memos, etc. – Rove went on to do his number for the Texan right (while also handling other clients, including Phillip Morris), working his black magic as required. Just hours before the one guber- natorial debate in 1986, Rove charged dramatically, and with no evidence, that he had found a hidden microphone in his office, and accused the incumbent, Democratic Governor Mark White, of having had it put there. (The campaign of Rove's boss, Republican Bill Clements, was in trouble.) Four years later, Rove made news again when it emerged that he'd been meeting privately with ultra-right FBI agent Greg Rampton, who had been supplying him with secret infor- mation on Agriculture Commissioner Jim Hightower. (Rove was working then for State Representative Rick Perry, who wanted Hightower's job.) Such Watergate-style operations have recurred since Rove began to work full-time for W. The crude attempt to tar the Gore campaign before the first debate (by anonymously mailing them a training video that only Bush, supposedly, was meant to see) appeared to be pure Rove – and certainly was vintage Nixon.[31]

So much for our President's Nixonian abilities and personnel. But *what* makes W run that way? It seems anomalous indeed that Richard Nixon – who 'went up the walls of life with his claws,' as Bryce Harlow once remarked – should have exerted such an influence on this or that George Bush, who, to quote Ann Richards, 'was born on third base, and thought he hit a triple'. The simple answer to this mystery is quite important, since it will help us understand exactly what we're living with today. Surprisingly, the large and very wealthy House of Bush, with its sterling fourteenth-century pedigree (the Queen of England is a distant cousin) and its decades of high influence on Wall Street, is driven by much the same resentment that compelled – and in the end destroyed – the threadbare Californian, son of Hannah and the loser Frank. That shared hostility explains the otherwise bizarre entanglement between the golden Poppy and the brazen Nixon, who evidently saw Bush as the son he'd never had: 'A total Nixon man – first,' he enthused, at the outset of his second term. 'Doubt if you can do better than Bush.' And yet the heart of Nixon beats more strongly in the breast of our new President, who lacks those dated scruples that he once had to talk his father out of honoring.[32]

The Bush resentment is more complicated than the plain class grudge that drove the under-privileged Nixon. Like him, they were angrily fixated on the Kennedys – not out of thwarted aspiration, certainly, but from dynastic envy, George the Elder having longed for years to transform Prescott, retroactively, into an American patriarch like Joe Kennedy: 'Just wait till I turn these Bush boys out,' he promised proudly, back when Jack was President.* Over the years after Camelot, the cult of JFK became more galling than inspiring, as it appeared to leave the Bush ménage forever in the shade, and grumbling tightly on the patio of their own mammoth seaside compound. Seeking to define themselves as somehow better than the competition, they took, preposterously, to trumpeting the family's modest origins, their frontier diligence and pluck – just like Nixon. 'While Kennedy was running for the Senate in 1952 with a healthy inheritance to back him,' wrote Bush friend Fitzhugh Green, in an early presidential hagiography, 'Bush was struggling to build his own bankroll,' a 'struggle' that in fact entailed much generous investment by the folks back home (primarily Bush's dad and uncle Herbie). Such invidious mythology loomed large in Poppy's presidential spectacle, what with the pork rinds and the cowboy boots, and the canny exploitation of his clumsy way with words ('I may not be eloquent,' etc.). And yet, while disavowing the Camelot mystique, Bush Sr – like Nixon – also tried at times to reproduce it, strongly echoing JFK in his own inaugural address (penned by Peggy Noonan, who as a girl had been 'in love with the Kennedys'), and even picking Dan Quayle as his running mate in part because he thought the

---

* Decades later, on the eve of the 1996 Republican convention, George Bush suddenly brought up the haunting model of Joe Kennedy, and pointedly dismissed it, a gratuitous outburst that betrayed how much the model really meant to him: 'It'd be wonderful' if his first son were ever to be President, he told a reporter. 'But it's not – I'm not like Joe Kennedy sitting there: "Here's a couple of hundred thousand – go out and win the West Virginia primary." I, you know, it's not a scheme. It's not a dynasty. It's not a legacy.' Given what would later happen down in Florida, the father's protest that 'it's not a scheme', and his reference to the elder Kennedy's theft of an election, stand out as obliquely, and suspiciously, prophetic.

Indianan's youthfulness would call Jack Kennedy to mind. (He was wrong.)*[33]

Worked up by their lesser status as a rival house, the Bushes, once they'd settled down in dusty Midland, also found themselves offended by the high disdain that many Eastern liberals felt toward Texas. Unlike Nixon, who never longed to go back where he had come from, the transplanted Bushes loved their adoptive neighborhood as they loved themselves; and that allegiance sharpened their Nixonian hostility toward sophisticated coastal types. Barbara writes of one telling face-off at a Georgetown dinner party in early 1968, when she and George had just moved to Washington for his first stint in Congress. Sitting next to her was some nostalgic Camelot survivor who kept taking shots at LBJ, then said, 'I hate all Texans.' When Barbara told him she was one, he said that she was obviously different, having grown up in the East. 'I said that he was right, but that he was talking about my children, who were lucky enough to be born Texans. I turned my back and never spoke to that whining, pompous man again.' With that, 'George and I crossed "inside Washington" dinners off our list.'[34]

Fed by his clan's imperial ambitions, and shaped by his

---

* In *George Bush: Man of Integrity* (1988), a family-sponsored propaganda volume meant to sell the Christian right on Bush's presidential bid, there is this revealing passage, at the start of Chapter 7, 'Family Comes First':

It is impossible to understand the Vice President outside the context of his own family. There is an electricity, a special magic, when Barbara and the children are nearby.

When all four boys recently appeared with their father on a morning television talk-show, the telephone lines lit up for hours. Some said that they were reminded of the Kennedys, that they had never seen so many young men in the same family so bright and handsome and personable.

George Bush with Doug Wead, *George Bush: Man of Integrity*, (Eugene, Oregon, 1988), p. 111.

experience as a very wealthy kid in segregated Texas, the eldest son could only come to hate the East, or any other precinct outside Nixon country. This had to do primarily with the sixties. Bush's time away from home – at Andover, then at Yale – was tolerable only insofar as he could replicate the sort of non-stop fun-time, and homogeneous companionship, that he had known when he was growing up in Midland. As head cheerleader at Andover, and then as president of Delta Kappa Epsilon, Yale's most drunken frat-house, and as a member of Yale's ultra-secret order Skull and Bones (like his dad), Bush had a ball. The currents of the time, however, were all against such puerile institutions – and, eventually, against his father, and against the President his father was now serving with that anomalous steadfastness. The elder Bush became a Nixon surrogate as soon as he joined Congress in 1968 – the year of the Tet offensive, the Chicago Seven, *Soul on Ice* and the *White Album*, to name just a few manifestations of the global trends that seemed to spell the end of everything that Nixon *and* the younger Bush had both believed in.

And yet there is, of course, a difference between Bush's anti-sixties beef and Nixon's. For the thirty-seventh President, as for millions of other Americans, the schisms and innovations of that decade were apocalyptic, threatening everything with mere destruction, and so requiring a defensive movement *back* toward that exclusive tidy Eden that 'we' enjoyed before the rise of Lyndon Johnson, Martin Luther King, the Beatles. 'The country – we turned away from the Great Society,' Nixon raved to Alexander Haig in May 1973. 'It turns away from an obsession about the blacks. And it's starting to turn away from the crime and drug syndrome, the dirty movies, etc. It turned away from, you know, the whole [unintelligible] peace thing. I mean, it turned a little character.'[35] The villains of the piece were not 'the blacks' *per se*, and not even the Communists, but all those affluent liberals who had made things go so wrong – the permissive parents and their snotty college kids, the pompous bleeding-hearts who let the reds and Negroes get away with murder, the pseudo-intellectuals with their big words and 'dirty movies'. Nixon's rage at that élite expressed, among other things, a class-based sense of grievance, piqued to fury by the spectacle, or thought, of privileged types who, even though they had it all, were blithely dumping on the values that had made this country great, and that he'd worked his whole life long to honor (or so he liked to think).

For George W. Bush, on the other hand, the sixties represented not a vast barbarian invasion but a pretty big impertinence. The turmoil was annoying to him largely for its threat of interference with his *faux*-aristocratic life of buddy rituals and heavy drinking; but he was most irked by the general disrespect for George Bush Sr, a famed alumnus whose support for Nixon and the war in Vietnam were naturally well known at Yale. Of course, it was also a matter of taste for young Bush, who didn't groove to *Sgt. Pepper* any more than Nixon did. ('The Beatles went through that kind of a weird, psychedelic period, which I particularly didn't care for,' confessed the Governor, who went on to have Wayne Newton help inaugurate him.) But it was all the somber questioning that most aggrieved him – the sudden vocal skepticism toward the wisdom of the Fathers, for their errors, or crimes, in Vietnam and on the ground at home. The younger Bush could not abide such anti-paternal sentiment, much less share it, since his own dad was (and still is) his guide in everything. 'There is an arrogance about some Ivy League connections that is bad,' the father wrote the son in 1974, referring to the student enemies of Richard Nixon. 'I saw an intellectual arrogance that I hope I never have,' said W in 1992, describing Yale precisely as his dad (and Nixon) did.[36]

That there was some 'arrogance' among the campus left is surely true (although far less so than in the White House at the time).* To thus write off that whole explosion of dissent, however, itself betrays a certain smugness, especially considering Bush's own frank lack of any intellectual *or* moral engagement in those painful years: 'I don't remember any kind of heaviness ruining my time at Yale.' To be that cavalier about the war, the global influence of US corporate power, the plight of blacks and the demands of 'women's liberation' was to be absurdly out of step – a careless Bourbon among Jacobins, Girondists, fretful moderates and active royalists. His own beloved dad was more affected by the issues of the day: Representative Bush voted, bravely, for the Civil Rights Act of 1968, with its 'open housing' provision (a stand that won him lots of hate mail from his native Houston); and, although a dedicated hawk, he took the protestors seriously, meeting with them often in DC, and even standing up for them before Republicans at home, pointing out the moral basis of the demonstrations, and reminding his constituents that 'we in Texas certainly can't stand to be without the right to dissent'. (That respectful view was very different from the absolute

---

* As a freshman, Bush was shaken by a rude encounter with Yale's liberal chaplain, William Sloane Coffin. It was shortly after George Bush (who had tapped Coffin for Skull and Bones in 1948) had lost the Texas senate race to Democrat Ralph Yarborough. The younger Bush asked Coffin what he thought about the contest: 'Oh, yes. I know your father. Frankly, he was beaten by a better man,' the chaplain said. Although Coffin claims to have no recollection of that cruel remark, it was by all accounts a shattering moment for the boy.

contempt that would pervade the Nixon White House.)* For his part, the son, through all his years in Jim Crow Texas, was never moved to take a stand on civil rights – unlike Joe Lieberman, Pat Schroeder, Edward Garvey, Barney Frank, Clinton, Gore and many other white members of the generation that our President has often deprecated for its selfishness. Nor did the younger Bush say anything, pro or con, about the war back then. His silence on the subject struck his brothers in the DKE house as remarkable, since he was not the silent type, and they were talking endlessly about it. He refused to sign an anti-war petition, but otherwise did nothing about Vietnam, other than to keep from going there by taking full advantage of that soft assignment to the Texas Air National Guard.[37]

Thus was all the era's idealism quite lost on our President, who staggered through that fiery epoch partying and making good connections. (When they first saw *Animal House*, some of Bush's college pals were struck by his strong undergraduate resemblance to the woozy, boozy 'Bluto', played by John Belushi.) The chaos and the disrespectfulness he noticed, and deplored, while simply tuning out the grand utopian impulse that was throbbing everywhere. Indeed, his only impulse *vis-à-vis* 'the [unintelligible] peace movement' was – just like Nixon

---

* Roger Morris recalls the Nixon team's dismissiveness: '"Look," [they might have said], "these people in the streets are thoughtful, they may have *a point* about the war, it may behoove us to rethink some of our assumptions." They never did that. They thought [the demonstrators] were insubstantial and capricious, they thought it was basically a draft protest, they thought they were cowardly, they thought they were there for frivolous reasons . . . They just never took the protest seriously in an intellectual sense . . . And their disdain and their contempt for the anti-war movement was part of the defense mechanism for keeping them out . . . If you could dismiss them as a bunch of flukes and phonies and kids, you didn't really have to think seriously about what they were saying.' Quoted in Tom Wells, *The War Within: America's Battle over Vietnam* (Berkeley, 1994), p. 307.

– to *attack* it. For its 'arrogance' in challenging his own complacent views, and in dissing his beloved father, Bush became a surly and half-conscious sort of counter-revolutionary, who would ultimately work that grudge into his platform. This explains the basis of his own relationships with other bitter sons (and daughters) of the lower middle class – Nixon's spiritual children, whose hard alliance with the wealthy W is but the next step down from George the Elder's more ambivalent (and less destructive) partnership with Tricky Dick himself. Our President's most devoted operatives are those ex-kids who saw their parents' values spat on by the *haut-bourgeois* protesters of the sixties, and who are now still seething after all these years: the toxic Rove, mad Mary Matalin, and other livid shadow-boxers. Long ago Rove provided Bush, moreover, with some simple broadsides that enable the illusion of an intellectual basis for the anti-sixties fervor that impels the whole cabal: Myron Magnet's *The Dream and the Nightmare* and David Horowitz's *Destructive Generation*. Such screeds offer a veneer of sober doctrine (a very thin veneer, in Horowitz's case) for what is nothing more than a belated, and gratuitous, assault against the vanished counterculture – that is to say, an endless venting of self-righteous wrath *for its own sake*.

BULLY PULPIT

Such, after all, is Nixon's spiritual legacy: 'Study of revenge, immortal hate, / And courage never to submit or yield,' as Milton's Satan puts it. Our President's continuation of that legacy is manifest not only in his firm reliance on such implacable destroyers as Rove, Matalin and Horowitz, but – as this *Dyslexicon* makes clear – in his own language. Both in his gaffes and in his lucid statements, Bush consistently betrays the raging animus that also drove our thirty-seventh President, and that Nixon also tried, and failed, to keep concealed from public view.

While Nixon's rage is famous, Bush's boiling anger is (as of this writing) still known only to insiders, and to the readers of his best biographers. That anger was, in fact, his salient feature back when he was working in his dad's campaigns. As George Bush's self-styled 'loyalty enforcer', W took on the job of blowing up at those reporters who may have been, or seemed to be, 'unfair' in their coverage. He evidently did that job with zest, if not with much lucidity: 'You no good fucking son of a bitch, I will never fucking forget what you wrote!' he ranted at Al Hunt of the *Wall Street Journal*, who was sitting down to dinner in a Dallas restaurant with his wife, Judy Woodruff, and their four-year-old son. Such pique is not unusual, of course; Bobby Kennedy was also known to lose it, often, in defense of Jack. Bush's tantrum was unusual, however, for its complete irrationality. Hunt recalls that Bush was 'quite clearly lubricated', but this was, in itself, not so remarkable (although it was a year since Bush's famous pledge to give up drinking). More striking was the fact that Hunt had written nothing to offend George Bush. It was April 1987. In the most recent issue of the *Washingtonian*, Hunt was one of many journalists offering a forecast of the next year's presidential line-up: 'Kemp and Indiana Senator Richard Lugar against Hart and Robb' was all he wrote – an item whose exclusion of George Bush might seem offensive only to a mind unhinged by filial devotion. (The Vice President had not declared his candidacy yet.) 'This,' Hunt thought, 'is a guy who's got problems.'

Bush thus allowed his wrath to carry him away throughout

his father's presidential quests. ('I'm a warrior. I'm not very objective,' he confessed to Larry King in 1992.) By the time he ran against Ann Richards for the Texas governorship, however, Bush had learned to bite his tongue and smile, a deliberate feat of self-restraint that he terms 'feisting out'.* Considering how hot he burned within, it was an astonishing achievement – especially since the caustic Governor Richards went all-out to try to piss him off. (So amazed was Bush's cousin, Elsie Walker, at the sight of the contender calmly taking all those blows that she cabled her aunt Barbara: 'WHAT HAS ... WHAT DID HE DO?') Such self-discipline has so far served him well. Although he did at times get snappish during the campaign – especially at those moments when Al Gore ripped into him – he never flared up right on camera, as Nixon did. Taken all in all, however, his language gives the game away, almost as clearly as those tapes incriminated Nixon.[38]

For Bush, despite his many howlers, is *not* always inarticulate. There are, in fact, two kinds of speech at which he does quite well. First, he can be good at talking policy, albeit not at length. When he is entirely confident about his subject, and wholly comfortable with those around him, he can be just as clear and well informed as any other politician. He seemed to know what he was saying, for example, at his gubernatorial debate with Garry Mauro in 1998 (although he also came across as slightly nuts, jabbering as if on speed and violently listing to the side, eyes rolling skyward); and he did well at the little 'education forum' he chaired on C-SPAN during the

---

* 'It was, some people in Texas later said, an odd way of putting it – "*feisting out*" – something you might hear in the South when someone was talking about feisting curs, small mongrel dogs that could corner wild boars or snarl for hours at a squirrel they had sent up a tree.' Minutaglio, *First Son*, p. 229.

transition. That round-table was clearly modelled on the 'economic forum' that Clinton held in 1992, and Bush did suffer by comparison. He could not talk for very long, and often got so fidgety when others spoke that they got nervous. Still, the sight of him so ably nattering was rather a surprise, considering how incoherent and ill-at-ease he often is in other circumstances.

Second – and more commonly – Bush is almost always clear when he's speaking cruelly. For example, when his subject is the punitive infliction of great pain, there is no problem with his syntax, grammar or vocabulary, even if he happens to be lying. There was the sudden clarity of his aside, at the Winston-Salem face-off with Al Gore, on the fate of James Byrd's murderers in Texas, which the Governor brought up by way of a response to Gore's remarks about the need for hate-crimes legislation. 'You have a different view of that,' Jim Lehrer prompted him.

BUSH: No, I don't, really.

LEHRER: On hate-crimes laws?

BUSH: No. We've got one in Texas – and guess what? The three men who murdered James Byrd. Guess what's going to happen to them. They're going to be put to death. A jury found them guilty, and it's going to be hard to punish them any worse after they get put to death. And it's the right cause, so it's the right decision.

The speech stood out for its rare pithiness – and for the joyous leer with which the Governor made that statement (which was disingenuous as well as scary, since he had in fact opposed the hate-crimes law that James Byrd's family had wanted him to pass).* His bald pleasure at the prospect of those executions – a gleefulness so flagrant that he was asked about it at the next debate – had everything to do with the unwonted clarity of those remarks. Like all the rest of us, however well or badly educated, Bush can talk quite clearly on the subjects that most interest him: baseball, football, campaign tactics, putting men to death.

On the other hand, our President is extraordinarily tongue-tied when he's trying, off the cuff, to sound a note of idealism, magnanimity or – especially – compassion. For all the maudlin yammering about his 'heart', and his success at vending that Orwellian oxymoron 'compassionate conservatism', the higher sentiments – Judaeo-Christian or chivalric – are so completely foreign to his nature that he can't even express them in plain English, much less make them sound convincing. For example, minutes after his plain-spoken promise to despatch James Byrd's murderers, the Governor, in yet another move to play down gun control, said this about the need to get ourselves a kinder, gentler culture:

> '. . . Columbine spoke to a larger issue, and it's really a matter of culture. It's a culture that somewhere along the line we've

---

* The Governor displayed the same stone-heartedness in turning that petition down. Renee Mullins, James Byrd's daughter, travelled from Hawaii to Austin to ask Bush to approve the law. She was escorted by Diane Hardy-Garcia, Texas lobbyist for the Lesbian & Gay Political Caucus. 'According to Hardy-Garcia, who accompanied Mullins to the meeting, the governor seemed very uncomfortable. Mullins asked Bush why he opposed the bill, and he told her he hadn't read it. "She gave him a copy and he threw it on his desk," Hardy-Garcia said. Then she asked, "Will you help us?" He said, "No."

'She was crying, and he didn't try to console her or even offer her a Kleenex, Hardy-Garcia said. "He was cold, icy, to her."' Molly Ivins and Lou Dubose, *Shrub: The Short But Happy Political Life of George W. Bush* (New York, 2000), p. 100.

begun to disrespect life. Where, for a child can walk in [sic] and have their heart turn dark as a result of being on the Internet, and walk in and decide to take somebody else's life. And so gun laws are important, no question about it. But so is loving children and character-education classes and faith-based programs being a part of after-school programs. Somebody, some desperate child that needs to have somebody put their arm around him and say we love you and so there's a – this is a society of ours that's got to do a better job of teaching children right from wrong. And we can enforce law, but there seems to be a lot of preoccupation on, not necessarily in this debate, but just in general in law, but there's a larger law [sic]: Love your neighbor like you'd like to be loved yourself. And that's where our society must head if we're going to be a peaceful and prosperous society.'

While he speaks pure gibberish when he tries to *care*, Bush is clear not only when he's frankly brutal, but also in his jokes (which aren't exactly kind). The President does boast a certain ready wit, but has a hard time flexing it on stage, unless he trusts the audience. At his ease – or in his cups – the guy can be a riot. For example, there's a website (thesmokinggun.com) that features sixty seconds of a 1992 wedding video, which shows Bush, 'quite clearly lubricated', ad-libbing a deadpan mock-testimonial to the happy couple, as the interviewer, some other wedding guest, cracks up at the insulting spiel. What's most interesting about the tape is not his drinking (although it was now six years since his pledge to give that up), but his offbeat and sardonic putdown humor. You can see from that surprising bit (which, as of this writing, no one from the mainstream press has ever mentioned) why Bush was always such a hit at frat parties, and finally made it as a politician.

His humor has an edge to it; and always has, reportedly. As a child, Bush was a relentless tease, and then went on to other funny places. At Andover – where he was nicknamed 'Lip' – the drollery of choice was sarcasm, which the future Chief Executive wielded with unusual frankness. 'He would call people names, derogatory nicknames,' one classmate recalls. 'Other people would use them behind people's backs, but he was more open about it.'[39] During the campaign, Rove and Co. spun that habit as another sign of Bush's natural ease with all folks great and small; but in fact that teasing edge connects with something truly nasty in the President's sense of humor. There is, of course, his snickering mockery of Karla Fay Tucker's final plea for life – the sort of joke that she herself would probably have enjoyed, back when she was killing folks with pickaxes. Although his other public jests have not been quite as shocking as that one, his humor often tends toward the sadistic, seeking chuckles in the most unlikely situations – David Letterman's heart surgery, the slaughter of animals, the Russians massacring Chechnyan women and children, the perdition of the Jews, etc. (See 'The Wit and Humor of George W. Bush'.) The candidate once claimed that his taste for laughs reflects his interest in 'the lighter side of life', but that *Reader's Digest* way of putting it does not do justice to the man's peculiar wit, which smacks of very different magazines.

Bush has often protested that we cannot see or judge what's in his 'heart', and he gets testy when observers try. Like his father – and, indeed, like Nixon – he abhors psychologizing, often using 'psychobabble' as a term of grim opprobrium. (He abhors such treatment of himself, but not of others: John Rocker's mandatory 'counselling' didn't bother him a bit: see 'Freedom of Expression'.) However, it takes no Freudian speculation to perceive that there's a bit of darkness in that famous heart of his, as we can tell not only from his language, but from the grisly bits of his biography. As a lad in Midland, for instance, George and all his little pals had fun despatching frogs, shooting them with BB guns and stuffing lit firecrackers into them. ('It was gruesome,' one chum reminisces.) Of course, boys will be boys, and maybe it's a Texan sort of boy thing to kill harmless amphibians. (One local biddy often felt compelled to preach the virtues of St Francis to those children, urging them to join the ASPCA.)* But Bush was a boy no longer when, as president of DKE, he went public in defense of the fraternity's sadomasochistic hazing rituals, which included branding each initiate just above and in between the buttocks with the red-hot tip of a wire coat-hanger. The on-campus stir over such practices inspired some coverage in the *New York Times*, which quoted the young Bush as pointing out dismissively that 'the resulting wound is "only a cigarette burn"'.[40]

Such biographical details confirm the rather kinky picture that we also get from Bush's language, his fuzzy discourse snapping into focus at the gratifying thought of someone else's punishment. ('We added beds./We're tough!/We believe in tough love!' he crowed poetically in Winston-Salem, referring to the expansion of Texas's prisons.) The point here is not to hint at as-yet-undiscovered sins. Some day there may be tawdry news about this President's private life, or, of course, there may be none. Such revelation is forever likely in the culture of TV.

---

* 'In west Midland there was always a gaggle of children, usually led by George W., a knot of kids rolling from one house to the other, patiently enduring the no-cruelty-to-animals lectures when they were summoned to the home of the elderly, childless neighborhood fixture whose husband ran the Honolulu Oil Corporation: *Now, children, we must respect all living creatures.*' Minutaglio, *First Son* pp. 38–39. (Emphasis in original).

For our purposes, what matters is the evidence, in Bush's language (and life story), of a rage that *will* keep coming out, no matter how ingeniously he tries to mask it, either with religious turns of phrase, or with pacific promises of 'unity' or 'healing'. That inner wrath is what we'll see, and what we'll hear, despite its endless efforts to conceal itself. Thus the Bush team's showy gestures of conciliation always ended up exploded utterly, and pretty quickly: 'I'm a uniter, not a divider', a reassurance not convincing to begin with, turned into an easy punchline from the morning of 8 November, as all Bush/Cheney's mighty propaganda forces started working overtime to demonize Al Gore, and all his fellow-Democrats, and everyone who voted for him (or who tried to vote for him). Likewise, on 13 December, Bush grandly vowed a spirit of 'reconciliation and unity', promising to be the President of *all* the people, when he made his first acceptance speech – a pledge he quickly followed up by nominating the fanatic John Ashcroft to be Attorney General, and James Watt's protégée Gale Norton to be Secretary of the Interior. Throughout the transition, meanwhile, Bush continued taking shots at the departing team, as if the race had not been settled in his favor. But when he took the national spotlight yet again on 20 January 2001, yet again he hailed 'our unity, our union', giving his 'solemn pledge' to 'work to build a single nation of justice and opportunity', etc. (That day, Karl Rove grinningly announced 'the return of civility and respect'.) And then, as if he'd never made that pitch for 'unity', his team continued hunkering down, working just as hard as ever for an ultra-rightist victory, smearing every effort to find out the truth in Florida, and other-wise pursuing the *attack* – which, finally, is the only thing they really want to do. And that, of course, was also Nixon's way. On the night he won in 1968, he, too, postured as an altruistic mediator – pledging solemnly to 'bring us together' – while also longing to take care of 'them' once and for all.

ON MESSAGE

However, there is one crucial difference between Bush's show and Richard Nixon's. Back then, the President's hypocrisy, while dimly apprehensible to the untrusting audience, did not become explicit until Watergate, which finally made his falseness unmistakable to all – even his most fervent champions. (Trent Lott was an exception.) By contrast, this President's hypocrisy is so apparent that, when he says things like 'unity', 'bipartisan' and 'reconciliation', he might as well have on a sandwich board that says, 'I'M TALKING BULLSHIT.' The same was true of the whole rightist propaganda mill that ran the country ragged following Election Day. Its bad faith was so blatant, and the propaganda so pervasive, that you couldn't *not* notice the hypocrisy – unless you were a part of it, in which case you believed that the hypocrisy was wholly on the other side. Thus it is, of course, with all hermetic propaganda systems, be they democratic or authoritarian. Indeed, that big, loud network of Republicans – shifting ground from one hour to the next, bitterly attacking principles that they had just now bitterly defended, and screaming at the Democrats for doing things that they themselves had done, or were about to do – behaved exactly like their erstwhile enemies in Moscow (and New York), executing endless swift volte-faces to toe the party line.

Thus we had the GOP – the long-time bastion of 'states' rights' – now demanding, then defending, the use of federal power to overturn a ruling by the high court of the state of Florida. The party that had long decried – and was *even now* decrying – 'judicial activism' was also gratefully applauding the Supreme Court's highly activist decision itself to elect the nation's President. The party that was *even now* decrying judicial interference with the legislative branch was also now applauding the Supreme Court for having halted a state recount on the grounds that there was 'no clear standard' for the process – when the standard had been written by the Florida legislature. The party that was vehemently arguing that hand recounts are wholly unreliable and absolutely not to be allowed was *at the same time* calling for hand recounts in New Mexico, and was supporting, as its leader, the very man who had approved the passage of a Texas law permitting hand recounts in close elections. The party that had just pulled off a massive keep-out-the-vote campaign in Florida's (and Tennessee's) most heavily Democratic precincts, disenfranchising tens of thousands of black, poor white and Hispanic voters, now hailed the Supreme Court's decision to abort the recount under the equal protection clause in the Constitution. And even as they frantically demanded, then defended, all those shifts and gimmicks, the Republicans assailed Al Gore as one 'who would do anything to get elected', and the Democrats as fiendishly intent on making some historic 'mischief'.

Such flagrancy was quite a shock – a show of overt, unapologetic propaganda that was certainly unprecedented in our history. And yet the weird transparency of that manipulative drive was not entirely new; for the candidate, in his own laid-back way, had always been transparent in *his* daily propaganda effort; and when he talks to us as President, he is transparent still. In short, his public speech has always blandly advertised the fact that it *is* propaganda, this insincere and incoherent politician selling us by telling us how hard he works at selling us – as if he merits our support exclusively because of what a first-rate job he's done at acting like he merits our support. Thus he spoke at the beginning of the race. 'So it should be gruelling?' Larry King asked him. 'Yes, it should be gruelling,' he replied: 'I'm not so sure length necessarily equates to gruelling, but it should be a tough process. You need to be scrutinized and questioned. There needs to be debates, like we're going through. There needs to be town-hall meetings. There needs to be travel. This is a huge country. And a candidate's got to be able to travel the country with a consistent message that rallies people for a better tomorrow.'

As a statement of political intention, that bit was, typically, as empty as it was illiterate. As a simple overview of the most effective propaganda practice, on the other hand, it made some sense, since it is sadly true that, to get elected in the culture of TV, 'a candidate's got to be able to travel the country with a consistent message that rallies people for a better tomorrow', and that's about it. That thin truism won't take us very far. What *else* should a candidate 'be able' to do, aside from fly from state to state and say the same thing every day? Can a 'message' that 'consistent' really tell us anything? And how can our 'tomorrow' be any 'better' than today, if we're all out there getting 'rallied' – hypnotized by buzzwords and catch-phrases?

Bush never ceased to push his message, or to keep us posted on how it was going. After the controversy over his appearance at Bob Jones University, he thought about the implications of his having worked that hateful room, and realized the error of his ways – he hadn't sent the proper message. 'I readily concede I missed an opportunity at Bob Jones; I [could] have been a hero,' he said in March. 'If I had gone down there and said, "We're all God's children; we can receive redemption in all different kinds of ways; the Catholic religion is a great religion, Judaism is a great religion," it's all I would have needed to have said. One sentence.' Things eased up by the summer, when he looked forward to the big event in Philadelphia, and to the upbeat message that the show would send the audience, if all went well: 'The convention is important because it gives a sense of who I am, and I think if we do our job right, to lead our party and lead the country, I think what you are going to find is that this is going to be a convention that spells out what we're for,' he told Fox-TV's Carl Cameron, who seemed to understand that statement. At the debates, Bush did a fairly good job staying on message, even though that pushy know-it-all did kind of rattle him. From time to time he managed to highlight a 'theme'. Explaining, at the third debate, why he is 'absolutely opposed to a national health care plan', he told us this: 'I trust people. I don't trust the federal government. It's going to be one of the themes you hear tonight. I don't want the federal government making decisions on behalf of everybody.'

That last one was a pip, considering the 'trust' that Bush's operation ultimately showed in 'people' over 'government'. In retrospect, it's all too obvious that that 'consistent message' was completely false – a pseudo-PC circus meant to mask the true intentions of a deeply anti-democratic movement. He has 'opposed . . . a national health care plan' not out of a populist concern for individual freedom, but because he's resting comfortably inside the pocket of Insurance. The 'message' of the GOP convention was no less deceptive: a prime-time picture of 'inclusiveness', with many folks of color at the podium (albeit very few out on the floor) and lots of eager music black and brown, making for an antiseptic mini-series that could have been entitled, *It Takes a Potemkin Village*. This from the party of Strom Thurmond, Jesse Helms and Bob Barr, a party managed by Trent Lott and Tom DeLay, and dedicated to the proposition that all men of color were created for the slammer.

If Bush was ever troubled by the gap between his democratic 'message' and the hard élitist interests backing him, it was because his 'message' hadn't been illusory *enough*. He'd 'have been a hero' after speaking at Bob Jones, if he had only had the foresight to have Rove or Karen Hughes cook up 'one sentence' for the cameras – just a quick I'd-like-to-give-the-world-a-Coke type sentiment, and he would have been a Visionary. Of course, the school itself would still have been the place it was: a fortress of medieval bigotry, and – worse – a crucible of just the sort of theocratic ideology that drove the forces of Team Bush, however bright and tolerant his 'message'. (For more on Bush's 'message', see 'Message: I'm Real'.)

And yet it almost seems a waste of time to set the record straight like this, because the candidate was always so disarmingly upfront about the crafting of his misimpressions. He tended not so much to say that he *believed* in this or that, as to make clear to us that this or that would be, or was, his 'theme' or 'message'. The actual point of all such propaganda – the matter that we now call 'substance' – comes up only as an afterthought, if it comes up at all: 'Well, there'll be a health care debate, and there'll be a health care issue that I'm going to – I mean, a health care speech and policy that I lay out. I talk about health care all the time at these one-on-ones when asked. It's on people's minds.'

WHAT YOU SEE IS WHAT YOU GET

If Bush had won legitimately, we could say that we'd got the President we deserve. His 'message' having played well on TV, and the audience having picked him by a clear majority (both electoral *and* popular), he would be the people's choice, and there would be no ambiguity about it. But the situation now is highly complicated – and not just because of the shenanigans in Florida and on the Supreme Court. For Bush owes his unlikely victory not only to those party spinmasters and goons who forced the issue, nor only to the Rehnquist Five, but also to TV. Although he never played well on the medium *per se*, TV was very, very good to him; because the network that controls the medium, from above, and from the anchor-desks and pundit-chairs, embraced him, and implicitly endorsed him, for several reasons.

First of all, there is the great extrinsic factor of the media's corporate ownership, the top managers and major shareholders preferring the aggressively big-merger-friendly GOP to the less-aggressively big-merger-friendly Democrats. Al Gore had many champions in Hollywood, of course, including all the top pro-Clinton heavyweights from Michael Eisner on down. A tough New Democrat somewhat to Clinton's right, Gore was never threatening to the interests of the corporate media, for all his pulpit-thumping with Joe Lieberman. (Indeed, even Rupert Murdoch was a quiet Gore supporter, the Democrats having used the Staples Center – 40 percent-owned by News Corporation – as a gift for their convention.)*[41] Nevertheless, the media's parent companies will do much better, and clean up much faster, now that they have Bush to play with, since he's for corporate concentration above all (literally), nor will his

---

* After the election, Gore taught a course at the Columbia School of Journalism. For the class on 28 February, which he devoted to the ills of media concentration, Gore recruited Murdoch as guest lecturer. The blunt Australian – who had prepped himself, in part, by reading some of my own writings on the subject – assured the students that the current corporate domination of the media is not a problem. With something like sincerity, he also boasted of the 'objectivity' of Fox News – an odd assertion, what with Al Gore sitting there beside him.

FCC – now chaired by Colin Powell's son Michael, an adamant free-marketeer – discuss even the feeblest sort of regulation, whereas his predecessor, Bill Kennard, did try now and then. (Under Bush, we will soon see the final merger of newspaper chains with media corporations, a move that Gore would not have made without a lot of prior shilly-shallying.) The media-corporate bias toward the Governor was evident, for example, in MSNBC's decision to show repeatedly, throughout the five-week civil war in Florida, its dubious Hail-Caesar documentary on Desert Storm – an obvious stroke of pro-Bush programming, certainly approved, if not dictated, by the network's corporate Dad and Mom: General Electric (a huge defense contractor, likely to do well from 'missile defense') and Microsoft (whose anti-trust woes Governor Bush did not approve of, and will surely end).

Certainly such bias at the top does not translate directly into bias right on camera. The influence is, for the most part, atmospheric rather than direct, the smartest, most ambitious employees inferring how the wind blows from on high, and suiting up accordingly. This is true of all large corporations (including universities), but such impact is especially momentous in the culture industries, from which we tend to garner all we know about the world. In TV's case, the problem is compounded by the rightist conquest of the news divisions – a sweep that Nixon long ago envisioned, and took some steps to realize, bullying the networks into mere cheerleading. ('ABC and CBS have improved considerably over the past couple of months since my visit with them,' Chuck Colson reported to Bob Haldeman in late 1970.)[42] The system once assailed by Spiro Agnew (his tirades penned by William Safire and Pat Buchanan) as pro-Red is now solidly right-wing, its frequent talking heads including Ollie North, Bob Novak, Peggy Noonan, William

Bennett, George Will, Tucker Carlson of the *Weekly Standard*, Rich Lowry of the *National Review*, Alan Simpson, William Kristol, John Sununu, Paul Gigot, Ed Rollins, David Frum, David Brooks, Linda Chavez, Andrew Sullivan, John McLaughlin, Tony Blankley, Armstrong Williams, John Reilly and the whole prime-time ménage at Fox, John Fund of the *Wall Street Journal*, *Time*'s paranoid Hugh Sidey and Reagan Democrat Chris Matthews. (Mary Matalin has gone back to work directly for the Bush machine.) Opposing that dark legion are a few wan pseudo-liberals, like Bob Beckel and Bill Press, some genuine articles like Eleanor Clift, Mark Shields, Joe Conason and Robert Reich and, here and there, some genuine – and very lonely – person of the left, such as Katrina van den Heuvel of the *Nation*, the provocative Christopher Hitchens, Jim Hightower, and (on weekends) Jeff Cohen. Otherwise, TV's punditocracy (like radio's, and like the brain trust in the think tanks) is firmly on the right – i.e., *not* conservative, but *radical* in its support for private privilege and, to some extent, a theocratic state.

Always well armed with Bush/Cheney's talking points, that chorus worked efficiently to change the subject when the Governor's incapacities came up (which was not often). And their canned views were generally seconded by those nervous nellies who worked with them – the anchors and reporters who, although not necessarily on the right themselves, could not afford to seem unsympathetic. Certainly the national press corps in DC is, on economic matters, largely to the right of the American majority (a fact documented by Fairness and Accuracy in Reporting), because those members of the Fourth Estate are in some pretty high tax brackets, and would therefore benefit from a return to Reaganomics.[43] And yet even the moderates and liberals of the press deferred to the pro-Bush consensus, for their careers depend on such compliance. What mainly drives them is a general fear of seeming 'liberal', as countless rightists (many of them *in* the media) have long been charging, notwithstanding the abundant counter-evidence, from TV's long love affair with Ronald Reagan, to the coverage of the 1988 campaign, to the news divisions' loud huzzahs for Operation Desert Storm, to the journalistic drives to make 'Whitewater', 'Filegate', 'Travelgate' and 'Chinagate' look like genuine stories and not propaganda fabrications. The media's refusal, during the recent coup, to call a spade a spade reflected the anxiety of those professionals, who all keep bending over backward not to be accused of 'liberal bias.'* Such a tag would be a killer in the corporate news biz, since it would mean that you'd have no more *access* to those Inside Players who tell you what the news should be.

And yet there is another, deeper reason for TV's support of Governor Bush. On the one hand, as we have noted here, he is himself not telegenic, unless his turns are very tightly choreographed, and he sticks closely to his script and shows no tension or bewilderment. It is worth noting here that Bush's incapacity is so apparent that it was conceded, gently, by his own supporters, once he had the job sewn up. 'He has made sure that he has a high-powered team around him to make up for any deficiencies, though I'm not saying he has big deficiencies,' said the GOP's Robert Michel *vis-à-vis* the President-select's

---

* The media's marked deference to the Bush team following Election Day was also an expression of mere arrogance. In many instances, the power exerted by the telestars has gone straight to their heads – a self-regard that has, of course, been heightened by their whopping salaries. Such conceit may help explain the quickness of Tim Russert and Chris Matthews, among others, to instruct Al Gore to pack it in, even though the ballots were still being counted. In an editorial, the *New York Times* gave Gore the same premature advice, for whatever reasons.

impending cabinet. And William Safire, in a piece on the relationship between Donald Rumsfeld at Defense and Colin Powell at State, offered this not-comforting conclusion: 'What happens in those crises when State and Defense disagree? Bush can consult Dick Cheney or get George Shultz on the phone or, in due course, trust his own judgment.'[44]

And yet while Bush *per se* plays badly on the medium, the TV system as we know it is his natural ally, because both it and he are all about mere 'message'. Both of them are all *about* TV, and nothing else. This is nothing new for him, a calculating sort from way, way back, but on TV it was not ever thus. For many years – indeed, from McLuhan's day – both observers and practitioners of campaign propaganda entertained the question of exactly where to find the proper balance between word and image, argument and spectacle, issue and impression. The comfortable assumption was that those two categories were entirely separate, fixed, alike resilient and both perfectly amenable to expert handling by the news professionals, who, if they were sober, civic-minded and meticulous enough, could strike the crucial balance, and so at once instruct and entertain their audience.

But now there is very little place for 'substance' – or, indeed, for any rational discourse – on TV (or, indeed, throughout the other large commercial media), for formal, political and economic reasons. As the networks have developed it, the medium is far too speedy, loud, disjunctive and sensational to permit even the resonance, much less the discussion, of a complex sentence, much less an idea. The heavy pressure of the advertisers, furthermore, forbids the airing of whatever issues might be either too depressing or too complicated (or too threatening) for the venue's crucial atmosphere of light festivity – a non-stop pseudo-carnival that never can slow down, or else someone might lose money. Into this tightly regulated riot of commercial propaganda every politician has to fit his/her own propaganda 'message' – and, if s/he's lucky, also has to fit him- or her*self*, looking 'nice' enough (with just the right amount of Self-Effacing Humor) and sounding 'clear' enough (without alarming anyone) to keep from standing out as 'stiff', 'robotic', 'wooden' or in any other way ridiculous. With such smooth integration all 'political' success has everything to do – which, by and large, leaves out telling truth, or making sense.

Thus Bush belongs here in the culture of TV. He fits in, not despite his open calculation and the utter superficiality of his (overt) concerns, but because of them. Such defects don't disturb the pundits of today, most of whom, whatever medium they work in, cannot even see what's wrong with Bush, so steeped are they themselves in TV's trivial world-view. Our President's most calculating predecessors weren't so lucky, their over-concentration on mere spin arousing strong objections back in those less TV-saturated days.

For example, Emmett John Hughes, one of Eisenhower's top assistants, was blown away by Nixon's straining effort to project a natural identity. Hughes quotes from Nixon's own account, in *Six Crises*, of his resolution following the first debate with JFK: 'I went into the second debate *determined* to do my best to *convey . . . sincerity . . .* If I succeeded in this, I felt my "image" would take care of itself.' Hughes (who added those italics) found the contradiction there amazing, and yet typical: 'Only the most shallow exercise in self-scrutiny could conclude with such a resolve to appear "sincere". Yet it was characteristic of the candidate, the politician, and the man.' Like his mentor, George H. W. Bush conceived 'sincerity' as a performance. 'I can't be as good as Ronald Reagan on conviction,' he confessed, during the 1988 campaign. 'There's nobody like him at conveying what it is like to strongly feel patriotism and love of country.' Such ingenuous theatricality marked much of that failed President's public speech, just as it marks his son's – a self-reflexiveness that many journalists noted at the time. 'Bush is always telling you how to look at what he is doing, or what the impression is that he is trying to create,' Meg Greenfield wrote in *Newsweek* back when George I was king. That tendency got lots of laughs when Bush, in the middle of a campaign speech in New Hampshire, accidentally read one of his stage directions: 'Message: I care.' And yet he did that all the time, and quite deliberately: 'We have – I have – want to be positioned in that I could not possibly support David Duke, because of the racism and because of the bigotry and all of this.' Such dim transparency amounted almost to a kind of honesty, as Michael Kinsley wrote in 1992: 'What these tics share is a clear view of the mind at work. Bush's mental processes lie close to the surface.'[45]

As do our Presidents, this Bush also endlessly explaining what the 'theme' or 'message' is – but in the new millennium our journalists don't seem to notice it. While Bush's comic flubs did get some press, his constant commentary on his own self-presentation raised no qualms or questions. 'I think probably the best thing I've done is interface with the press,' he told *Brill's Content* in September 2000. 'They get to see the human – that I'm a human person, that I've got feelings, I care, I've got priorities. It gives them a better sense of who I am as a person . . . I think the more somebody gets to know a person the more likely it is they'll be able to write an objective story.' The entire interview went like that, the candidate discoursing at great length on what a dandy job he had been doing keeping the whole press corps off the subjects of his record, his sponsors, his affiliations and his ultimate intentions – and the *Brill's* reporter, Seth Mnookin, played right along, asking Bush no question that might spoil the mood of chummy candor. As any journalist should know, 'the more somebody gets to know a person' the *less* likely it is that he or she will write objectively about him. If Mnookin had been listening to the candidate instead of watching him, he might have asked Bush to explain the meaning of 'objectively' or, for that matter, what his 'feelings' really had to do with anything, or what he meant by that all-too-familiar 'message', 'I care'.

By now, the mainstream press has quite forgotten the important differences between what's on TV and (what we might call) reality. Instead of trying to interrogate the photo op, asking what it *isn't* saying or how it's fiddling with the truth, the journalists – or those who have been granted the appropriate credentials – often actively *collaborate* with those who set the picture up, so as to help the audience discern the proper 'theme'. When Bush presented certain choices for his cabinet, a reporter asked him, helpfully, if his 'diverse' selection might not indicate 'a message that you're sending to America'. 'You bet,' replied the President-select, without missing a beat: 'That people who work hard and make the right decisions in life can achieve anything they want in America.' At another such unveiling two weeks later, Bush was once again helped out by a reporter: 'You've now named a cabinet that is very diverse in terms of gender and ethnicity and experience in the private sector and the federal government. What does your cabinet say, do you think, about your management style, about how you intend to make decisions as President?' 'It says I'm not afraid to surround myself with strong and competent people,' Bush shot back, and then expanded on that 'theme' by adding that he knows 'how to recruit people and how to delegate, how to align authority and responsibility, how to hold people accountable for results and how to build a team of people'. It was a memorable lesson, which Bush concluded with a stirring pledge: 'And that's exactly what we're going to do.'

The journalists' collusion has extended well beyond such servile prompting. On TV itself, the eternal 'expert' nattering on 'politics' deals mainly, and often exclusively, with what some still call 'image', but what is really just TV. TV's journalistic stars go on and on and on about the politicians' failure or success at pleasing, or at not displeasing, TV's viewers. Reflexive and impressionistic, such interminable yakking tells us nothing, dwelling on details of bearing, posture, makeup, voice instead of on what anybody did, or said, or failed to say. And yet such discourse is not merely empty. By reducing all discussion to the level of the taste test, wherein 'likeability' is all that counts, it tacitly discredits all intelligent discussion, while favoring those figures who can rile us without challenging or (as it were) taxing us. In other words, it is not just TV itself that works against the rational position, but those never-ending propagandists *on* TV who *tell* us who is 'likeable' and who is not. That influence will work on those inclined already to agree with it, especially when it manages to get in the last word.

Thus TV functioned after each of the debates. On CNN, for example, after the third encounter on 17 October, far-right motor-mouth Bob Novak got the ball rolling by suggesting that 'there might have been a defeat for Gore on the likeability factor. I haven't seen all the numbers, but I understand he didn't do well on credibility or likeability.' Of course, the wish was father to that thought, as Novak is among the steeliest of commandos, saying nothing that will not advance the Cause (cutting taxes). From there Jeff Greenfield took the ball and ran a long way with it, wondering whether 'Gore's clear decision to be aggressive, to try to define very sharp differences' might make him seem 'assertive and tough-minded' or 'rude and smug' – although 'we're going to have to wait forty-eight hours or so to find out'. He then moved on to Bush, who 'clearly was trying to stage a conversation with both the people here and to [*sic*] the country, and, in effect, to say: "Look, I'm a regular, soft-spoken guy. And Al Gore just wants this too much,"' *Time*'s Tamala Edwards then weighed in: Gore had learned the 'lesson' that he can't 'out-soften George Bush on compassion and talking about his heart', and therefore worked, this time, to 'strike a contrast'. She seemed, however, to differ with Bob Novak: 'In this forum, where he was answering questions and being that aggressive, it will be interesting to see whether or not it plays as [if] he was a little terrier running out and trying to answer this person's question, vs. standing back and saying: "You know, let me talk down to you."' Bill Schneider then talked for what seemed like a week, about a snap poll CNN had done just then. Novak summed up: 'I don't think it's a win for Al Gore,' and as to Bush: 'I don't think that Governor Bush is very good in this kind of a format . . . But I don't think he hurt himself.'

That Novak would admit that much about the Governor's inane performance confirms how bad it really was. Bush was vague on the details of his own voucher plan, his own position on the patient's bill of rights, and on affirmative action, among other issues, while Gore was certain, and relentless. It was at that third debate that Bush's various evasive tactics were most blatant – crying out that he was being attacked, using ancient lines that didn't answer ('Well, you know, it's hard to make people love one another; I wish I knew the law, because I'd darn sure sign it,' he said, on making schools accountable), and at one point even had to have Jim Lehrer rescue him from Gore's persistent inquisition. Nevertheless, the 'analysts' at CNN said not one word about the *substance* of the candidates' exchange, but just kept harping on the general 'statements' that the candidates were putatively 'trying' to make about themselves, through their tone and body language.

Although a waste of time, that post-debate bull session was at least not strongly biased, nor was its anti-intellectualism too pronounced. On ABC, there was a far more noxious session on the subject of that third debate. We will do well to reproduce that episode in its entirety, because it captures perfectly the barbarous synergy between the right and TV news, each feigning populism for its own élitist purposes. It took place two weeks before Election Day, on the 22 October broadcast of *This Week*, with Sam Donaldson and Cokie Roberts, joined by George Will and George Stephanopoulos. The topic was the Dingell-Norwood bill, which would provide a patient's bill of rights, including the right to sue your Health Maintenance Organization. In the debate, Bush had claimed to be in favor of a patient's bill of rights, and Gore then challenged him to say if he would back that piece of legislation.

DONALDSON: Well, talk about the message. I mean, remember during the last debate, Gore kept talking about 'the Dingell/Norwood bill, the Dingell/Norwood bill.' And we thought, as a public service, we'd just show you who Dingell and Norwood are. Let us tell you about them. Representatives Dingell and Norwood introduced the Patient's Bill of Rights favored by Gore and the House of Representatives. John Dingell, from Michigan, is the longest-serving Democrat in the House. His father, who was a House member before him, was a sponsor of Social Security in the thirties, and pioneered the idea of national health insurance back in 1943. Charlie Norwood, from

Georgia, a Republican, is a dentist. He served in Vietnam and was first elected to the House in 1994 as part of the Republican revolution.

So that's who Dingell and Norwood are. Now I'll tell you—

STEPHANOPOULOS: But the important—

ROBERTS: Yeah, but—

DONALDSON: But there's a guy named Greg Ganske who's also on the bill. It's actually the Dingell/Norwood/*Ganske* bill!

STEPHANOPOULOS: But the import – the *important* point—

DONALDSON: But I don't have time to start telling you about him!

ROBERTS: He's from Iowa!

STEPHANOPOULOS: The important point there is that George Bush didn't answer the question about the Dingell/Norwood bill, which is a patient's bill of rights that allows people to – the right to sue.

ROBERTS: Actually, I don't think that *is* the important point there.

STEPHANOPOULOS: Why not?

ROBERTS: Because that's not what comes across when you're watching the debate. What comes across when you're watching the debate is this guy from *Washington* doing *Washington-speak*.

STEPHANOPOULOS: But it's—

ROBERTS: And you know, it's having an effect not just at the presidential level, but at the congressional level as well.

Because the Republicans did a very smart thing, which is that they voted for *their* version of a patient's bill of rights, and they voted for *their* version of prescription drug coverage. So they get to go out and tout all these issues, and then the Democrats are left saying, 'But you didn't do *Dingell* and *Norwood*!'

STEPHANOPOULOS: Well, then they – but what gets lost there – wait a second, what gets *lost* there is that George Bush *did* oppose a patient's bill of rights in the state of Texas. And he did – and he's *not* for the Dingell/Norwood bill.

ROBERTS: It was lost because Al Gore didn't *say* it.

STEPHANOPOULOS: Yeah, well, he did say it, actually, in the course of the debate.

DONALDSON: This is very cerebral. George Will, you are, but it doesn't be – helping Gore [*sic*].

WILL: It's not helping Gore in part because people find him overbearing and off-putting and all the rest. But also the fact – I think the issues are beginning to break, finally, for George W. Bush. The reports in the papers are that – that Gore is going to stress social security from now on. I think he's going to find that when p– I'm surprised that Bush hasn't been stressing his plan to allow people to invest a portion of their social security taxes in the stock market. Since 1992, Sam, the number of Americans with – owning stocks, largely through mutual funds, has doubled. Two point two million more Americans joined the stock-holding ranks last year alone. And I think you're going to find, and he's going to find, that it helps.

THE POWER OF FORGETTING

Amid all that sparkling repartee, Stephanopoulos's earnest efforts to *recall* and to *explain* could not go anywhere – and neither could the issue of the Patient's Bill of Rights, a total bore as far as Sam and Cokie were concerned (and, in George Will's eyes, a portent of Communism). Stephanopoulos's colleagues couldn't possibly relate to Dingell/Norwood, since they're far too wealthy to concern themselves with HMOs, and therefore wouldn't ever need to sue one. However, Stephanopoulos's problem wasn't just the privileged superciliousness of his particular co-workers, but the heavy anti-democratic bias of the entertainment system that employs them all. The partnership of Donaldson and Will reflects the perfect union of two com-plementary pro-business forces. On the one hand, there's the relentless upscale emphasis of ABC News, which, like every other TV network (and news magazine, and national news-paper), is an advertising medium pitched at shoppers and investors, and so devoid of labor coverage (unless a strike should inconvenience the commuters) and serious consumer news. (The born-again anti-consumerist John Stossel does his let's-be-fair-to-agribusiness 'exposés' on ABC.) On the other hand, in Will we have the outright plutocratic presence of the GOP, which doesn't want too many of the natives getting restless (or voting). Although Dingell/Norwood is not even slightly leftist – Charlie Norwood, Republican of Georgia, was a Gingrich ally – the issue of the Patient's Bill of Rights, with its allowance for litigation by the masses, was just a bit too Bolshevik for the gang on ABC. And so the effervescent Sam and Cokie laughed it off, and the grave Will deftly changed the subject – to the stock market, and all those glad Americans who own a piece of it, which upbeat subject Sam and Cokie and both Georges all discussed until the next commercial.

Thus that broadcast, in its chortling way, attempted to preserve the status quo by getting everybody to *forget* a democratic possibility, and just go back to sleep. Whether they work brutally or entertainingly or both, *all* anti-democratic forces see the people as extremely thick, and basically oblivious – and work on them accordingly. 'The receptivity of the great masses is very limited, their intelligence is small, but their power of forgetting is enormous,' Hitler wrote.[46] As that example will remind us, the effort to exploit the masses' feeble memory can be violently crude, with just one party taking over all the nation's media, its hooligans attacking dissidents, and all contrary books turned into 'furnace fodder'. Here in the USA, the mass forgetfulness is (by and large) more peaceably exploited, as those in power – economic or political – do not just overwhelm the audience with their own propaganda, or send their own thugs to trash books and beat up writers. Rather, those powers rely upon the media to carry out such labors for them – and to do it with finesse, hyping the authorities and killing off the opposition without violence (and without having to be told). This is a distinction that our President understands. Asked by Mnookin if there 'should be some kind of redress in the courts' when writers such as Hatfield publish 'rumors and gossip', Bush first answered that there should ('Yeah, I would hope so at some point'), then came up with a subtler, smarter answer:

> 'Well, I don't know that, I don't know that question [*sic*] . . . I think there ought to be some – I think the press corps ought to self-police, and I think there ought to be – in order to enhance the integrity of the press corps, it seems like to me that

when they catch, when they catch these fraudulent acts, these scurrilous attacks, they ought to rise up in indignation, and I don't know if that – you know, I think that maybe might have occurred when they started condemning this guy for writing the story.

'There's a little – you know there's kind of a deep – in the consciousness of the press corps there's still this gotcha element. It seems like it's improving.'

It did improve, as we have seen, the mainstream press consistently forgetting all the Governor's weaknesses and thereby urging us to do the same. And yet the telejournalists' oblivious work on his behalf throughout the race was nothing by comparison with what they managed after his inauguration. Once installed, and having made the proper 'unifying' gestures at his swearing-in, Bush was born again again, as all of his past history went straight down the memory hole. Not only was his record utterly forgotten, and with it all his ultra-rightist ties, but so was the chicanery in Florida, and so was all the party's brazen post-election propaganda, and so was the Supreme Court's arbitrary and unprecedented move to choose the nation's President. Once Bush had been enthroned, it was as if all that had never happened, so ravishing were his new clothes. On CNBC's *Hardball* just a week into the Bush regime, Chris Matthews gave historian Robert Dallek and *USA Today* reporter Doris Page his view on why the Democrats had 'lost': Gore did not blast Clinton for his Oval Office dalliance back in '96 (Matthews meant '98), and then Gore/Lieberman's campaign was too left-wing. Page tried politely to remind her bumptious host that Gore had actually not lost the national vote, and that there was even some question as to whether he had lost in Florida; but Matthews was unfazed by those reminders – or, rather, couldn't hear them, but kept explaining why the Democrats had 'lost', while Page and Dallek sat there, their perplexity apparent through their smiles.*

Such forgetfulness, it seems, should not be quite so easy in the culture of TV. After all, there's so much stuff on tape, and so much of that is all so readily available, at least to those of us who can afford to be online, that journalists have no excuse for blanking out on what occurred, say, twenty years ago, or just last week (as long as what occurred was televised). Equipped with such an archive, journalists could do a lot to fight the institutional tendency to prettify our past. Indeed, unless they do such crucial work, that tendency will soon take over absolutely, hiding our whole history in a fog of fragrant myth. Certainly the videos can shed no light on matters too complex to have been televised (e.g., the savings and loan association scandals of the eighties), or that were largely hidden from the public (e.g., Iran/contra), or that took place long, long ago, before the advent of TV. A grasp of history requires, of course, a knack for understanding things that were complex *and* secretive *and* happened long ago (e.g., Prescott Bush's business dealings with the Nazis).[47] And yet there's still a great deal that the videos can teach us, if we will bother to look closely at them. They tell us much that books cannot, about the character of certain men, and certain times.

---

* The telejournalists were not the only ones afflicted with amnesia. 'I think one of the key reasons he won is because people could relate to his style a lot better than they were able to relate to Al Gore, and I think that's continuing in the presidency,' said Leon Panetta, formerly Bill Clinton's Chief of Staff, three weeks after the inauguration. 'Presidency Takes Shape With No Fuss, No Sweat', *New York Times*, 10 February 2001.

There are, for instance, many telling moments of the Nixon era that you can't appreciate by reading, in part because they go unmentioned in most books, and in part because the cold print doesn't do them justice. There was, for example, the Senate floor fight over Nixon's nomination of G. Harrold Carswell, a judge from Georgia, to the Supreme Court in early 1970. Rankling over the Democrats' rejection of Clement Haynsworth (who had opposed desegregation efforts in Virginia, and shown an anti-labor bias), Nixon sought to 'shaft' the liberals by picking Carswell, an unrepentant white supremacist and patent mediocrity. The national outcry was immense; and yet what finally finished Carswell was the statement made in his defense by Senator Roman Hruska of Nebraska, the Republican floor manager. 'Even if he is mediocre,' grumbled Hruska on 8 April 1970, 'there are a lot of mediocre judges, and people, and lawyers. They are entitled to a little representation, aren't they? And a little chance? We can't have *all* Brandeises, Cardozos, and Frankfurters, and – stuff like that there.'

That truculent assessment, which showed up on the network newscasts, proved a fatal blow to Carswell's chances. Its defiant lowbrowism, its weird assertion that the Supreme Court ought to include a special seat to represent the stupid, and its not-so-tacit thrust against the Jews ('stuff like that there') were too much even for the Nixon White House, so Carswell went down to defeat. Although the system certainly survived the episode (the next man chosen by the President was Harry Blackmun), Nixon's scorched-earth move to nominate so base a candidate, and Hruska's shocking testimonial, were just a few examples of the vengeful spirit of the White House in those years – a spirit that *did* do harm to the Republic. Like the image of the President accepting, with a smile, an honorary hard-hat from a delegation of construction workers visiting the Oval Office – shortly after many of their buddies had punched out a lot of demonstrators in the streets of New York City – the sight of Senator Hruska praising Carswell for his lack of any pertinent experience or intellectual distinction said all too much about the temper of those times.

And as TV has lately shown us, the simian spirit of those times is with us still – and even more predominant, for now the defects that disqualified a Carswell really aren't that big a deal, as long as the defective one can help the haves to get still more. Thus it was with Bush the Elder's nomination, and Congress's confirmation, of the undistinguished Clarence Thomas, whose prior judicial record was far skimpier than Carswell's; and thus it was, again, when Thomas helped appoint the younger Bush our President, and more Republicans approved the putsch.* Such widespread tolerance of clear unfitness represents a great leap *backward* from the mainstream principles of 1968, when even Roman Hruska's fellow party members knew that they should give it up. And yet the difference between then and now is still more striking. For it is not the GOP alone that drives the anti-intellectual reaction, but also, and ironically, the mainstream media – Nixon's biggest and most powerful enemy (or so he thought), and now a helpful and forgiving friend to President Bush. As his coverage has made clear, the media no longer minds the sort of mediocrity and inexperience that ruled out Harrold Carswell, nor do the telejournalists much disapprove the racist ideology that also told against that nominee. Far from looking down upon the ignorant masses, as Spiro Agnew memorably

---

* There were a few honourable exceptions, including John Delulio of Princeton University and the Supreme Court Justice, John Paul Stevens.

and wrongly charged, today the media itself applauds such ignorance, and does as much as possible to strengthen it, by gleefully indulging in the same snide pseudo-populism that the Nixon White House used to tar its public enemies, the media included. As Agnew (using Pat Buchanan's words) assailed the TV newsmen as an out-of-touch 'élite' whose views 'do *not* represent the views of America', so did Sam and Cokie loudly jeer Al Gore for even knowing what 'Dingell/Norwood' was, and for his tiresome 'Washington-speak', which, Sam and Cokie seemed quite sure, just doesn't interest average folks. And as Agnew (and Buchanan) lashed out at the 'intellectuals' as 'an effete corps of impudent snobs', so Sam dismissed Gore's point, and Stephanopoulos's attempt to clarify it, as 'cerebral'.

Thus TV's news stars, and the many pundits to their right, kept urging us, and urge us now, to lighten up and join the party – or at least to let the winners party on. In other words, they want us to forget what TV has itself made clear to us, thereby moving most of us to vote *against* that party.* TV revealed the candidate's unsuitability, although he claimed to be 'more suited', and revealed his constant calculation (which he kept imputing to his adversary). TV showed us how thin-skinned he really is – despite the endless hype about his 'likeability' – and even that sadistic streak, which stood out most when he was trying to show his 'lighter side'. TV, moreover, had already shown us what the movement backing him is really all about – the crazy hatred and fanatical resolve on full display throughout the great mock-epic of the failed impeachment (which

---

* The combined totals of the Democratic and Green votes put the anti-Bush vote at close to 52 percent of the electorate.

Governor Bush was always very careful never to bring up).*
That same crusading madness was apparent on TV throughout
the post-election crisis, a spectacle not easy to forget, whatever
TV's newsmen say, and however charming this new President
can be behind closed doors.

Given all that TV had to show us, it seems a little strange that,
in the culture of TV, it takes a book to emphasize the obvious.
And yet this book is only doing what TV did all along, despite
the efforts of its managers: urging you, through all of Bush's
'themes' and 'messages', his half-truths and his slick, distracting
lines, his endless shots at 'them' for being 'calculating', devious
and 'irresponsible', to look who's talking.

---

* Nor did any of the liberal media ever ask him to explain his own position on the
Republicans' long anti-Clinton drive, in light of Bush's many promises to end 'the
bickering and rancor', 'the finger-pointing', the 'partisan' hostilities in Washington,
which had cast the USA into 'a season of cynicism'. 'I know millions of Americans
are sick of the politics of personal destruction, when people are able to float rumors
in the political process with one thing in mind, and that is to destroy somebody,'
he said, on *Meet the Press* in November 1999 – referring to the pesky story of his
own past use of drugs.

THE MADNESS OF KING GEORGE

In the New World, the Bush heritage represented the mergers of well-established families. George's maternal ancestors, the Walkers, who were early arrivals in America, settled on the coast of Maine in the seventeenth century before moving on to Maryland and St Louis, which became central to their Midwestern dry goods business. Devout Catholics, they named the man who became George Bush's maternal grandfather after a seventeenth-century poet and Anglican priest, George Herbert.

Herbert S. Parmet, *George Bush: The Life of a Lone Star Yankee*

It is oddly fitting that the father of our President should bear the name of England's great religious poet; for the elder Bush is certainly the most poetic of this era's leading malapropists. Although they've been no less prolific, neither George W. Bush nor Dan Quayle – the one a natural, the other an adoptive son – has shown the older man's unique stylistic flair. While W has often had Quayle's flubs ascribed to him, and vice versa, no one could mistake the voice of Poppy Bush, who has always had a wacky lyricism all his own.

That style owed much to Bush's temperament – the unselfconscious gabbiness bespeaking, literally, his all-around hyper-activity. He talked the way he golfed and ran and fished, played tennis and tossed horseshoes. (As Michael Kinsley has observed, Bush is by no means 'a quiet man', which – thanks to Peggy Noonan – was what he called himself in his acceptance speech at the 1988 Republican convention.) His talk betrayed not just his natural speediness, however, but also the central fact of his biography – his hothouse adolescence in the wealthiest enclaves of the East. When Bush ad-libbed, those shorts of his would start to glow right through his suit, his monied past a-twinkle in the schoolboy references to 'deep doo-doo', the playful abbreviations ('the Big Mo'), and all the other blue-blood mannerisms. His generational affiliation had an influence as well. A very highly privileged man of yesteryear, Bush would make no bones about how hip he wasn't, but would often flaunt it with a certain proud abandon. Those factors – and, no less, his politician's sense of what he should or shouldn't say – all helped produce his weird patois: the pidgin English of an old preppy on acid.

And yet, as with the son, so with the father, it is unwise to notice only what might make us laugh. As funny as his gaffes have often been, there is a dark side to his clubby babble. The same stiff patrician who ingenuously burbled on about 'deep doo-doo' and 'the vision thing' was also capable, it seems, of doing anything to guard the privilege of his caste. His deeply anti-democratic instincts are quite obvious throughout his verbal record as they are in all his main achievements, from his dirty run in 1988 through his post-presidential efforts at a Restoration, by whatever means necessary, twelve years later. To apprehend his oligarchic impulse, we must look beyond his lightest verse, and take note also of his darker works.

First, however, we should pause for an appreciation of those celebrated gaffes, wherein, despite himself, he showed the world his shorts.*

THE B'S KNEES

This Bush's gaffes were often striking for their sheer inanity, their metaphorical confusion, and/or their trivializing stream of consciousness.

> 'It's no exaggeration to say the undecideds could go one way or another.'
>
> At a campaign rally in Troy, New York, 21 October 1988

> 'I don't want to get, you know, here we are close to the election – sounding a knell of overconfidence that I don't feel.'
>
> On TV with David Frost, Election Day, 6 November 1988

> 'All I was doing was appealing for an endorsement, not suggesting you endorse it.'
>
> Meeting of the National Governors Association, 3 February 1992

Bush made this remark to Colorado's Governor Roy Romer, who had criticized the economic plan that the President had just pitched to the group.

---

* The best of George H. W. Bush's comic lines are all collected, and wittily presented in *Bushisms: President George Herbert Walker Bush, In His Own Words* (New York, 1992), compiled by the editors of *The New Republic*

'Please just don't look at part of the glass, the part that is only less than half full.'

On the outcome of the previous day's
gubernatorial elections, 6 November 1991

'I don't really think – I think I respected certain components of one's presidency – Lincoln for his fairness, his determination, I'm going to preserve the Union. Then his equity that came with the freeing of the slaves. That's so big and so strong that obviously it had to be inspiring. Teddy Roosevelt's commitment to the great outdoors, and his, you know, kind of zest for life. His kids were around this very lawn out here. We have ours out there now. I mean, there's some examples of that kind. In fact, I'm not going to be driven off the golf course. Didn't affect Ike, and it isn't going to affect me either. I can do two things at once – mind the country's business and then every once in a while play golf. So I – I think there's a lot of examples in previous presidencies, pros and cons.'

On how he had been influenced by other US presidents,
C-SPAN interview, 22 December 1991

Bush's ramblings were especially embarrassing when he would try to project sympathy for working people – an effort that would often end up demonstrating just how out-of-touch he really was.

'And the other thing, and I guess – is that I expect it's difficult for somebody working in a plant here in New Hampshire to wonder, to know if the President really cares about what's happening in the economy. And I think I know this state. I went to school a thousand years ago across the border and – would go up every summer of my life, except 1944, to Maine, spending a fair amount of time. Almost – you could see it, practically, coming in on the plane. So when you get clobbered on the seacoast by a storm, I get clobbered by a seacoast on the storm. It goes further than that. When you get hurting because you worry whether you're going to have a job or you get thrown out, I do care about it and I just wanted to say that.'

At a Davidson Textron plant in Dover, New Hampshire, 15 January 1992

(In his patent inability to empathize with those beneath him, the father was forerunner to the son, who also has a hard time showing that he 'cares'.)

The gaffes that hurt George Bush the most were those that reconfirmed his image as a sheltered ninny – or 'wimp', to use the epithet that so incensed him and his family. These included such slips as his asking for 'a splash more coffee' on the campaign trail, and other revelatory bloopers.

Often Bush's utterances turned comic at the end, as he would topple from the sentimental heights into an anticlimax that revealed the calculation underneath it all. Speaking in Ohio, Bush reminisced about his close call as the Navy's youngest flyer in World War II:

'I was shot down, and I was floating around in a little yellow raft, setting a record for paddling. I thought of my family, my mom and dad, and the strength I got from them. I thought of my faith, the separation of church and state.'

5 December 1987

Not yet taught to feign the sort of piety that would attract the Christian right, Bush was evidently worried that his reference to 'my faith' might sound unconstitutional, so he tossed in that last item.

The wackiness of Bush's monologues would often help to mask their propaganda purpose, which was usually not funny. Although it isn't likely that he meant to do it, his zanier improvisations sounded kind of cute – suggesting an ingenuousness that could disarm his inattentive listeners, while his critics sometimes concentrated less on what it was he was proposing than on how foolishly he put it.

'If you're worried about caribou, take a look at the arguments that were used about the [Alaskan oil] pipeline. They'd say the caribou would be extinct. You've got to shake them away with a stick. They're all making love lying up against the pipeline and you got thousands of caribou up there.'

Bush/Quayle fundraiser, Houston, 31 October 1991

Here Bush was trying to justify his plan to let the oil companies start drilling in the Alaskan National Wildlife Reserve, a controversial plan that Bush the Younger is now set to realize, with the help of his Secretary of the Interior, radical anti-environmentalist Gale Norton.

THE DARK SIDE

'I will never apologize for the United States of America – I don't care what the facts are.'

At a press conference introducing the Coalition of
American Nationalities, 2 August 1988

The Coalition of American Nationalities was not the most felicitous of venues for a promise never to apologize for any national misdeeds. An 'outreach' group established by the GOP to help get out the Bush/Quayle vote in certain ethnic neighborhoods, the Coalition was dominated by pro-Nazi emigrés, as the *Washington Jewish Week* reported on 8 September. The newspaper named several European fascist activists among the Coalition's Bush advisors, including Nazi collaborator Laszlo Pasztor, who had served as junior envoy in Berlin for the Arrow Cross regime in his native Hungary; Florian Goldau, who had been a recruiter for the Romanian Iron Guard; Bohdan Fedorak, who had headed a Ukrainian pro-Nazi group involved in wartime pogroms; and Croatian-born agitator Jerome Brentar, a fixture on the Holocaust denial circuit.

The bad press forced the resignation of seven Bush advisors (although some of them – including Fred Malek, who had compiled the infamous 'Jews list' for Richard Nixon – were soon back on the job). Weeks later, just before Election Day, yet another fascist had to quit the Coalition: Aleksis Mangulis, identified by the *Philadelphia Inquirer* as a veteran of the Latvian Legion, an affiliate of the Nazi SS.

'Boy, they were big on crematoriums, weren't they?'*

After touring the Auschwitz death camp,
Chicago Sun-Times, 29 January 1992

Although shocking, the relationship between Bush/Quayle and European fascism should come as no surprise, since it evidenced two subterranean traditions in post-war US history. Since the fifties, on the one hand, the GOP had quietly cultivated the most sympathetic elements in US emigré communities, as a way to win large blocs of urban votes, and so offset the Democrats' advantage among blacks and Jews. That partisan effort, moreover, grew out of an older venture by the CIA, which from the end of World War II deliberately absorbed large numbers of Nazi and pro-Nazi fugitives, to help out in the anti-Soviet crusade.[48] (The Soviets, too, relied on fascist brains and brawn.)

As both a ranking party member and long-time confederate of the CIA (which he ran briefly, and most sympathetically, for President Ford), George Bush was in an excellent position to recruit the sort of talent that it takes to pull off anti-democratic coups of various kinds. With such a background, Bush was well suited for his deep involvement in Iran/contra – the most serious of all the post-war presidential scandals, because its per-

---

* The superciliousness of that remark would seem to have betrayed a lifelong inability to grasp the immorality of fascism. His biographer recounts the following anecdote about Bush's years at Andover: 'One Latin teacher remembered by [Bush friend] George Warren was "quite a horror" and "rather a fascist." . . . He had his class depart from Latin one day of each month and spent the time instead on current events and politics. "He was a Nazi. He'd talk glowingly of Hitler. This was in 1939, 1940, the Battle of Britain had been fought and we were going into that period of the Phoney War." All this was no problem for Poppy, who "seemed to have enjoyed the teachers and accommodated himself rather easily to even the most authoritarian. Bush would never defy."' Herbert S. Parmet, *George Bush: The Life of a Lone Star Yankee* (Transaction), p.39.

petrators had turned US foreign policy into a massive private covert operation.

Questions about Bush's role in that affair continued to annoy him until 26 January 1988, when Dan Rather tried to interview him on the subject in a live exchange on the *CBS Evening News*. The candidate responded with a furious exhibition of indignant stonewalling, even going after Rather in a bold (albeit irrelevant) *ad hominem* attack:

BUSH: Now, Dan, let's be careful here, because you're trying—

DAN RATHER: Yes, I want you to be careful, Mr Vice President, because the problem here—

BUSH: I *am* being careful!

RATHER: The problem here is, you repeatedly sat in the meetings. You sat in the meeting in which Secretary Shultz in the most forceful way raised his objections – and then you said you never heard anybody register objections.

BUSH: I wasn't there for a most forceful way. If it was a most forceful way, I've heard George Shultz be very, very forceful and if I were there and he was very, very forceful at that meeting, I would have remembered that and I don't remember that and [unintelligible]—

RATHER: Then how do you explain you can't remember what other people at the meeting say [unintelligible]—?

BUSH: Because I wasn't there at that point!

RATHER: You weren't in the meeting?

BUSH: I'm not suggesting. I'm just saying I don't remember.

RATHER: I don't want to be argumentative, Mr Vice President—

BUSH: You do, Dan. This is not a great night, because I want to talk about why I want to be President. Why those 41 percent of the people are supporting me.

RATHER: Mr Vice President—

BUSH: And I don't think it's fair to judge a whole career, it's not fair to judge my whole career by a rehash on Iran. How would *you* like it if I judged *your* career by those seven minutes when you walked off the set in New York? Would you like that? I have respect for you, but I don't have respect for what you're doing here tonight.

RATHER: Mr Vice President, I think you'll agree that your qualifications for President, and what kind of leadership you'd bring the country, what kind of government you'd have, what kind of people you'd have around you, is much more important than what you've just referred to. I'd be happy—

BUSH: I just want to be judged on the whole record, and you're not giving me an opportunity.

RATHER: I'm trying to set the record straight.

BUSH: You invited me to come here to talk about, I thought, the whole record.

RATHER: I want you to talk about the record. You sat in a meeting with Secretary George Shultz. He got apoplectic when he found out that you and the President were being party to some of these missions to the Ayatollah Khomeini, the Ayatollah of Iran. Can you explain how you were supposed to be – you are the anti-terrorist expert. Iran was officially a terrorist state, and you went around telling [unintelligible] – in the—

BUSH: I've explained that. I wanted [CIA agent William] Buckley out of there before he was killed.

RATHER: Mr Vice President, the question is you've made us hypocrites in the face of the world. How could you sign on to such a policy? How could you [unintelligible]—?

BUSH: I'll tell you how I could. The same reason the President signed on to it. When a CIA agent is being tortured to death, maybe you err a bit on the side of human life. But everybody's admitted mistakes. I've admitted mistakes. And you want to dwell on them. And I want to talk about the values we believe in, and the experience and the integrity that goes with all of this. And what I'm going to do about education. There's nothing new here. I thought this was a news program!

RATHER: Well, I had hoped, Mr Vice President, that you would tell us to whom you expressed your reservations –

BUSH: Yes, I did—

RATHER: – when you expressed them, and what the reservations were.

BUSH: [unintelligible] – under oath!

RATHER: What were your reservations?

BUSH: Reservations about getting the control of an operation in the hands of a foreign power. Don Regan stated the other day – and I never heard a word of it on CBS – that the Vice President, in the presence of the President, spoke up about his concern about the whole cover of an operation being blown, and secrets and people which you're dealing with and putting their lives in jeopardy [unintelligible] every covert action—

RATHER: And you weren't concerned about selling missiles to the Ayatollah Khomeini?

BUSH: The President has explained that. The committee looked at that and so there is nothing new on this.

RATHER: Mr Vice President, I appreciate you joining us tonight. And I appreciate the straightforward way in which you engaged in this exchange. There are clearly some unanswered questions remaining. Are you willing to go to a news conference before the Iowa caucuses, answer questions from all comers?

BUSH: I've been to eighty-six news conferences since March—

RATHER: I gather that the answer is no. Thank you very much for being with us, Mr Vice President. We'll be back with more news in a moment.

CBS Evening News, 26 January 1988

'When Dan Rather had tried to pin Bush down on Iran-Contra, the candidate had blustered, said that it was old stuff, and accused Rather of unfairness. Bush's campaign telephone banks had then stimulated calls to CBS-affiliated stations complaining about Rather. As [Anthony] Lewis noted, "It was a carefully prepared gambit and it worked. Through the rest of the 1988 campaign, reporters hardly raised the Iran question. It is still working. President Bush brushes off questions on the subject as dated, unfair, silly. He makes the press feel uncomfortable for asking. . . . But this was the worst government scandal in years, a true violation of the Constitution that damaged the national interest. It matters whether Mr Bush is telling the truth about his part in it." '

Lawrence Walsh, *Firewall: The Iran-Contra Conspiracy and Cover-Up* (New York, 1997) p.456

That 'gambit' was, as we have seen, urged on the President by his canny eldest son, who saw the opportunity to boost his father's sagging effort for the nomination.* (Going *mano a mano* with Dan Rather helped Bush win the Iowa caucuses soon afterward.) In any case, the cover-up itself was finally covered up for good when Bush extended presidential pardons to Caspar Weinberger and several other major players in the scandal.

Here it's worth recalling that the elder Bush enjoys a well-earned reputation for politeness and considerateness. He has sent out gracious notes and letters by the tens of thousands and, in dealing with his peers, has always taken pains to do the decent thing. (He skipped Nixon's first inauguration, for example, to go and see off LBJ, who would otherwise have left DC with no farewells.)

Such thoughtfulness seems disconcertingly at odds with the insensitivity that has marked many of George Bush's public statements. Like his eldest son, Bush would frequently betray a disconcerting callousness when speaking from the 'heart'.

---

* When faced with a persistent questioner about his knowledge of world leaders, the Governor tried to use the most disorienting of his father's tactics: shifting the inquisitorial spotlight to the questioner. In the son's case, the gambit didn't work.

> 'Obviously, when you see somebody go berserk and get a
> weapon and go in and murder people, of course, it troubles me.'
>
> 17 October 1991

A gunman had massacred twenty-three people in a cafeteria in
Killeen, Texas. The President was explaining why the shootings
would not alter his position against gun control.

On the other hand, Bush could always muster towering
and infectious outrage when it was necessary to promote a
war:

> 'Look, if an American Marine is killed – if they kill an American
> Marine, that's real bad. And if they threaten and brutalize
> the wife of an American citizen, sexually threatening the
> lieutenant's wife while kicking him in the groin over and over
> again, then, Mr Gorbachev, please understand, this President
> is going to do something about it.'
>
> White House press conference, 21 December 1989

Thus Bush obliged a reporter who had asked him how he
planned to tell the Soviet leader why he had invaded Panama.
The President was always able to rouse vigilantist sentiment in
favor of a righteous cause. Such rabble-rousing is no less effective for its illogic, incoherence or falseness: on the contrary. For
getting audiences hot and bothered, there's nothing like the
image of some colored brute abusing a (white) woman – a
charge so potent that it tends to obviate the need for any
evidence.

Bush first deployed his talent for such Jim Crow dema-
goguery in the summer of 1988, when he introduced the tale of
Willie Horton into the campaign against Governor Michael
Dukakis:

'What did the Democratic Governor of Massachusetts think he was doing when he let convicted first-degree murderers out on weekend passes, even after one of them criminally, brutally raped a woman and stabbed her fiancé?'

Illinois Republican State Convention; *National Journal*, 18 June 1988

'Horton applied for a furlough. He was given a furlough. He was released. And he fled – only to terrorize a family and repeatedly rape a woman.'

National Sheriffs Association Convention, Louisville;

Washington Post 22 June 1988

Such accusations were just true enough to serve their purpose: Horton, serving a life sentence in a Massachusetts prison, had been convicted of first-degree murder, did flee while on furlough, and did commit those crimes against a couple down in Maryland. Otherwise, the story was a classic of disinformation, based on the sloppy coverage of the case by the *Lawrence Eagle-Tribune* (and first used to bash Dukakis nationally by Senator Al Gore, who raised the Horton issue in a hot debate before the New York primary). Contrary to the Bush/Quayle propaganda, the infamous furlough program had not been started by 'the Democratic Governor of Massachusetts', but by Governor Francis Jennings, a Republican, in 1972. Nor was it Dukakis who 'let convicted first-degree murderers out on weekend passes', but the Massachusetts Supreme Court that had ruled, in 1973, that such prisoners must be included in the furlough program.

Moreover – and more important – prison furloughs had dramatically reduced recidivism. Such effectiveness explains why thirty-five states were using similar programs (i.e., extending furloughs to first-degree murderers) by the time the

Bush/Quayle team had started to attack Dukakis/Horton. The furlough system also helped reduce escape attempts. When Horton fled to Maryland (which occurred on his tenth furlough), the escape rate for lifers who had committed murder was .0008 percent – a rate considerably lower than it was before the program started.[49]

Bush used the same old racist plot, and with the same regard for truth, in trying to mobilize the audience against Saddam Hussein:

'And that's what we're dealing with. We're dealing with Hitler revisited, a totalitarianism and brutality that is naked and unprecedented in modern times. And that must not stand. We cannot talk about compromise when you have that kind of behavior going on this very minute. Embassies being starved, people being shot, women being raped – it is brutal. And I will continue to remind the rest of the world that this must not stand.'

GOP campaign rally, Manchester, New Hampshire, 23 October 1990

'Will we insist that Saddam Hussein get out of Kuwait, that the Government of Kuwait be restored, that the rape and the pillage and the plunder of Kuwait stop, and that aggression not be rewarded? It isn't oil, it is aggression – naked, brutal aggression.'

GOP campaign rally, Los Angeles, 26 October 1990

'They literally – literally, not figuratively – literally raped, pillaged and plundered this once-peaceful land, this nation that is a member of the Arab League and a member of the United Nations . . .

'They've tried to silence Kuwaiti dissent and courage with firing squads, much as Hitler did when he invaded Poland.

They have committed outrageous acts of barbarism. In one hospital, they pulled twenty-two premature babies from their incubators, sent the machines back to Baghdad, and all those little ones died.'

GOP campaign rally, Mashpee, Massachusetts, 1 November 1990

'We are talking about brutal, naked aggression. We are talking about brutal, naked aggression.'

GOP reception, Cincinnati, 2 November 1990

At this point, it may seem a pedantic exercise to note that Saddam Hussein had lately been a big-time client of the Reagan/Bush administrations, which had generously answered the petitions of the US-Iraq Business Forum (a large consortium of major US corporations) by showering Iraq with covert aid – although back then Saddam Hussein had been no nicer than he was once he had rolled into Kuwait. (Moreover, that invasion had been pre-approved by Secretary of State James Baker.)

It may also seem irrelevant to observe that, although the forces of Iraq's dictator did indeed commit some heinous crimes against Kuwaitis, they actually committed *none* of the offenses that the US and Kuwaiti propaganda charged them with. No pregnant women were impaled on bayonets, no crowds of innocents were crushed by tanks, no firing squads killed groups of 'dissidents'. (The Iraqis worked with more efficiency – leaving a mangled body in a street where everyone would recognize it, for example.) Nor was there any widespread vandalism or dismantling of Kuwait City – until *after* the Iraqis started to retreat. That tale of the twenty-two discarded babies soon turned out to be a bald canard. The story had them shocked and ranting in the halls of Congress, after it was told, with much pathetic weeping, by the daughter of Kuwait's ambassador to the United States (the girl posing as your average patriotic teen from Kuwait City).

But there's no need to quibble: Operation Desert Storm was an extraordinary victory. Not since World War I had the American people been so expertly bamboozled. (Militarily, the war was by no means as clean a sweep as advertised – and, politically, the job was botched.) The campaign gave a huge boost to morale throughout the weapons industries and, therefore, inside the Pentagon, and also gave our national spirits – and the President's approval ratings – a major lift that lasted through the summer of 1991.[50]

> 'By God, we've licked the Vietnam Syndrome!'
>
> *Los Angeles Times*, 19 April 1991

And yet, for all that vast applause throughout the nation and the military (and the media), and despite his now-imperial standing – a rise in popularity so daunting that all hands predicted easy re-election in 1992 – the President was still burned up about what 'they' had said about him four years earlier.

> 'You're talking to the wimp. You're talking to the guy that had a cover of a national magazine, that I'll never forgive, put that label on me.'
>
> *New York Times*, 27 June 1991

Bush followed his achievement in Iraq with a far more lasting contribution to the American judicial system.

> 'I am very pleased to announce that I will nominate Judge Clarence Thomas to serve as Associate Justice of the United

States Supreme Court. Clarence Thomas was my first appointee to the US Court of Appeals for the District of Columbia, where he served for over a year. And I believe he'll be a great Justice. He is the best man for this position.'

President's news conference, Kennebunkport, 1 July 1991

Reporters could not help but notice that the nominee, a black Republican, had been a judge for all of fifteen months:

REPORTER: Mr President, last year you vetoed the Civil Rights Bill, saying it could lead to quotas. Today you've made a nomination that could easily be seen as quota-based. How do you explain this apparent inconsistency?

BUSH: I don't even see an appearance of inconsistency because what I did is look for the best man. And Clarence Thomas' name was high on the list when the previous nominee went forth, Judge Souter, Mr Justice Souter now.

And so, I don't accept that at all. The fact that he is black and a minority has nothing to do with this in the sense that he is the best qualified at this time. And we had a very thorough screening process then; we had one now that we put into forward gear very fast, but we didn't have to start from square one.

So, Clarence Thomas, seasoned now by more experience on the bench, fits my description of the best man at the right time, or the best person at the right time because women were considered as well.

REPORTER: But do you see how it could be perceived so?

BUSH: No, I can't see it.

REPORTER: Was race a factor whatsoever?

BUSH: I don't see it at all.

President's news conference, Kennebunkport, 1 July 1991

In his 1992 campaign against Bill Clinton, Bush replayed the Nixon card by hinting broadly that the Governor of Arkansas had been a youthful creature of the KGB. (That smear had entailed the Bush/Quayle team's illegal use of Clinton's State Department passport file.) While hammering away at his opponent's draft record, Bush also deplored the fact that Clinton had participated in an anti-war protest while studying at Oxford. The President did not say why it was especially reprehensible to stage a protest 'in a foreign land', but then the charge was meant merely to sound damning, not to make a lot of sense.

Although that effort to tar Clinton was a failure in the short term, it helped kick off the long Republican *jihad* that eventually dragged the nation through the near-impeachment farce, and that, two years later, helped defeat Al Gore.

On Larry King's show (which had a live audience that evening), Bush responded to a caller's question about Iran/contra.

KING: Iran-contra – fair issue?

BUSH: Fair enough. I've answered every question. If Bill Clinton would do on the draft what I've done on Iran-contra, we'd have the facts out there.

(Applause)

That Iran-contra has been looked at to the tune of $40 million of investigation. I've testified to the commissions and everybody else, and *leveled* with the American

128

people. Now, I see a lot of distorted campaign rhetoric, like this [caller's question], and I'm sorry, I don't – If this guy had a specific question instead of a speech—

KING: Yes, his question is trust.

BUSH: Well, trust. That's what this election is going to be about: Who do you trust to lead this country? I served this country, and I served it in uniform, and I believe I've earned the trust in that capacity from the American people.

I have made tough decisions. I have not waffled, been on one side or the other – on the war, or on right-to-work laws, or spotted owls, or NAFTA agreements. Every position these guys take, they're on one side – 'Oh, by the way, I see the point over here.' You can't do that when you're President. So, I think I have earned the trust of the American—

This guy, I mean, you know, he's part of the campaign apparatus or something like that. [Laughs]

KING: What do you make of the Clinton Moscow trip thing? Do you think that's a—

BUSH: Moscow?

KING: He says it was just a student trip.

BUSH: Larry, I don't want to tell you what I really think, because I don't have the facts. I don't have the facts. But to go to Moscow one year after Russia crushed Czechoslovakia, not remember who you saw, I think – I really think the answer is, *level* with the American people.

I've made a mistake. I've said, 'I made mistakes.' But don't try to – You can remember who you saw in the airport in Oslo, but you can't remember who you saw in Moscow—

KING: So, in other words, you're saying—

BUSH: I'm just saying, *level* with the American people –

KING: Say you're sorry you went?

BUSH: – on the draft, on whether he went to Moscow, how many demonstrations he led against his own country from a foreign soil [*sic*]. *Level*, tell us the truth, and let the voters then decide who to trust or not.

(Applause)

KING: How about the missing pages in the State Department records? He implied the other night that that may have been Republican hanky-panky. He didn't even know there *were* State Department papers.

BUSH: Well, I'm sure there are passport files. But why in the world would anybody want to tamper with his files, you know, to support the man? I mean, I don't understand that. What would exonerate him – put it that way – in the files?

KING: Do you really have deep-down suspicions about the Moscow thing? I mean, just gut suspicion?

BUSH: I'm just concerned about it. No, I don't have it as a federal case. I'm just concerned about it, because it's a pattern here.

KING: Judgment-wise?

BUSH: Yes. I'll tell you what concerns me, and I really feel viscerally about this: demonstrating against your own country in a foreign land. I have demonstrators in front of the White House every single day. If you go up there right now, there are probably some sitting out here.

KING: And that's fine.

BUSH: In the war, when I was trying to mobilize world opinion and United States opinion, we had a lot of people marching and demonstrating in front of the White House – ministers and guys that opposed the war. And I understand that. But I cannot, for the life of me, understand mobilizing demonstrations and demonstrating against your own country, no matter how strongly you feel, when you're in a foreign land. I just don't believe it. I don't think you should do that.

(Applause)

That's what gets me. Moscow – I don't know what he did in Moscow.

KING: Well, what you're saying is: 'Do it at home, OK. Over there, no'?

BUSH: Sure. I mean, but I just – Maybe I'm old-fashioned, Larry. But to go to a foreign country and demonstrate against your own country when your sons and daughters are dying halfway around the world? I'm sorry, I – I just don't like it. I think it is wrong. I think it is wrong to do that

Larry King Live, CNN, 7 October 1992

On 15 January 1993, the White House belatedly released a copy of Bush's diary, which the Independent Counsel, Lawrence Walsh, had been struggling to obtain for many months.

The White House yesterday released excerpts of a long-secret diary President Bush started the day after covert arms sales to Iran were first disclosed in November 1986 and in which he said, 'I'm one of the few people that know fully the details.' That private statement of Bush's knowledge while vice president was made on 5 November 1986, months before a newspaper interview in which Bush said he had been 'out of the loop' on the covert dealings with Tehran to gain the release of American hostages then being held in Lebanon by pro-Iranian terrorists.

The excerpts show Bush professing less and less knowledge as the furor over the Iran-contra affair intensified.

Washington Post, 16 January 1993

Later on the sixteenth, Bush held his last press conference, where he appeared with his old friend Brian Mulroney, Prime Minister of Canada. UPI reporter Helen Thomas asked the President about that coda to the Iran-contra tragicomedy.

THOMAS: Mr President, on your diary, do you think you got a fair shake?

BUSH: I don't like any stuff about that.

MULRONEY: Helen, what we want to do is read *your* diaries. That's what I'm waiting for!

(Laughter)

'I AM WHO I AM'

Dan Bartlett, deputy counselor to the president, said Mr Bush believed he owed his victory, 'despite the narrowness of the election, to the power of his ideas.'

New York Times, 2 July 2001

BUSH ON BUSH

MATTHEWS: When you hear Al Gore say, 'reckless, irresponsible', what do you hear from him, really? What's the real words, the real message there?

GOVERNOR BUSH: I hear a guy who's not confident in his own vision, and, therefore, wants to take time tearing me down.

Actually, I – I – this may sound a little West Texan to you, but I like it when I'm talking about what I'm – what I–

MATTHEWS: Right.

GOVERNOR BUSH: – when I'm talking about myself, and when he's talking about myself, all of us are talking about me.

MATTHEWS: Right.

Hardball, MSNBC, 31 May 2000

In the culture of TV, it is impossible to do the sort of absolute and lasting propaganda job that, say, Parson Weems did for George Washington (with a lot of help from the general's friends). The printed fiction of the lad who could not tell a lie would never have withstood TV's non-stop up-close-and-personal, with its childish preference for good looks and winning body language. If Sam and Cokie had gone back in time to cover Washington the man, they would have killed him for his frosty manner and big, ugly dentures. (On the other hand, they would have overlooked his business deals and military record, and any other complicated 'issue.') As many students of the media have noted, TV's easy and habitual intrusiveness and great de-glamorizing tendency do not permit the sort of mountainous charisma that was once possible through print, and then through radio and cinema (and also through TV itself, pre-1964). Thus the sort of monumental grandeur that we still associate with FDR and Winston Churchill (and, in certain circles, Hitler), and that Nixon always craved, is now passé.

Video's de-mythifying effect annoys the right, because it ravages their dearest myths. It's hard to feel that war is swell, for instance, when you can see the corpses smoking; and so the Pentagon has long forbidden all press coverage of the battlefield (a policy enforced with special vigor by Defense Secretary Cheney throughout Operation Desert Storm), while Rush Limbaugh, Ollie North *et al* routinely charge the telejournalists with treasonous intent, so that any unexpected gruesome sight will come across as enemy propaganda. Notwithstanding *Adam-12* and *ChiPS* and *Cops*, TV has also dimmed the sheen of law-and-order, by airing the explosive video of Rodney King's near-fatal beating by the LAPD – images assailed by Rush (and others), who charged, predictably, that they were 'taken out of context'. Likewise, any televisual revelation of high corporate crime – not that we see much on TV, these days – is automatically dismissed, by pro-business spinmasters, as 'gotcha journalism', the all-important images impugned as 'staged'. Thus TV gets battered by the right whenever it appears to balk the powers that be. (When TV's anti-glamor aids their cause, meanwhile, the right takes full advantage: Bush 'won' Florida in part because TV was there to make the recount look suspicious, what with all those shots of people lofting ballots and laboriously peering at them – an innocent display that Bush's propagandists loaded with malign significance.)

While disapproving of such inconvenient revelation, the right also dislikes TV's anti-imperial effect on the façade of leadership. Like certain of their forebears (like John Adams), they prefer a high monarchic finish to theatrics lower-key, and therefore put down Jimmy Carter's modest style, as well as Clinton's, much preferring the retro silk-top-hat-and-mink-coat grandiosity that made a big comeback with Reagan/Bush, and – with the addition of a lot of cowboy hats – Bush II, whose inaugural weekend was as ostentatious as it was unmerited.

The taste for kingly presidential style accompanies a preference for a wholesome and uplifting presidential story. Thus Bill Clinton was despised for the vulgar strain in his biography: the hard times, the alcoholic stepfather, the mother punched around, the ne'er-do-well half-brother in and out of clinics – and all in *Arkansas*! Such a background, for which Clinton tended to be unapologetic, would not be likely to appeal to moralists in search of pretty stories to beguile the nation's subjects. By stark contrast with the Clinton narrative, the Bush biography, as it has thus far been purveyed, is all pretty sunny, despite an early cloud or two. There was the devastation of his baby sister's death ('a sharp pain in the midst of an otherwise happy blur'), and then, in his twenties, a vague period of personal 'drift' that entailed a bit of boozing, a drunken drive over a neighbor's garbage can (followed by a tough-guy face-off between him and Dad, all soon forgotten), and now and then a reefer, maybe. But then the young man clambered out of that distressing puddle, with the help of Laura ('a rock') and Jesus Christ. He went straight, put his best face forward, got rich, then got elected Governor, and the rest is history.

The story is a little thin, and – given Bush's temperament, and lifelong license – too good to be true. (Our First Lady's bio is even emptier.) Given what hints have survived the propaganda blackout on this politician's past, it's possible that his biography would make Bill Clinton's seem like good clean fun from start to finish. Bush's whole life story may eventually come out – or it may not, since there are no Republicans to peddle it, and the watchdogs of the media have, oddly, lost the urge to sniff out scandal. Such silence – call it 'Teflon' – helps protect the President from TV's X-ray eye, which cannot do him harm as long as everyone refuses to discuss what it reveals.

Even if the lid stays clamped on tight, however, the official version of the Bush biography is at some risk, as long as Bush himself talks off the cuff. His statements variously contradict the slight and tidy narrative that the journalists have largely bought so far. Such statements start to limn the outline of the actual person there behind that Norman Rockwell/Billy Graham façade – a man who never tried, and doesn't care.

'HELL, NO, I DON'T KNOW'

'The other reality in spring of 1968 was Vietnam. The war became increasingly personal as friends who had graduated the year before went into the military. The war was no longer something that was happening to other people in a distant land; it came home to us.'

George W. Bush, *A Charge to Keep*, (HarperCollins), p. 50.

'I don't remember debates [about the war]. I don't think we spent a lot of time debating it. Maybe we did, but I don't remember.'

Washington Post, 27 July 1999

'I just don't remember much protest. The only protest I remember that had a big impact on the East Coast was the Columbia protest. That was in 1968. But maybe I just missed it. I wasn't looking for it. I wasn't much of a protester. I'll be frank with you, I don't remember any of my friends protesting.'

Ibid.

Of some dozen Bush associates from that time, none recalls a conversation with Bush about his views of the war.

Chicago Tribune, 18 January 2000

Among the questions Bush had to answer on his application forms was whether he wanted to go overseas. Bush checked the box that said: 'Do not volunteer.'

Bush said in an interview that he did not recall checking the box. Two weeks later, his office provided a statement from a former, state-level Air Guard personnel officer, asserting that since Bush 'was applying for a specific position with the 147th Fighter Group, it would have been inappropriate for him to have volunteered for an overseas assignment and he probably was so advised by the military personnel clerk assisting him in completing the form'.

During a second interview, Bush himself raised the issue. 'Had my unit been called up, I'd have gone . . . to Vietnam,' Bush said. 'I was prepared to go.'*

Washington Post, 2 July 1999

> 'I was prepared to do it . . . but no – if I'd wanted to, I guess I would have. It was in my control.'

Los Angeles Times, 30 July 2000

A HANDICAP

> 'That woman who knew I had dyslexia – I never interviewed her.'

New York Times, 16 September 2000

Bush was referring to Gail Sheehy, whose piece in *Vanity Fair* proposed the diagnosis of dyslexia. This gaffe was celebrated

---

* The article continues: 'But there was no chance Bush's unit would be ordered overseas. Bush says that toward the end of his training in 1970, he tried to volunteer for overseas duty, asking a commander to put his name on the list for a "Palace Alert" program, which dispatched qualified F-102 pilots in the Guard to Europe and the Far East, occasionally to Vietnam, on three- to six-month assignments.

'He was turned down on the spot. "I did [ask] – and I was told, 'You're not going,'" Bush said.'

for its inadvertent wittiness: a dyslexic denial of dyslexia. ('He did not appear to be making what would have been an incredibly clever joke,' wrote Frank Bruni of the *New York Times*.) Overlooked in all the merriment was the statement's inadvertent confirmation of the Sheehy thesis: 'That woman who *knew* I had dyslexia' makes clear that the reporter got it right. (Otherwise, Bush would have used 'said' or 'claimed'.) Moreover, the candidate's inverse assertion that she had never interviewed him was not true, since the profile begins with an exchange between them, and includes other quotations of his answers to her questions. (For more on the Bush/Sheehy relationship, see 'Freedom of Expression'.)

KING: The dyslexia thing, did that bother you?

BUSH: Oh, that was just fiction.

KING: But did it bother you? Because, first of all, millions of Americans have it.

BUSH: Of course they are. My little brother, Neil, is dyslexic.

KING: Successful people have it.

BUSH: Very much so. Winston Churchill, one of my—

KING: So how did you react when a thing like that made—

BUSH: I just smiled. I just thought it was silly, you know. We've got a writer who just made something up. And, you know, I'm – even if I were, I would be a good president. But I'm not.

Larry King Live, CNN, 29 September 2000

SAVE THE CHILDREN

Throughout the presidential contest, Bush was dogged by rumors of his past drug use – rumors that were only strengthened by his adamant refusal to discuss them. Rather than just bite the bullet and confirm them, with a televangelistic anti-sixties *mea culpa*, or deny them hotly *à la* Nixon ('I am not a crook') or Clinton ('I did not have sex with that woman'), Bush refused even to talk about them, on the grounds that doing so would do major moral damage to the nation's children.

It was an unsuccessful gambit, since it only dragged the whole thing out, the Governor having to address repeatedly – and, worse still, *defensively* – the very subject he was trying to avoid. At those moments, his was an image not too likely to impress the young, who were surely smart enough to see that he was hiding something.

Although it was a PR dud, however, that move exemplified a kind of fakery that pervaded Bush's propaganda overall – a tendency to ideologize his self-protective tactics. Rather than just dodge the question, he tends to cast his flight as a re-affirmation of some principle with which few could argue, although he probably does not believe in it. (See 'Bring Us Together'.) In this case, Bush was cleverly, if ineffectively, appropriating Myron Magnet's argument, in *The Dream and the Nightmare*, that the poor were catastrophically corrupted by the hedonistic 'message' of the bourgeois counterculture. (E.g., "'Turn on, tune in, drop out'" was the slogan of the sixties counterculture, and the underclass duly turned on.')[51] Thus Bush argued that he had a certain generational *responsibility* to lie about his past.

STEVE COOPER: What about alcohol?

BUSH: Probably no more so than others that you know. But I quit drinking. I quit drinking for a couple of reasons. One, I was drinking too much at times. But remember during this period of life I was a Sunday school teacher. I was a Little League coach. I was a husband. I was a dad, but alcohol began to compete with my energies.

COOPER: Have you ever used drugs? Marijuana, cocaine?

BUSH: I'm not going to talk about what I did as a child [*sic*]. What I'm going to talk about, and I'm going to say this consistently: It is irrelevant what I did twenty to thirty years ago. What's relevant is that I have learned from any mistakes that I made. I do not want to send signals to anybody that what Governor Bush did thirty years ago is cool to try.

CNN, 2 February 1999

TIM RUSSERT: Senator Bill Bradley was asked: 'Does it matter if a presidential candidate has used cocaine, an illegal drug?' Bradley: 'I do think that if someone violated the law, they should state whether they did or not.'

BUSH: Yeah.

RUSSERT: Do you agree with Senator Bradley?

BUSH: I've said all I'm going to say about what I may or may not have done. Here's the important thing that I think baby-boomer generations ought to be saying: If we've made mistakes, we've learned from our mistakes; if we made mistakes when we were young, that we've learned and we're responsible citizens. And we're willing to say to children, who are listening to words that people like me utter, don't use drugs. I don't want to provide any excuse, Tim, for your 14-year-old child to say, 'Hey, maybe if old Governor Bush did something, I think I'm going to try it, Dad.' That is irresponsible behavior. Those of us who have got positions of leadership must have a loud, unified voice, saying, 'Drugs will destroy you.' Secondly, 'Abusing alcohol will ruin your chances.'

Meet the Press, NBC, 21 November 1999

BARBARA WALTERS: I know you're going to hate this discussion, but I've got to do it anyway. The whole issue of whether or not you took drugs may not be as important as your refusal to discuss it. I mean, Al Gore has admitted he smoked pot. Bill Bradley admitted he smoked pot. Why are you afraid to discuss it? I mean, what's the difference between discussing drinking and discussing drugs – pot, for example?

BUSH: I made up my mind before I got into this race that I wasn't going to try to disprove negatives, because I know how the system works. People—

WALTERS: But you talk about alcohol.

BUSH: People will float a rumor. People have made me talk. And I've decided I'm not going to talk about it. And you know what? I'm not going to talk about it.

WALTERS: Even though – you know it's sort of the mystery became more important than whether you did it or not. You don't think so?

BUSH: No, I think it's time for people to hear this voice out of me. Drugs will destroy you. It's time to have somebody stand up to say to baby-boomer parents, 'Join me in saying to our children, drugs will ruin your life.' But I'm not going to talk about the gossip and rumors about my own – what may have happened years ago.

20/20 ABC, 5 May 2000

Shortly before Election Day, it came out – the story broken by a Fox-TV affiliate in Maine – that Bush had once been arrested for drunk driving. Again, the candidate explained his years of silence on the subject by invoking his parental obligations. (Note also how deftly Bush changed the subject of the question – 'Why wait till now?' – from *himself* to the perfidious 'they').

UNIDENTIFIED REPORTER: Governor, why wait till now? Why wait till now?

BUSH: Well, it came out now because a news TV station in Maine [*sic*] broke the story. But I made the decision that, as a dad, I – I didn't want my girls doing the kinds of things I did, and I told them not to drink and drive. It was a decision I made. I've been very upfront with the people of the state of Texas that I, you know, that I had been drinking in the past, that I had made mistakes. And the story broke. I think – I think that's an interesting question, 'Why now?' Four days before an election . . .

UNIDENTIFIED REPORTER NO.2: Governor, did the girls know about this?

BUSH: No, the girls did not know until tonight. . . . I've talked to them. I'm a dad. I'm trying to – trying to teach my children right from wrong. I chose the course that – that to my daughters I was going to tell them [sic] they shouldn't drive and drink and that's the course of action I took.

Press conference, CNN, 2 November 2000

A MESSAGE OF 'DISCIPLINE' AND 'FOCUS'

'On a summer night in 1986, spent with his wife and friends at the Broadmoor resort in Colorado Springs in celebration of his and some friends' 40th birthdays that year, Bush partied heartily. He woke up with a raging hangover. To his stunned friends, he simply began announcing that he had made a decision never to drink again.

'It was a spontaneous pledge but one he has kept, says Bush. As he put it to me a few years ago when I was preparing a story about the contrasting ways in which he and [Ann] Richards viewed addiction-treatment programs in the state prison system (in sum, he has much more faith in the cold-turkey approach): "I quit for the rest of my life and if you catch me drinking, it's not going to be a good sign for your old buddy George."'

Sam Howe Verhovek, 'Is There Room on the Republican Ticket for Another George Bush?' *New York Times Magazine*, 13 September 1998

WALTERS: Do you ever take, like, a glass of wine at a wedding or something?

BUSH: No, I've had no alcohol since I decided to quit.

WALTERS: Are you afraid you're an alcoholic?

BUSH: No.

WALTERS: Then why wouldn't – couldn't you take, you know, I don't know, a 'Happy New Year, here's a sip of champagne'?

BUSH: Because I just decided to quit.

WALTERS: Period.

BUSH: When I said I was quitting, I was quitting. And I think that speaks to my discipline and my focus.

20/20, ABC, 5 May 2000

'One afternoon [in 1987] at a Mexican restaurant in Dallas, [Bush] spied Al Hunt, the *Wall Street Journal*'s Washington Bureau Chief. Hunt and his family, including his four-year-old son, had just settled into their seats . . . Now Hunt spotted the thirty-nine-year-old Bush [*sic*] winding over to his table. "You no good fucking sonofabitch, I will never fucking forget what you wrote!" he heard the vice president's son sputtering as he stepped up to Hunt and his family.

'Hunt stared at him, nonplussed. He didn't know Bush very well, had hardly seen him around the campaigns or at the White House. Lingering for thirty seconds by Hunt's table, Bush mentioned the *Washingtonian*. Hunt was confused. He hadn't thrown any darts, let alone any hatchets, at Bush's father. He also assumed that Bush was drinking heavily, that "he was quite clearly lubricated".'

Bill Minutaglio, *First Son*, pp. 208–09.

(As this episode took place in the spring of 1987, 'the vice president's son' was not thirty-nine, as Minutaglio painstakingly asserts: Bush's fortieth birthday, with its famous vow of abstinence, had been on 6 July 1986.)

ON J. H. HATFIELD'S FORTUNATE SON

In October 1999, Bush's propaganda team swung into action to suppress an ugly story: that, in 1972, he had been busted for cocaine possession down in Houston, and that his dad then managed, with the help of a compliant local judge, to have the crime expunged from the record, on the condition that the 26-year-old perform a few months of community service at Project PULL, a non-profit-making organization that helps troubled youths in inner-city Houston.

Thereafter Bush would often rail against the author J. H. Hatfield, whose *Fortunate Son* had made the charge. In this passage from an interview with Seth Mnookin of *Brill's Content*, the candidate addressed the case again, and in the process made a few intriguing slips.

MNOOKIN: Now, speaking of rumors and gossip, the St Martin's Press, the book they put out. Should there be a legal, should there be some kind of redress, when publishers print that stuff, either in – should there be responsibility in the courts?

BUSH: Well, I don't know that, I don't know that question. You know, I would hope there would – *to save* – to protect the innocent, but the problem is I'm a public figure, and the question is, where do you draw the line?

I think there ought to be some – I think the press corps ought to self-police, and I think there ought to be – in order to enhance the integrity of the press corps, it seems like to me that when they catch, when they catch *these fraudulent acts, these scurrilous attacks*, they ought to rise up in indignation, and I don't know if that – you know, I think that maybe might have occurred when they started condemning this guy for *writing the story*.

Brill's Content, September 2000 (emphasis added)

Nowhere in his statement (or in any other statement) did Bush claim that Hatfield's story was untrue. In fact, he all but confirmed it. The press condemned Hatfield, Bush said, 'for writing the story' – not for inventing it, but just for daring to report it. Moreover, the Governor began his answer with a typically revealing slip of the lip: 'You know, I would hope there would [be some legal means] *to save* – to protect the innocent.' 'To save' implies not 'protection of the innocent', but mere damage control, as in 'save my campaign' (or 'my ass').

'Scurrilous' does not mean 'untrue', furthermore, but 'vulgar', 'low', 'indecent', 'mean'. Tellingly, the only word that Bush did use to denote untruth was 'fraudulent' – but it refers to 'acts' rather than writings; and the only 'acts' at issue were, of course, Bush's own.

Although Hatfield's standing has been hurt beyond repair (even champions of free speech joined in the media's assault on him), his story merits close attention. First of all, Bush's altruistic stint at Project PULL is wildly out of character – a charitable sojourn unlike anything he'd ever done before or has done since. (Sometimes, the story is that Poppy made him do it, as a lesson in *noblesse oblige*. But that soft father never made his eldest son do anything, except drop certain girlfriends who failed to make the grade; and such cold orders came from Mom and Dad together.)

What Bush doesn't say, moreover, is as telling as the things he says – and so it's noteworthy that he has so rarely mentioned, publicly, his time at Project PULL. For all his efforts to 'reach out' to African-Americans, and his heavy volunteerist pitch, as a candidate for Governor, then President, Bush seldom talked about his noble months of service to the poor – an odd silence for a savvy politician, who, one might think, would mine that bit of his biography for every ounce of credit.

JESUS LOVES ME

By his own account, Bush was transformed completely by his partnership with Jesus, Who, through the sturdy medium of Billy Graham, entered Bush's famous heart in 1985. It was a timely conversion. Vice President Bush was gearing up for his presidential run in 1988, and had a mammoth image problem with the Christian right, who had never thought him to be one of them; and it was the unofficial duty of the first son – Poppy's 'loyalty enforcer' – to rectify the situation. As the family's chief liaison to the Christian Coalition, Bush would clearly do way better as a born-again than as a wimpy main-line Protestant. Considering his own apt self-description as 'a political animal', it is hard to believe that his decision to get 'right with God' bore no relation whatsoever to his all-consuming drive to make his father President.*

---

* Similarly, George's brother Jeb, a Catholic convert, had fallen from the faith – but then came straight home to the Church right after losing his first bid to be the Governor of Florida: 'Starting in November 1994, two weeks after his bitter defeat, he attended classes under the Roman Catholic Church's Rite of Christian Initiation of Adults. He went once a week for five months to [wife] Columba's church, the Epiphany Catholic Church in Miami, and was received into the faith at Easter 1995.' *Time*, 8 June 1998.

To point out the political convenience of his spiritual move is not to hint that Bush was insincere in his profession of renewed belief. He is no doubt a deeply pious man, boasting long and close relationships with many other deeply pious men. Indeed, his political and spiritual commitments do not contradict but reinforce each other: 'I've heard the call. I believe God wants me to run for President,' he told James Robison, the right-wing Fort Worth televangelist, in 1998. Bush feels 'a sense of destiny', observes Ed Young, Bush's Houston pastor. 'It's mystical. He will look right at you and say, "I'm going to be the President of the United States." And there's no ego in it. He is just reporting facts.' Bush identified especially closely with Jesus' most devout apostle, and Christianity's greatest propagandist: 'We talked a lot about Paul,' Don Evans has recalled.[52]

Thus the authenticity of Bush's faith is not in doubt. Indeed, it would be better for us all if he were faking it, this being a constitutional democracy (whose greatest presidents have *not* been deeply pious men). While Bush's zeal is surely genuine, there's still good reason to approach his spiritual engagement with the utmost skepticism. Specifically, the deep convergence of his turn-the-other-cheek philosophy and kick-ass politics (and, of course, peculiar zest for executions) raises questions as to how he understands the Savior's 'message'.

This section pertains to Bush's own religiosity. For more on his views of Christianity (and other creeds), see 'That Old-Time Religion'.

The Governor boldly introduced his faith into the national campaign at the Iowa Republican debate on 13 December 1999. The contenders there were each asked, by NBC's John Bachman, to name 'the political philosopher or thinker . . . you most identify with, and why.'

BUSH: Christ, because he changed my heart.

BACHMAN: I think the viewer would like to know more on how he's changed your heart.

BUSH: Well, if they don't know, it's going to be hard to explain. When you turn your heart and your life over to Christ, when you accept Christ as the Savior, it changes your heart. It changes your life. And that's what happened to me.

(Applause)

No thoughtful Christian could be happy with that answer, since Jesus was, definitively, *not* a 'political philosopher or thinker' – as the Pharisees and Romans also failed to understand.* As a piece of worldly cunning, on the other hand, it was brilliant, since it turned the Governor's ignorance to his advantage, even making it appear to be a sign of grace that he could not 'explain' his transformation. Given the applause, his answer surely helped him with the Christian right throughout the nation – and especially there in Iowa, where Bush won big soon after the debate.

Of course, such secular advancement is not what Jesus ever had in mind – as we might recall from a pertinent passage in the Gospel of St Luke. Fearing that his words were threatening them with worldly not eternal punishment, the Pharisees despatched *agents provocateurs* to try to get the Savior to endorse a sweeping tax-cut plan – a verbal crime that would permit them to 'deliver him unto the power and authority of the governor'.

---

* 'God, of course, is the greatest philosopher of all' – Richard Nixon, quoted in Monica Crowley, *Nixon in Winter* (Random House), p. 341.

'And they asked him, saying, "Master, we know that thou sayest and teachest rightly, neither acceptest thou the person of any, but teachest the way of God truly:

'"Is it lawful for us to give tribute unto Caesar, or no?"

'But he perceived their craftiness, and said unto them, "Why tempt ye me?

'"Show me a penny. Whose image and superscription hath it?" They answered and said, "Caesar's."

'And he said unto them, "Render therefore unto Caesar the things which be Caesar's, and unto God the things which be God's."

'And they could not take hold of his words before the people: and they marvelled at his answer, and held the peace.'

Luke 20:21–26

Three weeks later in New Hampshire, Bush was given an opportunity to reconfirm his piety, when Tim Russert, in a multicultural spirit (and somewhat dyslexically), asked about the millions of believers in the nation's other faiths.

RUSSERT: Governor Bush, in the last debate, when you talked about Jesus being the most philosopher thinker that you respected [sic], many people applauded you. Others said, 'What role would religion have in the Oval Office with George W. Bush?' Fifteen million atheists in this country, five million Jews, five million Muslims, millions more Buddhists and Hindus – should they feel excluded from George W. Bush because of his allegiance to Jesus?

BUSH: No. I was asked what influenced my life and I gave the answer the way – an honest, unvarnished answer. It doesn't make me better than you or better than anybody else, but it's a foundation for how I live my life. Some may accept the answer and some may not. But, Tim, I really don't care. It's me. It's what I'm all about. It's how I live my life. It's just a part of me.

GOP debate, Durham, New Hampshire, 1 June 2000

Here again, 'they marvelled at his answer, and held the peace' – even though Bush had gone on record with his personal belief that non-Christians will not make it into Heaven.

Bush's fervent claim to have been made anew by Christ – 'It's what I'm all about' – does not quite square with the abundant evidence of a bitterly unChristian temperament.

Several months after his father lost the 1964 Texas Senate campaign to Ralph Yarborough, the incumbent Democratic populist, Bush said he met Yale's prominent campus chaplain.

'I ran into William Sloane Coffin, who was the preacher at Yale, supposedly the guy that was there to comfort students,' said the Governor. 'I introduced myself and he said, "Yeah, I know your father, and your father lost to a better man."'

Even today, 33 years later, Bush is clearly offended by the statement, and it is one of the many reasons, he says, that he couldn't wait to get back to Texas, after his graduation in 1968: 'Texas people are more polite. I don't think a Texan would do that to a son.'

Sam Howe Verhovek, *New York Times Magazine,* 13 September 1998

Coffin's offhand comment to the boy, if he made it, was indefensible. Nevertheless, the lingering ferocity of that grievance does raise questions as to just how thoroughly Jesus Christ had purified Bush's heart twelve years before. Indeed, the record indicates that Bush's whole career in politics was motivated by a thirst for a payback that belies the candidate's assertion that Christianity is 'how I live my life'.

When Bush first announced his plan to run for governor, Randy Galloway, sportswriter for the *Fort Worth Star-Telegram*, asked him why. Ann Richards was 'too popular', said Galloway. 'You can't beat her.'

'Randy, I'm not runnin' against her,' Bush said. 'I'm runnin' against the guy in the White House.'

The venom in his voice conveyed a very personal motive: Bush had to avenge his father's humiliation in losing to Bill Clinton. Galloway remembers, 'The way he said it was like a blood oath.'

. . . Lacey Neuhaus, a Houston friend, agrees with this analysis. 'His dad had just lost. It ate him up. He was driven to go after the people who had trashed his dad. Ann Richards was tied to Clinton – or a surrogate for him – and therefore a perfect target . . . Running gave George a way to vent.'

Gail Sheehy, 'The Accidental Candidate', *Vanity Fair*, October 2000

The chasm between Bush's Christian scruples and Nixonian vindictiveness does not suggest plain old hypocrisy, but a profound blindness to the meaning of the Sermon on the Mount.

'There are some great admonitions in the Bible, talking about, you know, don't try to take the speck out of your neighbor's eye when you've got a log in your own. I'm mindful of that.'

Sam Howe Verhovek, *New York Times Magazine*, 13 September 1998

'Judge not, lest ye be judged.

'For with what judgment ye judge, ye shall be judged: and with what measure ye mete, it shall be measured to you again.

'And why beholdest thou the mote that is in thy brother's eye, but considerest not the beam that is in thine own eye?

'Or how wilt thou say to thy brother, Let me pull the mote out of thine eye; and, behold, a beam is in thine own eye?

'Thou hypocrite, first cast out the beam out of thine own eye; and then shalt thou see clearly to cast out the mote out of thy brother's eye.'

Matthew, 7:1–5

That verse bears directly on the great self-contradiction at the heart of Bush's whole political career – i.e., his own lifelong immunity to punishment for crimes that, as the Governor of Texas, he enthusiastically nailed others for committing. The busts for brawling (as an undergraduate), and drunk driving (in his twenties), and his own post-graduate drug use (a practice that, he claimed, he had not indulged past 1974), may well have meant the end of him, if he had been a poor young fella living under Bush's rule, and not the child of privilege that he was.

Whatever the true history of Bush's crimes (and punishments), he could not discuss the contradiction even hypothetically, when Larry King attempted to engage him on the subject. Rather than approach the issue of hypocrisy abstractly, and acknowledge, in a Christian spirit, the inequity that King was trying to address, Bush could only treat the questions tactically – that is, as attempts to worm something out of him.

The tension between King's emotional inquiry and the Governor's impatient wariness spoke volumes about Bush's 'heart'. (It also suggests that, as Bush reads it, Matthew 7:1–5 pertains not to himself and his rash judgments, but to anyone who would judge *him*.) Faced with a question that pertained directly to the Christian 'admonition' which he mentioned to the *New York Times*, Bush could only keep on parroting his Christian *message*.

KING: You took a hit on the drug issue.

BUSH: Yes.

KING: And one of the things that was raised was that, I guess, the hypocrisy question. If you did – and it's none of our business if you did or didn't – if you did, is it fair to have anyone in prison who did [get arrested on a drug charge] in Texas?

BUSH: I – you see—

KING: Now, that's a fair hypothetical.

BUSH: No, but I think – look – no – what you're trying to do is to get me to talk about my past, and I respect your attempt to do so. I'm not willing to do so.

KING: [Unintelligible]

BUSH: Here's what's important in life. Here's what's important in life for a parent or a leader is that you learn from your mistakes.

KING: Correct.

BUSH: That's important, and that's the most important thing for leadership.

KING: So if I were – let's say – I don't want to make it personal – if I'm Governor and I did something illegal, whatever it was, and anyone in my state is in jail for doing the same thing, and I didn't get caught and they did, I'd go nuts.

That would bother me – it was hypocrisy. That guy sitting behind the bar who did the same thing I did and I – he got caught and I didn't, and I'm the Governor. It would drive me nuts.

BUSH: Yes, well—

KING: If that's true, seriously.

BUSH: Well, I appreciate your attempt to get me to talk about my past and—

KING: But that wouldn't bother you?

BUSH: Here's what people need to know about me, that I'm going to bring honor and dignity, that I've learned from mistakes made, that I am prepared to send a message of personal responsibility, and that's what I'm going to do.

Larry King Live, CNN, 16 December 1999

BUSH FAMILY VALUES

Like his Christianity, Bush's fierce devotion to his big happy family is as political as it is personal. This is, in part, a propaganda matter. Bush uses his big happy family to send the 'message' that he comes from a big happy family – the same big happy message that Bush Sr sent the voters back in 1992 when, at the climax of the Republican convention, he (or someone) had the whole toothsome clan troop out onto the stage and affluently beam upon the hall of roaring delegates. It was a not-too-subtle dig at Clinton, whose wee ménage and fractious marriage seemed to mark him as unfit by contrast with the happy Papa Bush and all those happy sprouts.

Like that propaganda spectacle, our President's loud devotion to his family – and, specifically, his dad – is not just a cheery ad for 'family values' (or 'togetherness,' the coolly sentimental concept that *Barbara*'s father, Marvin Pierce, who ran *McCall's*, promoted through the magazine back in the fifties). Bush's grand fixation on his father speaks profoundly to the right, whose longing for a more paternal kind of Chief Executive has much to do with their weird loathing of the boomer Clinton, and of the kids-are-all-right sixties. Thus our President's obsessive emulation of George Sr – servicing Big Oil, employing Baker/Cheney/Powell, having Laura stump for reading (just like Barbara), choosing 'education' as a way to soften the agenda, battering Iraq, and so on – expresses more than his ambivalent desire to shore up Poppy's masculinity. This Bush's desperate father-worship speaks to all of those uncomfortable souls who wish that Dad – whether he might look like Ronald Reagan, or like someone else – would come back home to lead them, and the rest of us, in straight paths for his name's sake.

Of course, such motives are unconscious. Bush's service to and for the Family is, first of all, dynastic. As J. H. Hatfield meticulously demonstrates (which may have been another of his sins), our President's selection was apparently the upshot of a long-term plan that used the family's full financial and political resources to attain the Oval Office. That plan entailed (1) Bush's landslide re-election as Governor in 1998, with (2) a major push to win a strong majority of the Hispanic vote, and (3) a drive to get Rick Perry, a Republican, elected as Lieutenant Governor (to make sure the GOP retained control of Texas's government, if and when Bush should win the big prize). The plan's final step was the election of Jeb Bush as Governor of Florida, so as to lock up those twenty-five electoral votes. To ensure Jeb's victory, the Big Oil machine in Texas, at W.'s urging, gave the Florida campaign over $1 million (that we know of) – a move that many Democrats, and environmentalists, deplored. 'Why would anyone in Texas want to give money to Florida?' asked Florida's Democratic Party chairman. 'Obviously, it's his brother. They're playing politics with Florida's future.' The first son responded to such carping with a message of fraternal loyalty. 'If the Democrats in Florida don't understand brotherly love then they better reassess their emotions. I help my brother because he is my brother. If he asked for help, I'm more than willing to help him.'[53]

With Florida-and-Texas always on his mind, the latter's Governor was prone to certain gaffes.

BUSH: I talked to my little brother, Jeb – I haven't told this to many people. But he's the governor of – I shouldn't call him my little brother – my brother, Jeb, the great Governor of Texas.

JIM LEHRER: Florida.

BUSH: Florida. The state of the Florida.

News Hour With Jim Lehrer, PBS, 27 April 2000

Bush has always been as eager to deny his clan's ambition as he has been to gratify it:

' "Dynasty" is the wrong word. There's a history, but dynasty has got this sense of royalty.'

USA Today, 28 July 2000

By 'the wrong word', Bush meant 'the wrong message', since 'dynasty' reminded viewers of everything about this Bush that he would like them to forget: the deep pockets, the fancy schools, the lifelong easy ride. Above all, 'dynasty' would have implied that the Bush family *wanted* him to be our President – assuming that post to be *theirs*, as a sort of birthright. Typically, George H. W. Bush betrayed that feeling by denying it: 'I'm not like Joe Kennedy sitting there: "Here's a couple of hundred thousand – go out and win the West Virginia primary,"' he told CBS in 1996, about his son the Governor's presidential chances. 'I, you know, it's not a scheme. It's not a dynasty. It's not a legacy.'

Karl Rove, on the other hand, had been less coy about the family's dynastic longings. 'On this day, George W. Bush clearly comes into his own, and no one can dispute that,' Turd Blossom told the *Dallas Morning News* the day of Bush's swearing-in as Governor of Texas. 'We really do have a generational passage here. Sort of like Joe Kennedy handing off to young John.'[54]

A FOLLOW-UP QUESTION, PLEASE?

'You mean to tell me, Mr Vice President, you're retracting your concession?' Mr Bush asked, his tone incredulous, one aide said. The Texas Governor had already begun preparing his victory remarks.

'You don't have to be snippy about it,' Mr Gore responded, according to several of those who heard Mr Gore's side of the conversation.

Mr Bush told Mr Gore that his brother Jeb, the Governor of Florida, had just assured him that Florida was his, Gore aides said.

'Let me explain something,' Mr Gore said. 'Your younger brother is not the ultimate authority on this.'

New York Times, 9 November 2000

Here Bush's tendency to blurt things out might well have gotten him in trouble, if any members of the press had bothered paying attention. The vote was still in doubt, with many tens of thousands of Florida ballots still uncounted, and the exit polls all pointing to a victory for Gore. How, therefore, did Florida's Governor know that Bush had won?

THE WIT AND HUMOR OF
GEORGE W. BUSH

One of the things in the public arena, a lot of people take
    themselves so seriously.
And they've got the sullenness.
And everything is so heavy.
And humor, I think, is such a key ingredient to life.

> George W. Bush, January 2000

Q: When you're not talking politics, what do you and
        [your father] talk about?

BUSH: Pussy.

> To David Fink of the *Hartford Courant,* at the 1988
> Republican Convention, *Salon,* 9 April 2000

'Desert Storm. We sold a lot of tickets.'

> Joking about the commercial advantages of being George Bush's son,
> and part-owner of a baseball stadium
> *Larry King Live,* CNN, 16 August 1992

'[You're all] going to hell.'

> Joking about what he would say to Israeli Jews upon arriving in
> the Middle East in 1993, Austin-American Statesman, 1 December 1998

Republican gubernatorial candidate George W. Bush admitted Thursday he was guilty of a fly-by shooting when he mistakenly killed a bird that is on the protected-species list. Bush received a $130 misdemeanor fine in the Case of the Badly Bagged Bird.

'I killed a killdee,' confessed Bush, who was hunting with a borrowed 20-gauge shotgun on the opening day of dove season. 'I thought it was a dove.'

What Bush actually killed was a killdeer, known colloquially as a killdee because that is the cry the tiny plover makes. Asked the difference between a killdee and a killdeer, Bush said, 'One's dead and one's alive.'

Houston Chronicle, 2 September 1994

'In the end, it did not hurt, and it may have helped. I think it showed a side of me that voters had not seen. I was able to laugh at myself, to make a mistake, admit it, and poke fun at it. People watch the way you handle things; they get a feeling they like and trust you, or they don't. The killdee incident helped fill in blanks the voters may have had about what type of person I was. Plus it gave me great joke material.'

George W. Bush, *A Charge to Keep*, pp. 37–38

'I'm glad it wasn't deer season, I might have killed a cow.'

Associated Press, 17 October 1994

'Please . . . don't kill me!'

Mocking what Karla Faye Tucker said when asked, just before her execution,

'What would you say to Governor Bush?' *Talk*, September 1999

'If the Russian government attacks innocent women and children in Chechnya,' Bush told an Associated Press reporter, 'it cannot expect international aid.' The reporter asked the Governor if such attacks were taking place. Phone in hand, Bush turned to foreign policy advisor Condoleezza Rice: 'They *are* attacking women and children, aren't they?' Rice nodded yes.

When Rice appeared on ABC's *This Week* the following Sunday, she said that Bush's question was a 'little joke'. 'One thing that I've learned about the Governor,' she said, 'is that he has quite a sense of humor. So you have to be ready for that.'

Associated Press, 17 November 1999; This Week, 28 November 1999

(Bushwatch.com)

DAVID LETTERMAN: Let me remind you of one thing, Governor: the road to Washington runs through me.

BUSH: It's about time you had the *heart* to invite me.

Late Night with David Letterman, 1 March 2000;

taped shortly after Letterman's open-heart surgery

'I'm a uniter, not a divider. That means when it comes time to sew up your chest cavity, we use stitches as opposed to opening it up.'

Ibid. (This joke – which makes no sense –

was booed by the studio audience.)

'If this were a dictatorship, it'd be a heck of a lot easier, just so long as I'm the dictator.'

CNN, 18 December 2000

Bush had also used that gag in 1996, in a speech before a business group in Texas: 'It would be a heck of a lot easier to work in a dictatorship than a democracy' (Hatfield, p. 173).

'Who's that goosing me with that stick?'

> George H. W. Bush, when his eldest poked him in the rear
> end with a fishing rod, *Washington Post*, 28 December 2000

How do you rib a man for his failings and foibles if he spends much of his time ribbing himself? That is a question that President Bush and his aides have clearly asked and just as clearly answered, and what they have decided is that there is no armor or inoculation as effective as self-effacement . . .

[I]f you want to tease him for his tortured use of the English language, well, Mr Bush is already on top of that as well. His speech at the annual Radio and Television Correspondents Association dinner in Washington on Thursday night steered the event's tradition of comical presidential commentary in a mischievously masochistic direction. In fact, Mr Bush took out a copy of *George W. Bushisms* (Simon & Schuster), a collection of so-called *Accidental Wit and Wisdom of the 43rd President*, and reveled in his own ruminations.

> *New York Times*, 1 April 2001

As you know, we're studying safe levels for arsenic in drinking water.

(Laughter)

To base our decision on sound science, the scientists told us we needed to test the water glasses of about 3,000 people.

(Laughter)

Thank you for participating.

(Laughter)

> Radio and Television Correspondents Association dinner, 29 March 2001

CURIOUS GEORGE

BUSH ON BOOKS

Your mom loves books, and the Vice President does too. I've had conversations with them about their favorites. Did she get the boys reading or did that happen on their own?

G.W.B.: 'I think it kind of happened on our own. I was never a great intellectual. I like books and pick them up and read them for the fun of it. I think all of us are basically in the same vein. We're not real serious, studious readers. We are readers for fun.'

George Bush with Doug Wead, *George Bush: Man of Integrity*
(Eugene, Oregon, 1988), p. 132. (The interviewer was Wead,
a Christian political operative working for the Bush family.)

'I love history. I just finished reading *The Sword of San Jacinto*, about Sam Houston. I like occasional social commentary. I say occasional; I occasionally read social commentary. But I love history. I was a history major in college and I spent a lot of time on history. I'm trying to wrack my brain now that you asked me to think of all the great history books. Well, I mean, *The*

River Also Rises, the book about the Mississippi River that flooded; the '27 flood, I believe it was, of the Mississippi. It's a great book . . . It's amazing to be interested in history and living – making history. It's an interesting coincidence.'

C-SPAN interview, quoted in *Jewish World Review*, 5 February 1999

'When I was growing up, I preferred reading biographies about historical figures and baseball players. I still enjoy books about history, especially Texas history: *The Raven: A Biography of Sam Houston*, by Marquis James, is one of my favorites.

'I also like studying forces that helped shape today's economy and social structure. *The Good Life and Its Discontents: The American Dream in the Age of Entitlement, 1945–1995*, by Robert J. Samuelson, and *The Dream and the Nightmare: The Sixties' Legacy to the Underclass*, by Myron Magnet, each provide food for thought and discussion.

'Laura and I often read to our daughters when they were young. One of their top requests was *The Very Hungry Caterpillar*, by Eric Carle. A few more of my favorite books for children are: *Sarah's Flag for Texas*, by Jane Alexander Knapik; *James and the Giant Peach*, by Roald Dahl; *My Side of the Mountain*, by Jean Craighead George; *Tuck Everlasting*, by Natalie Babbitt; *The Wind in the Willows*, by Kenneth Grahame; *Just So Stories*, by Rudyard Kipling.

'Our capacity for discovery is never lost as long as we continue to read.'

American Spectator, December 1998

'He reads at night, another habit (current bedside books, according to former librarian Laura: *The Color of Night*, the latest thriller by David L. Lindsey; *Hadrian's Walls*, a novel by Robert Draper; and John C. Waugh's *Reelecting Lincoln*).'

Texas Monthly, June 1999

'I can't remember any specific books.'

Associated Press, 26 August 1999

Bush replied thus when asked, by a schoolchild in South Carolina, to name the book he liked the most when he was small.

'The Bible has influenced me a lot. I read it every day. I've sought redemption and believe I've found it. I get great strength from the Bible. There's a book called *Modern Times* by Paul Johnson, which had an effect on my thinking. It's just one of those books that catches your attention, and you go, Whoa – this thing is powerful.'

National Review, 31 December 1999

He reads the Bible every morning. 'I've got what's called the *One-Year Bible*, and I read it every other year all the way through. In the off years I'll pick and choose different parts of the Bible.'

Aaron Latham, 'How George W. Found God,' *George*, September 2000

Despite the high importance of his faith in his political agenda, Bush's daily reading of the Scriptures seems rarely to have been reflected in his speeches. In this he is remarkably unlike other fundamentalist politicians, who routinely quote the Good Book in their homilies, both written and extemporaneous.

BRIT HUME: Governor, there are a great many people who have said that they couldn't have done any better on that pop quiz on world leaders than you did. But it does seem, fairly or not, to have raised the issue of your knowledgeability of the world and your interest in that. Could you tell us, sir, what do you read every day for information?

BUSH: What do I read?

HUME: What do you read for information?

BUSH: Well, I read the newspaper.

HUME: Which?

BUSH: I read the *Dallas Morning News*, I read the *New York Times*, I read the *Wall Street Journal* and I read the *Austin-American Statesman*. I'm not so sure I get a lot of knowledge out of there, but I read them every day.

HUME: And what else?

BUSH: Well, I read books all the time. I'm reading a book on Dean Acheson right now. I like to read mysteries, I like to read novels.

But look, here's the test of a leader. A test of a leader is when given responsibility, can you perform? And I've got a record of leading. It's the second biggest state in the Union. If it were a nation, it would be the eleventh largest economy in the world. And I've had confirmation about my leadership style. The people of Texas overwhelmingly voted for me for the first time – for a person to be elected for the first time to back-to-back four-year terms. I've been able to reach across racial lines in my state. I got nearly 50 percent of the Hispanic vote. I got a significant part of the African-American vote. People appreciate the fact I know how to lead.

New Hampshire GOP debate, 2 December 1999

(Bush had said the same thing earlier in the same debate, in answering a question on his lack of foreign policy experience.)

I ask this national candidate what he reads in the morning. '*New York Times*. For news. Good foreign coverage. I don't read stories about myself, which *sometimes* have news.' He smirks. '*Chronicle*, of course' – he nods to the *Houston Chronicle* reporter. 'Sometimes read clips from the *Wall Street Journal*. Course we get the wire service.'

Gail Sheehy, 'The Accidental Candidate', *Vanity Fair*, October 2000

'Sitting down and reading a 500-page book on public policy or philosophy or something.'

Talk, September 1999

Bush replied thus, without a pause, when Tucker Carlson asked him to name something he isn't good at.

JUDY WOODRUFF: Governor Bush, while we are considering America's place in the world. You volunteered at last week's debate that you were now reading the biography of Dean Acheson. And my question is: What lessons do you take from the successes and the failures of Acheson and George Marshall during that critical period in US history? And how would you apply that to a Bush international policy?

BUSH: The lessons learned are that the United States must not retreat within our borders – that we must promote the peace. In order to promote the peace, we've got to have strong alliances: alliances in Europe, alliances in the Far East. In order to promote the peace, I believe we ought to be a free-trading nation in a free-trading world, because free trade brings markets and markets bring hope and prosperity.

And in order to keep the peace, the United States must be strong militarily. In a speech I gave at the Citadel in South Carolina, I talked about the need to not only make sure that the morale in today's military is high, but also to make sure that we reconfigure our military. You see, if we get to redefine how war is fought, we get to redefine how peace is kept.

The lessons of Acheson and Marshall are – is that our nation's greatest export to the world has been, is, and always will be the incredible freedoms we understand in the great land called America.

(Applause)

CNN's Candy Crowley asked Senator Orrin Hatch about the World Trade Organization, and then:

JOHN KING: Senator McCain, tonight there is an emotional kind of diplomatic drama playing out about a 5-year-old boy from Cuba, who lost his mother as they tried to enter the United States by water. The boy's father back in Cuba says he wants his son back. If you were President of the United States, what would you do?

MCCAIN: I'd say to Mr Castro, let his father come to the United States and enjoy peace and freedom and be reunited with his son. We don't want his son to grow up under communist tyranny.

Let me talk about Dean Acheson a second. When Dean Acheson walked into Harry Truman's office in June of 1950 and said, 'North Korea's attacked South Korea,' Harry Truman didn't take a poll: Harry Truman knew what we had to do. If he'd taken a poll, maybe Americans wouldn't have let us go.

This administration is poll-driven and not principle-driven. We didn't have to get into Kosovo. Once we stumbled into it, we had to win it. And the fact is that this administration has conducted a feckless photo-op foreign policy for which we will pay a very heavy price in American blood and treasure.

You have to have a concept of what you want the world to look like, where our interests and our values lie and how we are going to bring this world into the next century and call it, again, the American century.

WOODRUFF: Thank you, Senator McCain.

GOP debate, Phoenix, 6 December 1999

The Senator's point was not exactly clear. (Invading Cuba wouldn't be too popular, but we should do it anyway?)* And yet the true purpose of his Great Leap Backward from Havana to Pyongyang was not to ace the question about Elian, but to embarrass the front-runner, by coming up with a *specific* from the book – James Chace's *Acheson* – that the Governor had so vaguely paraphrased.

McCain got high marks for that shot at Bush, who later bristled at the speculation that he hadn't read the book at all. 'I mean, what kind of world is this?' he lamented to the *Washington Post*. 'I guess people are so used to being lied to in Washington that they think I'd get up on national TV and

---

* This would have been in keeping with the novel foreign policy agenda that he pushed throughout the contest for his party's nomination: 'rogue state rollback'.

make up some book. Where have we gotten to?' The Governor then took a tardy counter-shot at Senator McCain's performance: 'Maybe I should have picked out one little bitty detail of the book. I don't think so. I thought my answer was the right answer, otherwise I wouldn't have given it. I don't get it. I don't understand this cynicism.'[55]

That defensive self-appraisal says it all, capturing what's wrong not just with Bush's way of reading, but also with his education plans, and with his sort of governance. There could be no one 'right answer' to the open-ended question Woodruff asked. There's much to say about 'the successes and the failures' of the Truman team throughout 'that critical period in US history'. Her further question – on how the 'lessons' of Dean Acheson's Cold War accomplishments pertain to US foreign policy today – was also quite a good one, meaning that it offered Governor Bush the opportunity to think aloud on a rich and timely subject (and one that he himself had raised). But all that Bush could do was quickly rummage through his little bag of 'themes' for 'the right answer' – coming up with a pastiche of lines he'd used a hundred times, loosely fitted to the circumstances.* Whereas he should have *entertained* the question, he only tried to *nail* it – Bush told the *Post* that he had 'absolutely hammered' it, as if he were a sophomore who'd been memorizing answers all the night before. Thus, if he *had* read Chace's book, he read it just as he has always read (or had his staffers read) the memos and reports that cross his desk – in search of simple, handy bits for later use. That is not the way to lead *or* read – or to teach children how to read; and yet the President

---

* Moreover, that bit about 'exporting freedom' ran directly counter to what Dr Rice, his tutor and prospective National Security Advisor, was saying at the same time.

sees 'education' mainly as intensive training for an annual test, a vision just as narrowly utilitarian as his approach to Chace's *Acheson*.

Bush blew it. His take on *Acheson* was obviously not germane, however clear his point was to himself. And yet his answer was no worse than Senator McCain's. The Governor's assessment was right on the money: McCain *did* just 'pick out one little bitty detail from the book', and run with it – ran all the way from Cuba to Korea, then to Kosovo and home again, then stood there panting praise for Henry Luce. The illogic of his riff begged many questions (e.g., didn't the Korean War exact 'a very heavy price in American blood and treasure'?), but the press asked none of them, so wowed were they by Senator McCain's apparent mastery of the text.

But then, no reporter, then or later, thought to question James Chace's *Acheson*. Because it was *a book*, one written by a *known historian*, and on the subject of *a great American*, all hands assumed it to be Serious Stuff. And yet the book itself – much like the answers of McCain and Bush – is weak throughout, a hagiography based heavily on secondary sources. Unlike other recent studies of the early Cold War, *Acheson* provides a highly partial view of its intriguing subject, and of 'that critical period in US history'. And here it was the very ground of a debate, between two would-be presidents, on US foreign policy today.[56]

Thus that moment could not possibly shed light on anything. Far from demonstrating only Bush's difficulties with the world of books, it was a propaganda triple-whammy, stupefying at every level.

'Reading is the basics for all learning.'

'All Things Considered', National Public Radio, 28 March 2000

The Governor made this statement in announcing his 'Reading First' initiative in Reston, Virginia.

> 'This is Preservation Month. I appreciate preservation. It's what you do when you run for President. You gotta preserve.'
>
> *Los Angeles Times,* 28 January 2000

Thus spake Bush in honoring 'Perseverance Month' at Fairgrounds Elementary School in Nashua, New Hampshire. But in the end, the candidate's illiteracy just didn't matter much, this being the culture of TV.

BUT SERIOUSLY, FOLKS . . .

Bush did some stand-up on the subject at the Al Smith Memorial Dinner on 19 October 2000:

> And I see Bill Buckley is here tonight, fellow Yale man.
>
> (Applause)
>
> 'We go way back and we have a lot in common. Bill wrote a book at Yale – I read one.'
>
> (Laughter)

LET ME MAKE ONE THING
PERFECTLY CLEAR

Intelligence is can you think logically.
Intelligence is do you have a basis from which to make decisions.
Intelligence in politics is do you have good instincts.

George W. Bush, *Washington Post*, 19 January 2000

As a creature of TV, Bush is prone to flashes of illogic of a kind not based in any neurological disorder. He is especially given to tautologies – 'A is A because A is A.' While this tendency may well bespeak an inability to reason, it's just as likely to reflect on Bush's understanding of the fact that reason isn't *needed* on TV. 'Talk on television isn't meant to be listened to,' writes Peter Conrad. 'The words merely gain for us the time to look at the talker.'[57] Any able propagandist knows this instinctively. He therefore orates not to make an argument but just to be there talking firmly on the screen – showing us that *he is talking*, and, ideally, emphasizing *just those words* that (focus groups have shown) make just *the right impression*.

Tautology is the inevitable product of such spectacle.

BRIT HUME: What if there isn't any unity at the Republican convention?

BUSH: I am confident there will be. I'm confident people are coming together. And the reason I believe this is because our party is united.

'Fox Special Report with Brit Hume', Fox TV, 19 July 2000

'A reformer with results is a conservative who has had compassionate results in the state of Texas.'

New York Times, 10 February 2000

'There is a lot of speculation and I guess there is going to continue to be a lot of speculation until the speculation ends.'

On whether he'll run for President;
Austin-American Statesman, 18 October 1998

KING: Only 1 percent of Americans are even affected by [the death tax], right?

BUSH: Well, if that's the case, let's do it.

KING: Yes, but when 1 percent convinces 99 percent that it's in their best interest to lower their—

BUSH: Well, maybe we ought – maybe we ought – I don't know the figure of 1 percent or 99 percent, but if that – if it's good public policy, it's good public policy.

Larry King Live, CNN, 20 July 2000

'If you don't stand for anything, you don't stand for anything. If you don't stand for something, you don't stand for anything.'

Austin-American Statesman, 2 November 2000

'Dick Cheney and I do not want this nation to be in a recession. We want anybody who can find work to be able to find work.'

60 Minutes II, CBS, 5 December 2000

'One of the common denominators I have found is that expectations rise above that which is expected.'

Los Angeles Times, 27 September 2000

Some tautologies are very subtle, embedded in a single word:

'It is clear our nation is reliant upon big foreign oil. More and more of our imports come from overseas.'

Beaverton, Oregon, 25 September 2000; *Slate*

'Now, by the way, surplus means a little money left over, otherwise it wouldn't be called a surplus.'

Kalamazoo, Missouri, 27 October 2000; FCDH Transcripts

Bush tends also to surprise the audience with a bald self-contradiction. For this tendency there may be some physiological explanation; or it may express the muffled protests of a very deeply buried conscience.

'I don't care what the polls say. I don't. I'm doing what I think what's wrong.'

New York Times, 15 March 2000

Bush was referring here to his economic policies.

'Well, I think if you say you're going to do something and don't do it, that's trustworthiness.'

CNN online chat, 30 August 2000

'If you're sick and tired of the politics of cynicism and polls and principles, come and join this campaign.'

Hilton Head, South Carolina, 16 February 2000; *Slate*

'I'm a strong candidate because I come from the baby-boomer generation recognizing that we've got to usher in an era of responsible behavior.'

News Hour with Jim Lehrer, PBS, 27 April 2000

That inversion of the Myron Magnet thesis was the opposite of what Bush had meant to say – and what he did say all the time. For example: 'The culture of my generation, our generation, has clearly said, "If it feels good, do it, and be sure to blame somebody else if you have a problem"' (*Vanity Fair*, October 2000).

THE EDUCATION PRESIDENT:
THE SEQUEL

Each student should leave twelfth grade reading English at a twelfth-grade level or better. He should have read great English writers such as Shakespeare, Dickens, the Brontës, and, in translation, great Russian writers such as Tolstoy, Spanish writers such as Cervantes, Latin American writers such as Borges. Black students should know something about Hobbes, Locke, and Rousseau, and white students should know about Gandhi and Martin Luther King, Jr. In short, every student should know a little bit about everything, so he can make an intelligent decision about what he wants to study in greater depth in college.

Richard Nixon, *In the Arena: A Memoir of Victory,*
Defeat and Renewal (1990), pp. 99–100

'I had to read *War and Peace* when I was like 16 or 17. Don't give me a quiz on the thousands of characters in it, but I guess it had an influence because it was a discipline. It was more that than remembering anything in it. And of course, we had to read Shakespeare in school. It was required.'

George H. W. Bush, *New York Times*, 27 October 1988

179

'Higher education is not my priority.'

George W. Bush, *San Antonio Express-News*, 22 March 1998

As noted above, Bush's view of education is over-focused on 'results' – a clear reflection of his fierce pro-business fundamentalism. Students must be educated *for the workforce*, and that's it. They must have the basic skills, and solid 'character', to be reliable employees and (therefore) energetic shoppers. Any higher instruction, and they might turn 'arrogant', or 'uppity', as some folks used to put it.

Throughout the campaign, Bush took lots of credit for the great improvements in Texas's once-abysmal school system. As Molly Ivins, Paul Begala and others have demonstrated, those great improvements all predated Bush's term in Austin. The best that can be said for him is that he didn't interfere with them, although he did place an inordinate new emphasis on standardized tests – an innovation that leaves some kids behind, since not all children test as well as others, regardless of their gifts. In any case, the state's school system was impoverished by the Governor's tax cuts, although that fact was not apparent until after he had moved on to the White House (where he has been aggressively promoting similar tax cuts for the nation overall).

As to education, the biggest questions are these: Can an ill-read and semi-literate president really grasp the meaning, or importance, of true education? And is it possible for one so tightly bound to corporate interests to promote education at its best? (As chief of Houston's independent schools, Rod Paige, Bush's Secretary of Education, was quick to give the corporate marketers, like Channel One, full access to the classrooms.)

'If you don't measure, if we're having to guess whether or not our children are learning, by the time it's too late we're going to find out that they're not, if they're not.'

Campaign speech, MSNBC, 15 February 2000

'Laura and I really don't realize how bright our children is sometimes until we get an objective analysis.'

Meet the Press, NBC, 15 April 2000

'My education message will resignate amongst all parents.'

New York Post, 19 January 2000

'Governor Bush will not stand for the subsidation of failure.'

Ibid.

'How do you know if you don't measure if you have a system that simply suckles kids through?'

Beaufort, South Carolina, 16 February 2000, *Slate*

'We want our teachers to be trained so they can meet the obligations, their obligations as teachers. We want them to know how to teach the science of reading. In order to make sure there's not this kind of federal – federal cufflink.'

Milwaukee, 30 March 2000; *Slate*

'What's not fine is, rarely is the question asked, are, is our children learning?'

Los Angeles Times, 14 January 2000

'As Governor of Texas, I have set high standards for our public schools, and I have met those standards.'

CNN online chat, 30 August 2000

'One of the reasons I came to this school was because I love to highlight beacons of hope, centers of excellence that challenge the odds. One of the common denominators I have found is that expectations rise above that which is expected.'

Los Angeles, 27 September 2000; FDCH Political Transcripts

'The federal government ought to have maximum flexibility.'

Washington Post, 1 October 2000

Bush was referring to education funds. By 'federal government', he meant 'the states'.

CREATIONISM

Evolution is as well documented as any phenomenon in science, as strongly as the earth's revolution around the sun rather than vice versa. In this sense, we can call evolution a 'fact'. (Science does not deal in certainty, so 'fact' can only mean a proposition affirmed to such a high degree that it would be perverse to withhold one's provisional assent.)

Stephen Jay Gould, *Time*, 23 August 1999

In August 1999, the Kansas Board of Education voted to remove the subject of evolution from the state's science curriculum – a stroke of faith-based censorship much more effective than an outright ban, which would have been unconstitutional. The 6–4 decision was the upshot of a propaganda drive spearheaded by Celtie Johnson, a Christian Fundamentalist completely innocent of scientific training. 'To Johnson, evolution simply makes no sense', the *Kansas City Star* reported. 'She rejects the evidence most scientists say supports the theory that all living things share common ancestors'.

As 'young Earth creationists', Johnson and her co-religionists on the state's Board of Education believe that our multi-billion-year-old planet was created about 7,000 years ago, and, of course, in just six days. They seek to spread this superstition not by means of rational discourse but through intimidation and a pounding sophistry. Aside from their insistence on the literal truth of Scripture, they offer nothing but inflammatory rhetoric ('Do you want to believe your ancestors were monkeys?') and a heady potpourri of partial truths. For example: it takes up to 1,000 years to form an inch of topsoil. The average worldwide depth of Earth's topsoil is 7–8 inches. Ergo, the Earth has been around for just a few millennia. As evolutionists point out, that tidy proof ignores the crucial factor of erosion.

Such outright propaganda tactics have no place in any proper classroom – a fact apparent to most Kansans, who were and are embarrassed by the move. (The state's Republican governor also deplored it.) And yet, because of its effect on textbook publishers, the local victory of those creationists is likely to hurt public education far beyond the state of Kansas. 'Developing any book is an expensive undertaking and publishers cannot afford to print separate texts to meet each curriculum', noted the distinguished naturalist Gerry Rising. 'For that reason most cover only the non-controversial concepts included in all curricula. So religious fundamentalists have won an important skirmish in their national battle with scientists'.

Bush responded to the zealots' coup as if he had been part of it. By implying that the vote had had broad popular support, and that its aim had been to broaden the curriculum, he merely made more propaganda for their cause – an odd move for a self-styled champion of education.

'It's a state issue. The people of Texas can resolve that issue as can the people of Kansas. Should the people choose in my state [to adopt a similar rule], I have no problem.

Kansas City Star, 9 September 1999

'I think it's an interesting part of knowledge [to have] a theory of evolution and a theory of creationism. People should be exposed to different points of view.'

Ibid.

'I believe children ought to be exposed to different theories about how the world started.'

Times Union, 30 August 1999

'I have absolutely no problem with children learning different forms of how the world was formed.'

New York Post, 5 November 1999

'I personally believe God created the earth.'

Kansas City Star, 9 September 1999

'After all, religion has been around a lot longer than Darwinism.'

George, September 2000

THE SHAPE OF THINGS TO COME

'You teach a child to read, and he or her will be able to pass a literacy test.'

Townsend, Tennessee, 21 February 2001; *The New Republic,* 5 August 2001

AT THE HELM

Washington, DC: The Committee for Education Funding (CEF), a non-partisan coalition of 100 education organizations, is concerned that President Bush's proposed 5.9% increase in the Education Budget FY 2002 falls short of growing needs and expectations.

CEF is responding to 'A Blueprint for New Beginnings', President Bush's budget plan released on Wednesday. According to the blueprint, when advance funding for FY 2001 is counted, the total increase for the Department of Education is not $4.5 billion or 11.5%, as widely reported, but $2.5 billion or 5.9%. This increase would represent the smallest percentage increase for the Department of Education in five years if enacted.

Press release, Committee for Education Funding, 28 February 2001

'BRING US TOGETHER'

'There is a problem with heart in America. One of the great frustrations of being a governor is I wish I knew the law to make people love one another, because I would sign it.'

George W. Bush, Des Moines, Iowa, 13 December 1999

Although the last two sections seem to reconfirm the general impression that Bush is just a dope, a careful study of his speech reveals a certain genius at equivocation.

Of course, all politicians must master that evasive art. Often Bush stands out, however, for the peculiar cynicism of his answers. In particular, when asked about one of his more divisive policies, he doesn't always merely tell a lie or change the subject. At his best, he takes the question of his party's homophobia or racism, or of his own hard line on gun control, and ends up answering by affirming his own *tolerance* and *love of children*. Although he does it with his usual West Texas quasi-mellowness, the move is reminiscent of the sort of propaganda that the Inner Party makes in *Nineteen Eighty-Four*. (For examples of a similar trick, see 'Save the Children').

DIANE SAWYER: Mrs Clinton has said it's time for the American people to write their senators and congressmen and say, 'Buck the gun lobby.' Do you want Americans to write their senators and say that?

BUSH: I don't know what that means. I do know that mothers and dads have got to say and understand the most important job they will ever have, they will ever have, is to love their children.

Good Morning America, ABC, 10 May 1999

In just saying no to some progressive cause, Bush would often cast his answer as a heartfelt pitch for universal brotherhood. He made this move a few times in dealing with the tricky issue of the Log Cabin Republicans, an affluent gay lobbying group.

RUSSERT: Would you meet with them?

BUSH: Oh, probably not.

RUSSERT: Why not?

BUSH: Well, because it creates a huge political scene, I mean, that this is all – I am someone who is a uniter, not a divider. I don't believe in group thought, pitting one group of people against another. And all that does is create kind of a huge political, you know, nightmare for people. I mean, it's as if an individual doesn't count, but the group that the individual belongs in is more important.

Meet the Press, NBC, 21 November 1999

KING: You didn't speak to the Log Cabin Republicans, the gay group. Was that – should you have?

BUSH: Well, they asked me of whether or not I'd meet with them [*sic*], I said, probably not, because I didn't want to create a ruckus. I believe someone's sexual orientation is their personal business.

KING: But they're Republicans. They want to vote for you.

BUSH: Sure. Of course, and I've got a lot of members of the Log Cabin Republican club that support me. I welcome gay support.

Larry King Live, CNN 16 December 1999

Bush was always quick to sound the *theme* of racial harmony, albeit as a way to keep from doing, or endorsing, anything specific. (See also 'The Color Line.)

KING: Can a president do something about [racial profiling]? There was a movement that Bill Clinton can sign an executive order dealing with it. To your knowledge, can you?

BUSH: I don't know about that, but yes, I think the President can call upon racial reconciliation in America.

Larry King Live, 26 September 2000

THAT OLD-TIME RELIGION

I know thy works, that thou art neither cold nor hot: I would thou
  wert cold or hot.
So then because thou art lukewarm, and neither cold nor hot, I will
  spew thee out of my mouth.

Revelation 3:14–15

Bush's true divisiveness is most apparent in his faith – despite
the crowds of nuns and imams at his photo ops. His blithe assertion that non-Christians cannot make it into Heaven – a tenet
of his creed that he has never disavowed – bespeaks a cold and
absolute self-righteousness that has always posed a danger to
democracy, whatever ideology may cloak or drive it. The mili-
tant Christian is as bad a democrat as any other true believer;
Marvin Olasky, Bush's chief fundamentalist guru and the
coiner of the phrase 'compassionate conservatism', was once a
hard-line Marxist-Leninist – and no doubt just as flexible and
open-minded then as he is now.

The risk posed by the President's religiosity is not an abstract
matter of the necessary separation of Church and State –
although Bush is unmistakably intent on breaking down the

wall between them – as when he made 'Jesus Day' an official holiday in Texas. Nor is the danger merely one of possible intolerance toward this or that minority (although the Jew-free zone that is his cabinet does not betoken an enlightened spirit). The real threat, rather, is that bone-deep conviction of almighty rectitude – the dead *certainty* that God Is On Our Side. Such martial piety divides the world in two, in the good old Manichaean tradition. 'When you have no king but Caesar, you release Barabbas – criminality, destruction, thievery, the lowest and the least . . . When you have no king but Jesus, you release the eternal, you release the highest and best, you release virtue, you release potential,' John Ashcroft told them at Bob Jones (adding, 'I thank God for this institution'). 'If America is to be great in the future, it will be if we understand that our source is not civic and temporal, but our source is godly and eternal.'

Against the Bad, all means are justified, since it is God's will that We do away with Them. Unless it is constrained by democratic ways and common sense, that world-view always leads to war, both beyond our borders and among ourselves. The same crusading spirit that impelled the drive to nail the Anti-Christ, Bill Clinton, also motivated W to seek the presidential chalice for the GOP. 'This is redemption time,' claimed Bush's pastor back in Houston, of the Governor's mission to reclaim the White House for his Father. Such piety spells trouble for the Constitution – just as it did when Bush's dad was in the White House. 'Sometimes you have to go above the written law,' as Fawn Hall put it in her blunt defense of the illegalities of Iran-contra.[58]

'Mother and I were arguing – not arguing, having a discussion – and discussing who goes to Heaven,' recalls the Governor, who at the time had religion very much on his mind. Having dealt with a gathering drinking problem by abruptly swearing off alcohol, he had vowed a renewed commitment to his family and his faith. Bush pointed to the Bible: only Christians had a place in heaven. 'I said, Mom, look, all I can tell you is what the New Testament says. And she said, "Well, surely, God will accept others." And I said, "Mom, here's what the New Testament says." And she said, "OK," and she picks up the phone and calls Billy Graham. She says to the White House operator, Get me Billy Graham.'

'I said, "Mother, what are you doing?"' Bush continues, chuckling at the memory. 'Seriously. And about two minutes later, the phone rings, and it's Billy Graham, and Mother and I are on the phone with Billy. And Mother explains the circumstances, and Billy says, "From a personal perspective, I agree with what George is saying, the New Testament has been my guide. But I want to caution you both. Don't play God. Who are you two to be God?"'

Sam Howe Verhovek, New York Times Magazine, 13 September 1998

(Bush had also told a version of this story to a *Houston Post* reporter back in 1994.)

TIM RUSSERT: In 1993 [*sic*], you suggested that unless you accept Jesus Christ as your Lord and Savior you couldn't go to heaven.

BUSH: No, no. What I said was, my *religion* teaches – my religion says that you accept Christ and you go to heaven. That was a statement that some interpreted that said *I* get to decide who goes to heaven. Governors don't decide who gets to go to heaven. No, sir. God decides who goes to heaven, Mr Russert.

RUSSERT: Even non-Christians?

BUSH: God decides. And far be it from the politician who tries to play God.

> GOP debate, Durham, North Carolina, 6 January 2000

'I mean, that's the Southern Baptists. But I don't think that this is a government function.'

> *Slate*, 6 December 1999

Bush was referring to efforts of the Southern Baptists to convert Jews. He evidently meant that the government ought not to do it (or at least he didn't think so).

'That school was based upon the Bible.'

> *Palm Beach Post*, 4 February 2000

'That school' was Bob Jones University, whose ban on inter-racial dating, strident anti-Catholic teachings and candid anti-Semitism were all justified by Holy Writ, according to the Governor.

The most glaring contradiction in Bush's personal/political religious program was, and is, his whole-hearted embrace of the death penalty.

DENNIS RYERSON: Here's the question: How do you post the Ten Commandments in schools without telling children who are not in the Judeo-Christian heritage that their form of religious expression is invalid?

BUSH: Well, it seems like to me 'Thou shalt not kill' is pretty universal. I think districts ought to be allowed to post the Ten Commandments, no matter what a person's religion is. There's some inherent values in those great commandments that would make our society a better place for everybody.

GOP debate, Johnston, Iowa, 15 January 2000

Here Bush was lauding that Commandment *not* as a 'universal' moral principle – which would require him to have followed it – but as a universal sort of 'message' to be tacked up in the nation's classrooms, along with all the other nine. Aside from violating the Constitution's anti-theocratic spirit, Bush's answer also evidenced his usual obtuseness on the subject of capital punishment. Fox-TV's Bill O'Reilly urged the Governor to meditate upon that subject:

O'REILLY: OK. Now in – so far in this campaign, the thing that sticks in my mind with you is the Jesus Christ political-philosopher remark. Everybody remembers that. It's been played many, many times. When I heard you say that, I – I had no problem with it. I said, you know, that's a legitimate answer. Certainly, Jesus Christ was a[ll?] that. But somebody might say, 'Gee,' you know, 'if Governor Bush has been so influenced by Jesus Christ, how can he support the death penalty –'

BUSH: Sure.

O'REILLY: '– for example, so *hard*?' Because Jesus Christ would not have. How do you answer?

BUSH: Well, first, let me say the question was really, you know, who influenced me the most, and I didn't – this was not a calculated answer. It's one of those moments of time where somebody – 'Who influenced you most?' And –

O'REILLY: Off the top of your head.

BUSH: – 'Christ' came out of my mouth because Christ has influenced me, thanks to Billy Graham. It planted a seed in my heart, and it changed my life. It really did. I'm – I'm – I take great solace – I recognize I'm a humble – I'm a lowly sinner who sought redemption.

O'REILLY: But what about the death penalty?

BUSH: Let me—

O'REILLY: Texas leads the—

BUSH: Yeah, we can have a lot of issues that relate to Christianity. I – you know, I don't want to put words in Jesus Christ's mouth. I believe that the death penalty when administered surely, swiftly, and chilling signal [*sic*] that if you kill somebody in my state in the commission of another crime, there's going to be a consequence and you're not going to like it.

O'REILLY: So you might disagree with Jesus on this one if he said –

BUSH: Well—

O'REILLY: – 'I don't believe in that.'

BUSH: Well, I – yeah, and I'm not so sure he addressed the death penalty itself in the New Testament. Maybe he did.

O'REILLY: No, he didn't, but I don't believe he would be for it if he were here today. But I could be wrong. I mean, I could be wrong. But he was one of those—

BUSH: This – this – we both can agree on this. Far be it from me and you to put our – put words into the Savior.

The Reilly Factor, Fox, 6 March 2000

TONY SNOW: Is the Nation of Islam a faith-based organization?

BUSH: I think it is. I think it's based upon some universal principles. It's certainly not the religion I accepted. But I believe that the folks – the Muslims who accept, you know, love your neighbor like you'd like to be loved yourself—

SNOW: So you wouldn't mind having taxpayer money go to the Nation of Islam for—

BUSH: Well, let's make sure you understand something. I don't like taxpayer money to support any religion. What I like is taxpayers' money to support people who are seeking some kind of help, people that are trying to find some kind of better answer to their lives. I don't believe government ought to fund religion. I believe government can and should fund people who are trying to help and programs that help change people's lives.

Fox News Sunday, 30 January 2000

A few weeks later, just before the New York primary, the Governor's spokesman, Ari Fleischer, sought to make clear what Bush would have said if someone had prepared an answer for him.

He answered about the religion of Islam. He has said previously he does not believe Louis Farrakhan preaches peace. He interpreted the question to be about Islam, not Farrakhan, not the Nation of Islam. The governor doesn't think anybody who preaches hate would qualify for the program's funding. And Farrakhan preaches hate.

New York Times, 24 February 2000

'Throughout the world, people of all religions recognize Jesus Christ as an example of love, compassion, sacrifice and service. Reaching out to the poor, the suffering and the marginalized, he provided moral leadership that continues to inspire countless men, women and children today.

'To honour his life and teachings, Christians of all races and denominations have joined together to designate June 10 as Jesus Day . . . Jesus Day challenges people to follow Christ's example by performing good works in their communities and neighborhoods.'

From Governor Bush's proclamation of 'Jesus Day'
as a Texas state holiday, 10 June 2000

AT THE HELM

At his joint press conference with Tony Blair, Bush was asked, by UPI's Helen Thomas, about the appropriateness of his 'faith-based initiative' to give federal funds to social programs run by religious groups.

THOMAS: Mr President, why do you refuse to respect the wall between the church and state? And you know that the mixing of religion and government, for centuries, has led to slaughter. The very fact that our country has stood in good stead by having this separation – why do you break it down?

BUSH: I strongly respect the separation of church and state.

THOMAS: Well, you wouldn't have a religious office in the White House if you did.

BUSH: I didn't get to finish my answer, in all due respect. I believe that, so long as there's a secular alternative available, we ought to allow individuals who we're helping to be able to choose a program that may be run by a faith-based program or can— will be run by a faith-based program. I understand full well that some of the most compassionate missions of help and aid come out of faith-based programs. And I strongly support the faith-based initiative that we're proposing because I don't believe it violates the line between the separation of church and state. And I believe it's going to make America a better place.

Thomas tried again, but Bush curtly interrupted her, and moved on to another questioner.

THOMAS: Well, you are a secular official—

BUSH: I agree. I am a secular official.

THOMAS: —and not a missionary.

REPORTER: Sir, on the air strikes in Iraq, the Pentagon is now saying that most of the bombs used in those strikes missed their targets.

New York Times, Washington Post, Los Angeles Times, 23 February 2001

FREEDOM OF EXPRESSION

'It concerns me. As much as I'd like to stifle it occasionally.'

Bush on 'stifling the press', *New York Times*, 14 January 2001

Bush's position on free speech is flexible. On the one hand, he supports free speech for media corporations and well-fixed political campaigns (i.e., his own). He is therefore opposed to campaign finance reform. Likewise – despite his sermonettes against the 'dark' stuff on the Internet, and peddled by 'big Hollywood' – Bush is utterly opposed to any regulation of the media for public interest purposes. This puts him squarely in the *laissez-faire* tradition of Ronald Reagan, whose FCC chairman, Mark Fowler, once notoriously claimed that TV is just an appliance, like a toaster. (On such issues Bush is also not that far from Clinton/Gore, whose record is an awful lot like that of Reagan/Bush. Colin Powell's son Michael, Bush's choice to chair the FCC, is an unabashed free-marketeer convinced that Clinton/Gore's pro-corporate policies on media were somehow bad for business.

While adamant in his support of 'free speech' for himself and friends, Bush has no qualms about silencing the opposition, or anyone who might mess with his 'message'. Like Nixon, he is quick to deny access to any publication that might dare to scrutinize his record or his policies. One reporter, who had tried to cover Bush in depth, told me that the campaign's iron curtain was unprecedented in his own professional experience: 'I can honestly say that I never encountered so much resistance in so many arenas in my twenty-three years of being a working journalist.'

As the Hatfield episode demonstrates, moreover, Bush will use whatever spooky stratagems it takes to 'neutralize' an inconvenient voice. In general, Bush favors the prerogative of management over the free speech rights of individuals who work for them, as his take on the John Rocker episode made clear.

'When it comes to the overall story, the long-term view of the campaign, it's so important for the campaign to set the long-term view.'

Brill's Content online, September 2000

'Obviously, the less publicity I'm able to achieve in California . . . the more I'm able to continue to send the message that my head and heart's right here in Texas.'

CNN, 12 May 1998

This was Bush's explanation of his decision to bar coverage of a recent speech of his in Hollywood.

In the course of researching her *Vanity Fair* profile of Governor Bush, Gail Sheehy found herself abruptly frozen out by his campaign – and long before she 'knew' he had dyslexia. Her crime was to have discovered the horrific consequences of the Governor's polluter-friendly rule. In Odessa, she saw the residents of that blue-collar city suffering the tortures of the damned – darkness at noon, soaring rates of respiratory illness, windows taped shut in the thick of summer – because of copious emissions by the Huntsman plastics factory right in the heart of town. 'The Huntsman operation in Odessa is not the worst case of alleged environmental recklessness in Texas, but it is a classic example of how the interests of the oil and power and petrochemical industries are protected by the Bush administration, while the population is virtually helpless against the dangerously mounting pollution levels.' As the conclusion of her article reports, her effort to get some germane response from Bush led to her immediate alienation from his Presence.

> I hoped to have an opportunity to ask Governor Bush about his learning difficulties, his religious awakening, and his environmental policies. Coming out of the celebratory Republican convention, I joined Bush's whistle-stop train tour through the Midwest, expecting a real grassroots trip. Instead, it was a long string of privately owned railroad cars. The campaign had hired a top Philadelphia caterer, who was told to 'take care of the press, first class', which meant laying on heavy hors d'oeuvres – smoked-salmon napoleons and caviar on crème fraiche – while the train purred through traditionally Democratic states. Crowds were huge and highly charged, but the faces were almost exclusively white.
>
> Running down the roadbed at one stop, I collared Don Evans. I asked him how Bush, as President, would balance his loyalty to the oil, gas and petrochemical industries with the nation's growing concerns about environmental policy. The pause was long. 'We'll have a policy position on the

environment and energy – it's being worked on.' Evans empha-
sized that the Governor has taken 'enormous constructive steps
to reduce pollution'.

The next morning I was told by Karen Hughes, 'The
Governor will not be able to participate in your profile.'

Gail Sheehy, 'The Accidental Candidate', *Vanity Fair*, August 2000

As he explained throughout the GOP debates, Bush has no
qualms about trade with China, whose repression of free speech
(and other) rights doesn't seem to faze him.

'Imagine if the Internet took hold in China. Imagine how
freedom would spread. I told – in my earlier answer, I said our
greatest export to the world has been, is, and always will be
the incredible freedom we understand in America.'

GOP debate, Phoenix, 6 December 1999

Such tolerance of the Chinese way is not surprising, since Bush
himself is no more tolerant of heresy than are the rulers in
Beijing:

'There ought to be limits to freedom. We're aware of this [web]
site, and this guy is just a garbage man, that's all he is.'

Associated Press, 21 May 1999

Thus the Governor explained his complaint filed with the
Federal Election Commission, to shut down a parody site,
gwbush.com.

Perfectly at ease with media concentration, and therefore quite
untroubled by the prospect of a few huge corporations ruling
all the culture industries, online and off-, Bush was typically

unable to use simple English in attempting to feign deep concern at such a threat to free expression:

> 'Will the highways on the Internet become more few?'
>
> Concord, New Hampshire, 29 January 2000; *Slate*

Bush often would lament the gross and exploitative product of the media, especially when it was aimed at children:

> 'It's important for us to explain to our nation that life is important. It's not only life of babies, but it's life of children living in, you know, the dark dungeons of the Internet.'
>
> Arlington Heights, Illinois, 24 October 2000; *Slate*

Such product doesn't bother him so much, however, that he would side with parents agitating for some non-commercial programming alternatives.

> 'Put the "off" button on.'
>
> Associated Press, 14 February 2000

Such was the Governor's advice to parents troubled by the graphic fare on television.

I MAY AGREE WITH WHAT YOU SAY, BUT I SUPPORT THE RIGHT OF MANAGEMENT TO TEACH YOU NOT TO SAY IT

In October, 1999, John Rocker, a gifted pitcher for the Atlanta Braves, created a huge ruckus when he gave *Sports Illustrated* a rich sample of the contents of his mind. He was especially vivid on the subject of New York, 'the most hectic, nerve-racking city', where he had found the Mets fans especially unlikeable – although the catcalls in Shea Stadium were not the only local color that offended him. 'Imagine having to take the [Number] 7 train to the ballpark, looking like you're [riding through] Beirut next to some kid with purple hair next to some queer with AIDS right next to some dude who just got out of jail for the fourth time right next to some 20-year-old mom with four kids. It's depressing.' The ebullient Georgian also noted, 'The biggest thing I don't like about New York are the foreigners. I'm not a very big fan of foreigners.' Although universally condemned for such remarks, Rocker later heatedly denied any kinship with the controversial Knicks guard Latrell Sprewell, who had taken similar heat for choking P. J. Colosimo, his coach, two years before. 'That guy should've been arrested, and instead he's playing basketball,' exploded Rocker. 'Why do you think that is? Do you think if he was Keith Van Horn – if he was white – they'd let him back? No way.' It was not just New Yorkers who got Rocker's goat, however. He casually referred to one black teammate as 'a fat monkey'.

Rocker's free-associations prompted many calls that he be sensitized ASAP. 'Something should be done about this, so that Mr Rocker is held accountable for his vicious and bigoted remarks,' said Mayor Rudy Giuliani, whose delicate regard for others' feelings is well known. The Mayor advised 'some kind of training, where he becomes more educated'. Such calls had their effect. Soon the management of the Atlanta Braves decided to have Rocker 'counseled' so that he might go and sin no more.

At the GOP debate in Michigan, journalist Suzanne Geha asked Governor Bush for his opinion on the Braves' decision. His approval of the company's position was remarkable. First of all, it indicated a departure from the libertarian ideals of most American conservatives, who generally deplore the tendency to treat hate speech as a crime or illness. Bush's take on the outspoken Georgian was a little disingenuous, moreover, inasmuch as Rocker's diatribe was not the sort of thing that a Republican would mind. (See 'The Color Line'.)

SUZANNE GEHA: As a former owner of a baseball team, the Texas Rangers, and as a candidate for President, would you defend Rocker's right to say whatever he wanted short of making a threat, or would you support and require him to undergo psychological testing? Would you call for his firing or demotion?

BUSH: Listen, I think it's a free – this is a case of a player needs help [*sic*]. And I appreciate the fact that the Atlanta Braves are getting him counseling. But this is a world of – in athletics, this is a world of some young men who make a lot of money who don't – who aren't responsible for their behavior.

What I'd like to do, as the President of the United States, is usher in the responsibility era, so that each American, whether you be a baseball player or a – anything, wear the uniform of the United States, are responsible for the actions you take in life; that each of us must understand with certainty that we are responsible for the decisions we make.

And it starts, by the way, with having a president who behaves responsibly in the Oval Office.

(Applause)

GEHA: Governor Bush?

BUSH: Yes.

GEHA: Do you think that it is fair to order someone to undergo psychological testing if that individual says something that is so offensive?

BUSH: I think in this case it made sense to do so, and I appreciate what the Atlanta Braves have decided to do. I appreciate that.

Geha asked the Governor if Rocker might have been immune to such forced 'testing' if he played for a publicly supported institution rather than a private corporation.

BUSH: Look, I think – I think that – I don't know the particulars about this particular person. I think the Braves made the right decision, though. I mean, they know the man better than you and I do. The fellow said some incredibly offensive things. He is a public person. And I appreciate them trying to get the man help. I understand in America we can say what we want to say, but that doesn't mean that if the man needs help, he shouldn't get it. And I appreciate their efforts to provide psychological counseling for him.

GOP debate, Grand Rapids, Michigan, 10 January 2000

CAMPAIGN FINANCE REFORM

'I'm trying to protect my invest – my contributors from unscrupulous practices.'

Houston Chronicle, 18 July 1998

The Governor was explaining why he had resisted having the names of his campaign donors posted online.

Although he'd vigorously resisted publicizing his donors' names, the Governor was all for public information of *some* kind – the vaguer and more limited, the better. Indeed, such unenlightening revelation was the one 'reform' that Bush would ever recommend.

> 'I think a good reform would be for any group that decides to put money up on TV, they need to let us know something about their group and who their treasurer is, for example.'
>
> *This Week*, ABC, 5 March 2000

> 'On the one hand he preaches campaign finance reform. On the other hand he passes the plate.'
>
> *New York Times*, 8 February 2000

Bush was here referring to Senator John McCain – who had received 'more money than anybody' from DC lobbyists, the Governor charged. In fact, the Governor, in working lobbyists and their immediate families, had raised almost five times as much as Senator McCain in the first three-quarters of 1999, according to the Center for Responsive Politics.

When Al Gore endorsed McCain's crusade, the Governor again responded with *ad hominem* derision – and an outright lie about his own unprecedented campaign war-chest.

GORE: This current campaign financing system has not reflected credit on anybody in either party. And that's one of the reasons I've said before, and I'll pledge here tonight, if I'm President, the very first bill that Joe Lieberman and I will send to the United States Congress is the McCain-Feingold campaign finance reform bill. And the reason it's that important is that all of the other issues – whether prescription drugs for all seniors that are opposed by the drug companies, or the Patient's Bill of Rights to take the decisions away from the HMOs and give them to the doctors and nurses, opposed by the HMOs and insurance companies – all of these other proposals are going to be a lot easier to get passed for the American people if we limit the influence of special interest money, and give democracy back to the American people. And I wish Governor Bush would join me this evening in – in endorsing the McCain-Feingold campaign finance reform bill.

LEHRER: Governor Bush.

BUSH: You know, this man has no credibility on the issue. As a matter of fact, I read in the *New York Times* where he said he co-sponsored the McCain-Feingold campaign fund-raising bill. But he wasn't in the Senate with Senator Feingold.

And so I – look, I'm going to – what you need to know about me is, I'm going to uphold the law. I'm going to have an attorney general that enforces the law, that if the time for – the time for campaign funding reform is after the election.

This man has outspent me. The special interests are outspending me. And I am not going to lay down my arms in the middle of the campaign for somebody who has got no credibility on the issue.

Presidential debate, 3 October 2000

Although beside the point (and false to boot), the crack about Gore's claim to have co-sponsored the McCain-Feingold functioned to distract us from the issue, by invoking the effective propaganda legend of Al Gore as a 'serial exaggerator'. Having thus used up his only ammunition on the campaign finance front, Bush flailed around, resolving vaguely 'to uphold the law', and urging the postponement of the whole discussion until 'after the election'. The Governor then made a desperate lunge for the high ground with his preposterous claim that his opponent, and 'the special interests', had 'outspent' him. In fact, Bush raised, and spent, more money than any presidential candidate in US history (just as he had both times he ran for Governor of Texas). In the last election season, Bush/Cheney raised $193,088,650, and spent a total of $132,900,252. For their part, Gore/Lieberman had raised $185,860,812 and spent $120,369,160. Although the Governor's almighty fund-raising apparatus was well-known to the telejournalists, his claim to have been 'outspent' by Gore inspired no snide remarks from them about his tendency to gild the truth.[59]

Bush partisans would have you believe that his $63 million (as of December 20 [1999]) represents nothing so much as a vast outpouring of public support. 'The media's monomania about Bush's fund raising,' wrote George Will in a recent column, 'reflects an obdurate refusal to recognize that Bush has lots of money because he has lots of supporters, not vice versa.' Will, whose penchant for Republican front-runners is legendary, may want to fire his research assistant: According to the latest Federal Election Commission filings, Bush has managed to raise more than twice as much as Al Gore with about 20,000 fewer donors. And it's no surprise that of Bush's top-10 fundraising zip codes, two are in Greenwich (his *père*'s home turf), one is on New York's Upper East Side, and eight are in Texas [*sic*]. Like any mainstream Republican, Bush gets most of his money from the usual collection of establishment and business types, with added boosts from Texas oil and gas interests and from his father's old fundraising network.'

American Prospect, 31 January 2000

The exchange on campaign finance at the first debate continued, with Al Gore suddenly reverting to a notion of reform far more effective than the weak provisions of McCain-Feingold (which would actually *raise* the limits on individual donations). The Governor's hysterical response to his opponent's sally is worth noting.

LEHRER: Senator McCain said in August that it didn't matter which one of you is President of the United States in January. There's going to be blood on the floor of the United States Senate, and he's going to tie up the United States Senate until campaign finance reform is passed that includes a ban on soft money. First of all, would you support that effort by him, or would you sign a bill that is finally passed that included soft—

BUSH: Well, I would support an effort to ban corporate soft money and labor union soft money, so long as there was dues checkoff. I've campaigned on this ever since the primaries. I believe there needs to be instant disclosure on the Internet as to who's giving to whom. I think we need to fully enforce the law. I mean, I think we need to have an attorney general that says if laws are broken we'll enforce the law, be strict about – be firm about it.

GORE: Look, Governor Bush, you have attacked my character and credibility. And I am not going to respond in kind. I think we ought to focus on the problems, and not attack each other.

And one of the serious problems – hear me well – is that our system of government is being undermined by too much influence coming from special-interest money. We have to get a handle on it. And, like John McCain, I have learned from experience. And it's not a new position for me. Twenty-four years ago, I supported full public financing of all federal elections. And anybody who thinks I'm just *saying* it'll be the first bill I send to the Congress, I want you to know –

BUSH: All right, let me just say one thing—!

GORE: – I care passionately about this, and I will fight until it becomes law.

BUSH: I want people to hear what he just said! He is for *full public financing* of Congressional elections! I'm absol-utely, adamantly opposed to that! I don't want the government financing Congressional elections!

Presidential debate, 3 October 2000

The Governor's outrage was understandable, since full public financing of federal elections would eliminate the vast electoral advantage of the rich, and finally cleanse our airways of the heavy fog of propaganda that benights our politics throughout every campaign season. (Such radical reform would irk the broadcasters no less than it would hobble certain politicians, since it's the media machine itself that takes in all that money – a pay-off that explains why the National Association of Broadcasters is the top lobbyist *against* campaign finance reform.)

Faced with that surprising challenge by Al Gore, Bush resorted to a bit of tacit red-baiting, by equating actual reform with Big Brother-type control of federal elections. (Of course, as things turned out, our electoral system was subverted by the Governor himself.)

JUST KIDDING

'Show me the money!'

Texas Monthly, June 1999

The Governor shouted out that cinematic jest on seeing two lobbyists on the steps of the Capitol in Austin, Texas.

MOVING RIGHT ALONG . . .

'This is an impressive crowd, the haves, and the have-mores. Some people call you the élite. I call you my base.'

(Laughter)

Al Smith Memorial Dinner in New York, 19 October 2000

GOD'S GREEN EARTH

Mammon led them on,
Mammon, the least erected Spirit that fell
From heav'n, for ev'n in heav'n his looks and thoughts
Were always downward bent, admiring more
The riches of heav'n's pavement, trodden gold,
Than aught divine or holy else enjoyed
In vision beatific. By him first
Men also, and by his suggestion taught,
Ransacked the center, and with impious hands
Rifled the bowels of their mother earth
For treasures better hid.

Paradise Lost, Book I, pp. 678–88.

Of all the blots on Bush's record (his 'victory' excepted), none is quite as large, or evil-smelling, as his six years of environmental work in Texas. A man of oil and gas, the Governor was – as it were by nature – always sympathetic to the planet's dirtiest polluters: the big oil, petrochemical and automobile industries. His innate sympathy was much intensified by the gigantic campaign contributions that those and other toxic interests dumped into his coffers when he ran against Ann Richards in 1994, and against Garry Mauro four years later. His favor thus secured, Bush did all he could to gut the state's regulatory apparatus, in order to enrich the likes of Exxon, BP Amoco, Phillips, Texaco and Mobil, Dow and DuPont, Lockheed and Apache – and, among the dirtiest, Alcoa (whose CEO, Paul O'Neill, Bush made his Secretary of the Treasury). Such collaboration paid off handsomely for his investors, which meant the vast contamination of the air and water throughout Texas – or rather, throughout its major cities and its poorest pockets, where the toxins leave no healthy child behind.

Under Bush, Texas had the nation's highest volume of air pollution, with the highest ozone levels of any state – while ranking 46th in spending on environmental problems. Moreover, after 1994 Texas was the nation's leading source of greenhouse gases, accounting for 14 percent of the annual US total (while boasting only 7 percent of the US population). Under Bush, Texas's oil refineries became the nation's dirtiest, with the highest level of pollution per barrel of oil processed. And because all such industrial effluvia are concentrated in or near the state's poorest neighborhoods, Bush's Texas also led the nation in the number of Title VI civil rights complaints against a state's environmental agency – in this case, the Texas National Resource Conservation Commission (TNRCC), which Governor Bush brazenly staffed with staunch anti-environmentalists like Ralph Marquez, a veteran of Monsanto Chemical, and Barry McBee, of the pro-business law firm Thompson & Knight.*

---

* For a detailed overview of Bush's true environmental record, see Rick Abraham, *The Dirty Truth: The Oil and Chemical Dependency of George W. Bush* (Houston: Mainstream Publishers, 2000).

However shocking, such statistics cannot quite convey the ugliness of Bush's legacy as steward of the environment in Texas – a story not just of poor numbers, but of townships darkened by thick toxic fogs, of schools shut down because of airborne poisons, of children suffering from damaged lungs, as if they were heavy smokers. Gail Sheehy, for example, offered up a vivid picture of Odessa as a city ravaged by the Governor's extreme indulgence of such outfits as Alcoa, Dow and Exxon (a crime for which she was forbidden access to the candidate).

While Bush's grim environmental record is his worst offense, it also could have hurt him badly as a national candidate, if it had ever been reported with due clarity. Most Americans are flaming liberals on environmental issues – as Bush himself was well aware, having helped to mount Bush/Quayle's strong assault on Governor Dukakis for the latter's putative neglect of the disgusting Boston Harbor.[60] If the viewers knew more about the Texas Governor's hard-nosed let-them-eat-smog approach to the environment – and his aggressive efforts to impose a radioactive waste dump on the unwilling citizens of Sierra Blanca way out West – his canned assurances about the perfect sweetness of his 'heart' would not have helped him much.

In Bush's playbook, then, the less said about his views on the environment the better. That policy explains why he said very little on the subject throughout his two years as a presidential candidate. Whenever he *was* forced to talk about it, his actual views were all too clear.

Campaigning in Saginaw, Michigan, the Governor tried softening his usual pro-business spiel with what he evidently thought to be a green improvisation.

Texas Governor George W. Bush has been using a TelePrompTer recently to help him sharpen his speech delivery. But why stick to a script all the time? In a speech, Bush said he would not tear down energy-producing dams merely to protect fish. 'I made it clear to the citizens of the Pacific Northwest that I oppose breaching those dams,' the Governor said. And then he ad-libbed: 'I know the human being and fish can coexist peacefully'.

Associated Press, 29 September 2000

That gaffe has been much ridiculed – and its true import therefore overlooked. The remark is striking not because it's silly, but because it casts a threatened creature as a national enemy. A relic of the Cold War, the phrase 'peaceful coexistence' was a pre-*détente* Soviet coinage, meant to pitch conciliation between the world's two rival superpowers; Bush would have heard the phrase a million times in Midland, and at Andover. Thus its application to 'the human being and fish' is, although bizarre, not terribly amusing. The candidate's preposterous call for 'peaceful coexistence' with the fish suggests that he now sees 'us' as being somehow *at war* with them. Here we could psychologize by mentioning his boyhood tendency to slaughter frogs for fun. It is more germane, however, to observe that such a warlike view of nature has for centuries defined the white man's progress through the world. Of course, that view has largely fallen into disrepute, its catastrophic consequences – for 'the human being and fish', God's other creatures, and the planet overall – having now become so clear. Only within Bush's moral universe is that view still respectable – among the zealots of the Christian right, and throughout the automotive and extractive industries, whose luminaries see the fish (and every other living creature that moveth) as nothing more than obstacles to further profit.

On those few occasions when the Governor was forced to

speak at length on the environment, his epic incoherence was, in its own way, as telling as his brief ad lib in Saginaw.

RYERSON: We have time for one more question, but we'll just have to have quick answers of thirty seconds each. This is from Burt Miller of Mount Pleasant [Iowa], and he asks, 'Do you think tougher laws are needed to protect our environment?' Governor Bush.

BUSH: I think we ought to have high – high standards and set by – by agencies that rely upon science, not by what may feel good or what sound good [sic]. And I think it's important to give people time to say we're going to conform to standards and if they don't, I think we ought to fine them. I mean, I think we ought to be tough when it comes to our environmental laws. But I don't – I don't believe that this administration has got it right when it comes to the environment. They try to sue our way to clean air and clean water or regulate our air – way to clean air and clean water [sic].

I think we need to lead our way by bringing stake-holders to the table and rely upon the new technologies that are coming—

RYERSON: Thank you, Governor.

BUSH: —so that we can have clean air and clean water.

GOP debate, Iowa, 15 January 2000

Once in office, President Bush remained incapable of sounding like he could appreciate the natural world as anything but an exploitable resource. A few weeks after his inauguration, Bush began a White House briefing to allege the fragile state of the economy.

'It's good to see so many friends here in the Rose Garden. This is our first event in this beautiful spot, and it's appropriate we talk about policy that will affect people's lives in a positive way in such a beautiful, beautiful part of our national – our national – really, our national park system, I guess, is you'd want to call it [sic].'

White House briefing, 8 February 2001*

On the environment as on so many other subjects, Bush spoke relatively clearly only when reciting certain lines.

'Gas is a clean fuel that we can burn to – we need to make sure that if we de-control our plants, that there's mandatory – that the plants are – must conform to clean air standards. The grandfather plants, that's what we did in Texas, no excuses, I mean, you must conform.

'In other words, there are practical things we can do. But it starts with working in collaborative effort with states and local folks. You know, if you own the land, every day is Earth Day. And people care a lot about their land and care about their

---

* That stammering salute betrayed the President's low esteem for 'our national park system'. Bush's Texas ranked 48th in the nation for spending on state parks, and his proposed federal budget of 2001 was likewise ungenerous in that regard. Most of the $4.9 billion allocated for the national parks was dedicated to road repair and other non-natural improvements – a big blow to conservationists.

'Since the presidential campaign, the National Parks Conservation Association has been lobbying the Bush team about a new vision for funding the parks that focuses on protecting and managing the wilderness and wildlife. The new administration gave the group hope that it would be the one big environmental winner in the Bush presidency. Instead, Ron Tipton, the Conservation Association's Vice President, said "This is sure the wrong direction to go. The plan spends 98% on roads and buildings and only 2% on birds and bunnies".' ('The Federal Budget; Bush's Parks Plan Worries Watchdog Group', *Los Angeles Times*, 1 March 2001.)

environment. Not all wisdom is in Washington, DC on this issue.'

Presidential debate, 12 October 2000

The first, most incoherent part of that statement culminates in an outrageous lie about what Bush called 'the grandfather plants' in Texas.

'The failure of George W. Bush's "voluntary" approach to environmental protection is . . . illustrated in Texas where it was tried with old, outdated industrial facilities for almost thirty years. When the Texas Clean Air Act was passed in 1971, existing power plants, refineries and chemical plants were "grandfathered" and exempted from the law. Facilities built later were covered by the law and required to have better pollution controls. In 1971 these "grandfathered" polluters said that, over time, they would voluntarily comply with the law, to the same standards imposed on newer facilities. Instead, most continued business as usual. By 1998 these industrial facilities, some of the oldest, biggest and dirtiest in Texas, were responsible for 36% of the state's industrial air pollution, or over 900,000 tons. They emit as much ozone pollution-causing chemicals as 18 million automobiles.'

Rick Abraham, The Dirty Truth, p. 36

Only when he found himself docked back in the safe harbor of his campaign bromides ('If you own the land, every day is Earth Day') could Bush speak anything like lucid English on the subject of the suffering Earth.

GLOBAL WARMING

While deaf to all that science has to say on the creation, Bush purports to be enormously concerned that something he calls 'science' very strictly guides our national policies on other issues. 'The science is still out on issues like global warming', he said in March 2000. Although he did claim to 'believe there is global warming', as he said a few months later, he also noted that a 'number of conservative people . . . disagree about its cause and impact.'[61]

Such excessive cautiousness should come as no surprise, given Bush's long devotion to the very system – fossil fuels and automobiles – that has lately warmed our planet to the point of crisis. Although he made a few progressive noises as a candidate, and even, for a day or two, after his inauguration, it soon became quite clear that, as long as he and Cheney are in charge, the giant oil and coal and petrochemical concerns will always win out over every other interest – civic, scientific, economic. On this issue, our president will no more heed the warnings of the health care and insurance industries than he will listen to the great majority of scientists, or the public.

It is not merely Bush who is the problem here, however, but the larger TV culture that in part produced him. In his second debate with Al Gore, when the discussion turned to global warming, Bush's obtuseness on the subject meshed quite nicely with the stupefying triviality of the entire production. What with Gore's agonized attempts at self-effacement after his flamboyant sighing in the first debate, and Jim Lehrer's niggling overemphasis on the ground rules of that particular non-confrontation, the spectacle itself distracted everybody from the clear and present danger that is global warming.

LEHRER: What about global warming?

BUSH: I think it's an issue that we need to take very seriously. But I don't think we know the solution to global warming yet, and I don't think we've got all the facts before we make decisions [*sic*]. I'll tell you one thing I'm not going to do, is I'm not going to let the United States carry the burden for cleaning up the world's air, like the Kyoto treaty would have done. China and India were exempted from that treaty. I think we need to be more even-handed as, evidently, ninety-nine senators – I think it was ninety-nine senators – supported that position.

LEHRER: Global warming, global warming. The Senate did turn it down.

BUSH: Ninety-nine to nothing.

GORE: I think that – well, that vote wasn't exactly – a lot of supporters of the Kyoto treaty actually ended up voting for that because of the way it was worded, but there's no doubt there's a lot of opposition to it in the Senate. [. . .] But I disagree that we don't know the cause of global warming. I think that we do. It's pollution, carbon dioxide and other chemicals that are even more potent, but in smaller quantities that cause this. Look, the world's temperature's going up, weather patterns are changing, storms are getting more violent and un-predictable. And what are we going to tell our children? And I'm a grandfather now. I want to be able to tell my grandson when I'm in my later years that I didn't turn away from the evidence that showed that we were doing some serious harm. In my faith tradition, it's written in the Book of Matthew: 'Where your heart is, there is your treasure also'. And I believe that we ought to recognize the value to our children and grandchildren of taking steps that preserve the environment in a way that's good for them.

BUSH: Yeah, I agree. I just, I think there's been some, some of the scientists, I believe, Mr Vice President, haven't they been changing their opinion a little bit on global warming? A profound scientist recently made a different—

LEHRER: Both of you now—

BUSH: But the point is—

LEHRER: Excuse me. Both of you have now violated your own rules. Hold that thought.

GORE: I've been trying so hard not to [violate the rules].

(Laughter)

LEHRER: I know, I know, but about – under y'all's rules, you are not allowed to ask each other a question. I let you do it a moment ago—

BUSH: Twice.

(Laughter)

LEHRER: Twice, sorry. OK.

GORE: That's an interruption, by the way.

(Laughter)

LEHRER: That's an interruption. OK. But anyhow, you just did it, so now we're—

BUSH: I'm sorry.

LEHRER: That's all right. It's OK.

BUSH: I apologize, Mr Vice President.

(Laughter)

LEHRER: No, you're not allowed to do that either, you see. No, no. I'm sorry, go ahead. Finish your thought. People care about these things, I've found out.

BUSH: 'Course they care about – Oh, you mean the *rules*.

Bush thought that Lehrer had meant global warming.

LEHRER: Right, exactly right. Go ahead, sir.

BUSH: What the heck. I – of course there's a lot of – I mean, look, global warming needs to be taken very seriously, and I take it seriously. But science – there's a lot of – there's differing opinions and before we react I think it's best to have the full accounting, full understanding of what's taking place . . .

LEHRER: New question.

BUSH: Yes.

LEHRER: Last question for you, Governor – and this flows some-what out of the Boston debate. You, your running mate, your campaign officials have charged that Vice President Gore exaggerates, embellishes and stretches the facts, etc. Are you – do you believe these are serious issues, this is a serious issue that the voters should use in deciding which one of you two men to vote for on 7 November?

BUSH: Well, we all make mistakes. I've been known to mangle a syl-*lab*-ble or two myself, you know.

(Laughter)

But you know what I mean. I think credibility is important.

Presidential debate, 12 October 2000

Impacts of climate change will be far worse than previously thought and beyond the capacity of mankind to adapt unless greenhouse gas emissions are cut substantially, 700 scientists say in a report published yesterday.

Loss of food crops, disappearance of fisheries, melting of glaciers which provide millions of people with summer water supply, and a rise in sea levels will cause massive economic disruption and migration, it says.

The Arctic, which is already known to be suffering ice loss, could be completely ice-free in summer and the melting giant icecap on Greenland may cause faster sea level rise than previously thought . . .

The Intergovernmental Panel on Climate Change report is intended to guide politicians on problems they face as temperatures rise. Yesterday's assessments mean the world is heading for disasters on an unprecedented scale.

'Climate change, amongst other issues, threatens basic human needs of food, clean water and a healthy environment,' said Robert Watson, co-author of the report.

Guardian, 20 February 2001

AT THE HELM

The Bush administration, some influential Republicans in Congress and several big owners of coal-burning power plants have joined in advocating something long sought by environmental groups and Democrats: cuts in the plants' emissions of carbon dioxide, a heat-trapping greenhouse gas widely thought to contribute to a global warming trend.

New York Times, 10 March 2001

Under strong pressure from conservative Republicans and industry groups, President Bush reversed a campaign pledge today and said his administration would not seek to regulate power plants' emissions of carbon dioxide, a gas that is widely considered to be a key contributor to global warming. White House spokesman Scott McClellan clarified the president's abrupt reversal: 'The president is following through on his commitment to a multi-pollutant strategy that will significantly reduce pollutants', Mr McClellan said. 'CO_2 should not have been included as a pollutant during the campaign. It was a mistake'.

New York Times, 14 March 2001

PROFILE IN COURAGE

BUSH AND LEADERSHIP

Campaigning, Bush would often stress the **theme** of his **decisiveness**, making sure that viewers received the **message** that, as President, he would never be afraid to **take a stand**:

> 'My opponent won't tell you where he stands on this issue. He is afraid to offend somebody, but that's not what a leadership is about. You got to stand strong. If you don't stand for anything, you don't stand for anything. If you don't stand for something, you don't stand for anything.'
>
> *Austin-American Statesman*, 2 November 2000

> 'Our leaders should be judged by results, not by entertaining personalities and cute soundbites.'
>
> *All Things Considered*, NPR, 8 November 1999

> 'I'm a decisive person.'
>
> *National Journal*, 7 August 1999

However, while his **message** was decisive, the **candidate** was generally **not**. By and large, his spine was obviated either by the need to keep his true position hidden from the rational majority, or by his fear of losing the extremist members of his base.

ABORTION RIGHTS

'Those are all questions that have to be answered given the context of the moment.'

New York Times, 15 July 1998

Thus Bush addressed the question of his possible support for an abortion rights candidate on the party ticket. Such cautiousness infuriated Gary Bauer, who, throughout the GOP debates, attempted endlessly, without success, to force the Governor to 'stand strong' against abortion.

BAUER: I want to ask you a simple yes-or-no question. Will you commit tonight to having a pro-life running mate? I'm willing to say that Governor Christie Todd Whitman of New Jersey, the pro-abortion Republican Governor, doesn't need to stick close to her phone. I won't be calling her to be my running mate. Are you willing to make a similar commitment for a pro-life running mate?

BUSH: I think it's incredibly presumptive for someone who has yet to earn his party's nomination to be picking vice presidents. I'll tell you what I *will* do. I'll name somebody – I'll name somebody who can be the President. That ought to be the main criteria for any one of us who has the opportunity to pick a vice president, Gary. It's going

> to be, can that person serve as President of the United
> States?

GOP debate, Des Moines, 12 December 1999

As things turned out, Bush did, of course, pick 'a pro-life running mate' in Dick Cheney.

GAY RIGHTS

> 'I have no idea whether the children ought to be removed or
> not removed.'

Dallas Morning News, 23 March 1999

This was Bush's comment on a Texas bill that would require the forced removal of children from foster homes in which parents are gay, lesbian, or bisexual.*

STAY, PAT, STAY

In the fall of 1999, Pat Buchanan was assailed by all sides for suggesting, in his book *A Republic, Not an Empire*, that Hitler waged his war against the West because the governments of

---

* As far as his own record was concerned, Bush had a lot to hide from gay Americans.

Many supporters characterize Bush as a gay-friendly presidential candidate who condemns discrimination in all forms and campaigns for gay votes. Yet in his six years as Texas governor, Bush has rarely met an anti-gay measure he didn't like, starting with the state's sodomy law, which he once defended as a 'symbolic gesture of traditional values'. Even more troubling for gay activists is state legislation that would have barred gays from adopting or serving as foster parents. The bill ultimately failed last year, but Bush never distanced himself from a provision that would have allowed the state to strip gay parents of the children who have already been placed in their homes. (*The Advocate*, 24 July 2000)

France and Britain forced him into it, and that the Führer had in any case not posed a threat to the United States.

Such revisionism was not a new thing for Buchanan, who had always shown a Reich-sized soft spot for the Nazis. What was new for the feisty commentator was his blunt stand against 'free trade'. That position was a late expression of his anachronistic isolationism – and, no doubt, the primary reason why his views were now so noisily condemned.

Whatever mainly drove it, the condemnation of Buchanan's views on World War II expressed a broad and firm consensus against Nazism. This created a dilemma for George W. Bush, who didn't want to alienate those members of his party who did not necessarily agree with that consensus.

BOB NOVAK: Pat Buchanan is considering leaving the Republican Party, becoming the nominee of the Reform Party. Would you personally ask Pat Buchanan not to take that step?

BUSH: Yes, I would.

NOVAK: Call him up and ask him?

BUSH: I may just decide to ask him today on the stage in Ames, Iowa. Because – we're standing next to each other for the photo op. I will turn to him and say, 'Pat, I hope you don't leave the Republican Party.'

'Evans, Novak, Hunt & Shields', CNN, 14 August 1999

'I don't want Pat Buchanan to leave the party. I think it's important, should I be the nominee, to unite the Republican Party. I'm going to need every vote I can get among Republicans to win the election.'

New York Times, 25 September 1999

After catching flak for such a frank admission of political concern, Bush retroactively invented a more civic-minded motive for himself:

KING: Let's touch a lot of bases. When Pat Buchanan thought about leaving, you said, 'Stay, we need every vote.' Were you wrong?

BUSH: Well, actually, what I said was, stay, I'd like to debate his philosophy of isolationism and protectionism. I wanted the Republican Party to hear what he had to say and to hear what I had to say. And I was convinced that my view of free trade and America leading the world to peace would be the philosophy that would be accepted. I wanted to reject his kind of politics in the primary.

KING: So are you – your father said, in the end, he was probably glad that he's not in the party. Are you?

BUSH: Well, now that he's chosen to go, you bet. I mean, see you later.

(Laughter)

Larry King Live, CNN, 16 December 1999

KING: Should the Reform Party candidate be a participant in the national debates when candidates are selected?

BUSH: You need to ask me that question later on.

KING: Well, you can have an opinion on it. If Buchanan's the nominee, should he be in the debates?

BUSH: I'll reserve my opinion. I will reserve my opinion.

Larry King Live, CNN, 16 December 1999

THE STARS AND BARS

TIM RUSSERT: South Carolina: big issue –

BUSH: Yes.

RUSSERT: – whether to fly the Confederate flag.

BUSH: Yeah.

RUSSERT: A flag [that] to many black Americans represents slavery. Should South Carolina take that flag down?

BUSH: It's up to the people of South Carolina.

RUSSERT: It doesn't bother you that they fly it?

BUSH: It's up to the people of South Carolina to make the decision as to what to do with their flag, just like it's up to the people of Texas to decide whether we're going to have a lottery or not.

RUSSERT: Do you think the Confederate flag represents slavery?

BUSH: I think the Confederate flag creates all kinds of emotions amongst different groups of people. But it is up to the people of South Carolina to make that decision.

Meet the Press, NBC, 21 November 1999

BRIAN WILLIAMS: Governor Bush, a few blocks from here, on top of the state capitol building, the Confederate flag flies with the state flag and the US flag. It is, as you can hear from the reaction of tonight's crowd of three thousand people from South Carolina, a hot button issue here. The question is: Does the flag offend you personally?

BUSH: The answer to your question is – and what you're trying to get me to do is to express the will of the people of South Carolina is what you're trying to get—

WILLIAMS: No, I'm asking you about your personal opinion—

BUSH: The people of South Carolina. Brian, I believe the people of South Carolina can figure out what to do with this flag issue. It's the people of South Carolina—

WILLIAMS: If I may—

BUSH: I don't believe it's the role of someone from outside South Carolina and someone running for President to come into this state and tell the people of South Carolina what to do with their business when it comes to the flag.

WILLIAMS: As an American citizen, do you have a visceral reaction to seeing the Confederate flag?

BUSH: As an American citizen, I trust the people of South Carolina to make the decision for South Carolina.

West Columbia, South Carolina, GOP debate, 7 January 2000

UNIDENTIFIED REPORTER: Here's your favorite topic: the flag. If you were to fly the Confederate flag outside the state-house of Texas – I think you said that you wouldn't because of the symbolism, but it was never followed. What symbolism?

BUSH: That means that – what that means is that some people have – people have strong feelings about that. Some people feel one way about it, some people feel the other

way about it. And the people of South Carolina can make
up their own mind. Yeah?

REPORTER NO. 2: But, Governor, if I could just follow that?

BUSH: My strong feeling is that the people of South Carolina can
make up their mind. I've answered that question all I'm
going to answer it today.

REPORTER NO. 3: Governor, one more time.

BUSH: No, no, no.

REPORTER NO. 3: You're aspiring to be a national leader, not the
Governor. You're trying to be the President, the leader of
the party of Lincoln. And yet you're concerned about the
Republicans getting labeled as being insensitive to
minorities. Don't you see that your position on that
Confederate flag sends that kind of signal?

BUSH: No, I don't see that at all. I don't think it reflects my heart
at all. It reflects the understanding that the people of
South Carolina can make up their own mind on that
issue, just like they can make up their own mind on the
lottery issue. I don't – I don't believe that.

Nightline, ABC, 12 January 2000

Pushed to the wall, Bush started breaking down. In this
exchange, the Governor's last word on the subject was a burst
of wild non sequiturs:

JUAN WILLIAMS: Well, Governor, one of the things that stood out to
me when I looked at the polls here in New Hampshire
was that 51 percent of the voters said that George W.

Bush says what we want to hear. He'll just tell us whatever it is that we want to hear in order to please us, in order to win this office. And I was reminded [of] your stand on the flag issue in South Carolina. You said, 'It's up to the people of South Carolina' – as if you have no historical context, as if you don't have a position there of your own.

BUSH: Juan, I've got a position.

WILLIAMS: Your position is, 'Leave it up to the people.'

BUSH: No, no, my position is the people of South Carolina can decide. You may not like my position. But that's a position. And I don't believe the polls said that. I don't read the polls. But I suspect that when you look closely at what the people of this state like, they like somebody who tells them exactly what my record is, what my philosophy is. I don't make decisions based upon polls or focus groups, Juan. I'm the person who laid out a tax cut plan that has stood the test of time. I'm not the candidate that, when the heat got on, started, kind of, fine-tuning the tax cut plan.

Fox News Sunday, 30 January 2000

BOB JONES UNIVERSITY

RUSSERT: 'Compassionate conservative.'

BUSH: Yes, sir.

RUSSERT: That's how you've described yourself. A lot of eyebrows were raised when you made an appearance at Bob Jones University.

BUSH: Yeah, yeah.

RUSSERT: Now, let me show you a picture of Governor George W.
           Bush and the gentleman there to your right. On the left
           of the screen is Bob Jones III. Let me show you what he
           said about your dad, which I think is rather chilling. And
           I'll put it on the screen for you and our viewers: 'I
           believe that Mr Reagan came to office with good inten-
           tions, but he broke his promise to us when he took on
           Mr George Bush, a devil, for his Vice President . . . Mr
           Reagan has become a traitor to God's people.' How
           could you sit with a man who called your dad a 'devil'?

BUSH: Well, you know, each of us change in life, and now he
           doesn't believe George Bush is a devil.

RUSSERT: Did he tell you that?

BUSH: No, he would have told me that, I presume. I presume he
           was an honest enough man if he invited a son who is –
           completely loves his dad like I do. As you know, I'm
           a warrior for my dad. I wouldn't stand for that. And as a
           matter of fact, he was very complimentary of my dad.
           People change, Tim. People change and—

RUSSERT: The reason he called your dad a devil is because your
           dad said that university should lose its tax-exempt status
           because it discriminated.

BUSH: Well, as I said, the man didn't bring up my dad at all. I
           was invited to go to the campus. There were six thousand
           students and voters there. I went because I wanted to get
           out my message of compassionate conservatism. My
           views on my dad haven't changed, just because he said
           that some eighteen years ago.

RUSSERT: But – well, let me show you what Mr Jones' current thinking is and put it on the screen, because this is just as disturbing: 'We believe that the Lord God created races with distinctions and that races are meant to be separate from one another. We basically accept that there are three races: Caucasians, Negroes and Orientals. Caucasians can't date Orientals. Orientals can't date Caucasians and neither of them can date Negroes.' That's what he believes in.

BUSH: Yeah. Well, I disagree with that, too. That was also said in 1983, if you notice on that one.

RUSSERT: It's still the policy of the university.

BUSH: Well, it's not a good policy. And I didn't – when I go to speak to voters, I don't necessarily have to embrace the policies of the university.

RUSSERT: But you're giving affirmation to that institution.

BUSH: I am not giving affirmation. I'm giving affirmation – quite the contrary. I'm giving affirmation to somebody who's going to unite our country. I stood up there and said, 'Let's march together toward a better tomorrow.' How can I go into a university like that and subscribe to those views when my little brother, the great governor of Florida, married a girl from Mexico in my own family?

RUSSERT: Why go, Governor? You wouldn't go to a Ku Klux Klan rally.

BUSH: That's exactly right. I sure wouldn't.

RUSSERT: You wouldn't go to hate groups?

BUSH: I would not go to hate groups. But this is a group that's based upon – this is a religious group.

RUSSERT: Well –

BUSH: This is not a hate group.

RUSSERT: – I checked their Internet [site] yesterday. You know what it says? That Mormonism and Catholicism are 'cults'.

BUSH: Well, I disagree.

RUSSERT: That's in the president's letter.

BUSH: You're not a cultist. I agree.

RUSSERT: No, I'm not. But let me show you what the chancellor said about the Pope. The Pope – I openly acknowledge I'm a Catholic. Let me put it on the screen: 'The Pope is the greatest danger we face today . . . He is doing more to spread anti-Christ communism than anyone around. The papacy is the religion of the anti-Christ and is a Satanic system.'

BUSH: But, Tim—

RUSSERT: Not just – What do you think the Catholic voters in Michigan and New York and California see or think when they read that, and know that you associate your-self with that school?

BUSH: Well, but look, I don't associate myself with the thought. First of all, that was a 1982 quote by a man who's now passed away.

RUSSERT: He's the chancellor. He was the chancellor.

BUSH: And I'm not – he's not – Mr Jones – I don't agree with that, Tim. Do not subscribe – I mean, you know, you cannot subscribe those views to me because I went to a university to speak to try to convince six thousand people to be on my team. Ronald Reagan went there and spoke. Do you think the Catholics in Michigan rejected Ronald Reagan when he asked for their vote for the presidency? Of course not. They listened to what Reagan had to say, and they looked at Ronald Reagan's heart. And I do not agree with this notion that somehow if I go to try to attract votes and to lead people toward a better tomorrow, somehow I get subscribed to some – some doctrine gets subscribed to me. I don't accept that, and neither should you. And it's unfair.

RUSSERT: But people who know you and respect you and like you say, 'George W. Bush, Thomas Burch and Bob Jones III aren't your kind of people. Why are you associating with them?'

BUSH: Well, first of all, Burch shows up because he represents a veterans group and he said, 'I want to support your candidacy.' You know, I've got thousands of supporters who support me for one reason or another. I went to Bob Jones University because I wanted to convince people that my brand of conservatism is the right brand of conservatism for the Republican Party and is the right brand of conservatism for the country. That's why I went. That's what a leader does. A leader doesn't shirk. A leader leads. A leader stands up and sets an agenda. And that's what I'm going to do.

Meet the Press, NBC, 13 February 2000

'I did denounce it. I de – I denounced it. I denounced inter-racial dating. I denounced anti-Catholic bigacy – bigotry . . . No, I – I – I – I spoke out against interracial dating. I mean, I support inter – the policy of interracial dating.'

CBS News, 25 February 2000

BUSH ON AMERICAN GOVERNANCE

'Many of them are good personal friends of mine. I'm confident that we'll be able to get along pretty well.'

National Journal, 7 August 1999

Bush was referring to his relations with Congress.

'The legislature's job is to write law. It's the executive branch's job to interpret law.'

Austin, Texas, 22 November 2000

'I am mindful of the difference between the executive branch and the legislative branch. I assured all four of these leaders that I know the difference, and that difference is they pass the laws and I execute them.'

Washington, DC, 18 December 2000; *Slate*

THE SHAPE OF THINGS TO COME

'I think it is a little early to project the amount of money the Legislature will be dealing with. And, as you know, I hope I'm not here to have to deal with it.'

Dallas Morning News, 14 July 2000

Bush was referring to the possibility of a shortfall in the Texas budget. As it turned out, the Governor's large tax cuts wreaked havoc with the state's economy, leaving a 'once-healthy surplus . . . nearly erased by budget overruns, particularly from health care costs like Medicaid', the *New York Times* reported on 12 February 2001. 'We made tax cuts because we thought we had this huge surplus,' recalled one Republican State Senator. 'I might have voted a little differently on all those tax cuts had I realized that we were only funding twenty-three months of these [Medicaid] programs.'

This testament to Bush's 'leadership' as Governor pertains directly to his presidential vision since, Reagan-like, he entered national office calling for the same kind of radical tax-cutting plan that had lately ravaged his own state (although it paid off nicely for the very richest people there).

A NEW BROOM

'The administration I'll bring is a group of men and women who are focused on what's best for America, honest men and women, decent men and women, women who will see service to our country as a great privilege and who will not stain the house.'

GOP debate, Des Moines, Iowa, 15 January 2000

'I've been consistent throughout the course of the campaign that my Supreme Court will be people that will not use the bench from which to legislate.'

USA Today, 3 November 2000

Following Election Day 2000:

REPORTER (off mike): At what point do you think this dispute [will end]?

BUSH: You know, that's hard to tell. I think it's – that this is
        certainly unprecedented in modern times. Now, the
        more quickly this gets resolved, the better off it is for
        the nation. And we believe that the responsible course of
        action is to be well prepared. It's in our nation's best
        interest that – that – that should I assume the presidency,
        that this is an administration that has planned well and is
        prepared to assume the highest office of the land. And it
        will be. And we will be prepared.

                        Bush campaign press briefing, 10 November 2000

'This morning I talked to Secretary Cheney. We had a very
good conversation. He sounded really strong, and he informed
me that, as a precautionary measure, he went into the hospital.
He was feeling chest pains, and turns out that subsequent tests,
blood tests, and the initial EKG showed that he had no heart-
attack. I'm pleased to report that I know all Americans join me
and Laura in wishing him all the best.

'Looking forward to talking to him this afternoon to continue
strategizing about this election and the election results. I am
disappointed with last night's ruling by the Florida Supreme
Court. We believe the justices have used the bench to change
Florida's election laws and usurp the authority of Florida's
election officials . . .

'Secretary Cheney will make a great vice president.

'And as I reported today – I'm pleased to report that he
sounded very strong on the telephone. And he did the right
thing. He felt some warning signs, and he went into the hospital
and had them checked out. And he's going to make a great vice
president. And America's beginning to see how steady and
strong he is . . .

'I'm looking forward to a good Thanksgiving meal, I might

add, with my family. And Dick Cheney is healthy. He did not have a heart-attack.'

Bush campaign press briefing, 22 November 2000

Secretary Cheney had, in fact, just had a heart-attack. Either Bush's staff had kept the truth from him, or he knew it and was lying.

TIM RUSSERT: How important is that for a president to be able to read people, understand the nuances – body language?

BUSH: Oh, it's incredibly important for a lot of reasons. First of all, it's important to be able to have a – a – s – be able to delegate to people whose instincts you trust. Micromanagers fail when it comes to big CEO positions. And in order to be a good manager, you've got to surround yourself with people who've got the right judgment, which means you better have the good judgment.

CNBC News, 30 December 2000

Presenting Al Gonzales, his new White House counsel, Bush used much the same Horatio Alger narrative that George H. W. Bush had used in selling Clarence Thomas, even though Gonzales did not need that sort of pitch. In any case, 'a two-bedroom house' is not a hovel, nor is it necessarily a sign of poverty to have a lot of siblings.

BUSH: But he's a guy who grew up in a two-bedroom house. His mother and daddy working, you know, as hard as they possibly can to bring up – six brothers and sisters?

GONZALES: I have seven siblings.

241

BUSH: Seven siblings. Eight in the family. And now he's going to be sitting at the right hand of the President of the United States. To me, these appointments – and each – each person has got their own story that is so unique, stories that really explain what America can and should be about. And so I welcome them. I can't tell you how good of folks they are, not only in terms of the jobs they'll have, but just in the quality of character.

Press conference, 18 December 2000

'The person who runs FEMA [Federal Emergency Management Agency] is someone who must have the trust of the President, because the person who runs FEMA really is the first voice oftentimes that someone whose lives have been turned upside down hears from.'

Press conference, 4 January 2001

On Linda Chavez, named as Secretary of Labor:

'She is a member of a labor union at one point.'

Press conference, 2 January 2001

A few days later, Chavez ran into trouble when it came to light that she had harbored an illegal immigrant as a household employee.

Q: Mr President-elect, all of your nominees have been asked a very blunt question late in the interviewing process – namely, is there anything in your past that would be an embarrassment if it became public? The question is, was Mrs Chavez asked that question and what do you know her answer to have been—

BUSH: I would have to ask the questioner. I haven't had a chance to ask the questioners the question they've been questioning. On the other hand, I firmly believe she'll be a fine Secretary of Labor. And I've got confidence in Linda Chavez. She is a – she'll bring an interesting perspective to the Labor Department.

Press conference, 8 January 2001

'I do remain confident in Linda [Chavez]. She'll make a fine labor secretary. From what I've read in the press accounts, she's perfectly qualified.'

Ibid.

THE SHAPE OF THINGS TO COME

BUSH: Yeah?

REPORTER: The European Union and Japan have filed a challenge in the WTO against a rule in the Agriculture Appropriations Bill that would allow steel companies to receive money from anti-dumping duties.

BUSH: Say again, now?

REPORTER: It's an Agriculture Appropriations Bill. President Clinton opposes this language in there that would allow companies to receive receipts from anti-dumping duties.

BUSH: I think the administration needs to do what they think is right, and I'll address all these issues once I'm sworn in as the President.

REPORTER: Thank you very much.

BUSH: Thank you.

Press conference, 22 December 2000

ALL THE WORLD'S A STAGE

BUSH ON FOREIGN POLICY

'I'm not going to play like I've been a person who's spent hours involved with foreign policy. I am who I am.'

News Hour with Jim Lehrer, 27 April 2000

Throughout the presidential race, Bush displayed an awesome unawareness of the wider world. Reporting and commenting on his princely ignorance at once became a major journalistic sport.

'Kosovians can move back in.'

Inside Politics, CNN, 9 April 1999

'Keep good relations with the Grecians.'

The Economist, 12 June 1999

'If the East Timorians decide to revolt, I'm sure I'll have a statement.'

New York Times, 16 June 1999

'The only thing I know about Slovakia is what I learned first-hand from your foreign minister, who came to Texas.'

Knight Ridder, 22 June 1999

Bush made that comment to a Slovak journalist. In fact, it was the foreign minister of *Slovenia* whom he had met in Texas.

Such gaffes inspired a local TV journalist, Andy Hiller of WHDH in Boston, to ask Bush the names of several foreign leaders. Hiller started out by asking Bush if he considered himself weak on foreign policy.

BUSH: Nah. I've got a clear vision of where I want to lead America.

HILLER: Can you name the President of Chechnya? [Aslam Maskhadov]

BUSH: No. Can you?

HILLER: Can you name the President of Taiwan? [Lee Tung-Hui]

BUSH: Yeah: Lee.

HILLER: Can you name the general who's in—

BUSH: Wait a minute, is this a – is this a *Fifty Questions*?

HILLER: No. It's four questions of four leaders in four hot spots.

Hiller asked Bush to name Pakistan's leader, Pervaiz Musharaf.

BUSH: The new Pakistani general has just been elected. He's not elected – this guy took over office. He appears he's going to bring stability to the country, and I think that's good news for the subcontinent.

HILLER: And you can name him?

BUSH: General – I can't name the general. General.

HILLER: And the Prime Minister of India? [Atal Bihari Vajpayee]

BUSH: The new Prime Minister of India is – no. Can *you* name the foreign minister of Mexico?

HILLER: No, sir. No, sir. But I would say to that, I'm not running for President.

BUSH: I understand. I understand, but the point I say to you is, is that, you know, if what you're suggesting is, is that – what I'm suggesting to you is if you can't name the foreign minister of Mexico, therefore, you know, you're not capable of what you do. But the truth of the matter is, you're is – you are, whether you can or not.*

Rebroadcast on *The News*, MSNBC, 4 November 1999

'When I'm the President, we're not going to obfuscate when it comes to foreign policy.'

New Hampshire GOP debate, 7 January 2000

During this period of heightened concentration on his foreign policy credentials, Bush was asked if he had 'any take at all' on Vladimir Putin, Boris Yeltsin's successor as Russia's head of state.

'I really don't. I will if I'm the President.'

Meet the Press, NBC, 21 November 1999

BRIT HUME: Do you think that President Bush could have done the job he did in assembling and holding together the Gulf War coalition, composed of many very varied nations, had he not had the knowledge of the world that he had from years of experience and diplomacy and politics at the UN?

---

* In thus turning the tables on his questioner – 'Do you?' – Bush was trying the tactic that his father had used so successfully against Dan Rather back in 1988.

BUSH: In order to be a good president when it comes to foreign policy, it requires someone with vision, judgment and leadership. I've been the governor of the second biggest state in the United States. If it were a nation, it would be the eleventh largest economy in the world. I was overwhelmingly re-elected because the people in my state realized I know how to lead and I've shown good judgment.

    A couple of weeks ago, at the Reagan Library, I talked about my vision for peace. My goal, should I become the President, is to keep the peace. I intend to do so by promoting free trade which, in my judgment, promotes American values across the world. I intend to do so by strengthening alliances, which says America cannot go alone [sic], we must be peacemakers not peacekeepers. And I intend to strengthen the military to make sure that the world is peaceful.

HUME: With all respect, sir, I don't think you answered the question.

BUSH: Well, I gave you my qualifications why I think I'll be a good foreign policy leader.

GOP debate, New Hampshire, 2 December 1999

Bush had just recited the same litany of his achievements in his answer to Hume's question about his daily reading.

'I'm honored . . . He understands our belief in free trade. He understands I want to ensure our relationship with our most important neighbor to the north of us, Canadians, is strong.'

Wall Street Journal, 3 March 2000

Here Bush was referring to 'Prime Minister Jean Poutine', who, according to a humorous questioner, had just endorsed the Governor's campaign. 'Poutine' was not Prime Minister of Canada, however, but a hearty French-Canadian lunch of french fries, cheese curds and gravy.

> Discussing terrorism and other foreign threats, Bush vowed to 'use our technology to enhance uncertainties abroad.'
>
> *New York Times,* 6 March 2000

> 'Oh. I thought you said "some band". The Taliban in Afghanistan! Absolutely. Repressive.'
>
> *Glamour,* June 2000

This was a reply to a question in another journalistic pop quiz. When asked about the Taliban, Bush shook his head and stood there mute until the reporter hinted: 'Repression of women in Afghanistan . . . ?'

> 'The fundamental question is, "Will I be a successful president when it comes to foreign policy?" I will be, but until I'm the president, it's going to be hard for me to verify that I think I'll be more effective.'
>
> *New York Times,* 28 June 2000

> 'We'll let our friends be the peacekeepers and the great country called America will be the pacemakers.'
>
> Houston, Texas, 6 September 2000; *Slate*

> 'I will have a foreign-handed foreign policy.'
>
> Redwood, California, 27 September 2000; *Slate*

'A key to foreign policy is to rely on reliance.'

Washington Post, 1 November 2000

Such howlers made for easy laughs – too easy. Hooting endlessly at Bush's elementary mistakes, the telejournalists ignored the crucial questions: what was the Bush/Cheney foreign policy agenda? Who would tutor Bush, or tell him what to say – and why? At times, Bush himself provided a clear foreglimpse of Dick Cheney's foreign policy, but the telejournalists would be too busy jeering to take any notice of it.

SAM DONALDSON: In Russia, the new acting president Vladimir Putin has made a deal with the Communists and the Duma, trying to bring them into the government. Is there a danger here, that bringing the Communists into the government will end up with a Communist once again running the government?

BUSH: The danger is that Russia doesn't have free and fair elections, and the danger is Russia doesn't accept the rule of law. The danger is Russia c – a – l – l – continues to favor corrupt élites. And a – so what I intend to do—

DONALDSON: I asked you about the Communists, Governor?

BUSH: Well—

DONALDSON: Are you—

BUSH: Sam, you can put a label on anybody. If they steal international aid, they're not – th – they're bad people. And my only point to you is that what Russia must understand is that a market-oriented economy with the rule of law is going to make – is going to make it much easier for them to deal with the United States. But we must deal with

Russia, regardless of what course they choose internally. On nuclear security, there is a post-Cold War era, and we must work with Russia not only on helping them dismantle tactical and strategic wea-weaponry, but we also must work with them on changing the anti-ballistic missile system, so that we can bring more certainty into an uncertain world.

DONALDSON: Well, Governor, it may be a fool's errand on my part, but I'm going to try one more time to see if you think there is a danger in the recent deal that Putin has made with Communists—

BUSH: There could be, Sam. And I'm concerned about that. But I am more concerned about larger issues. And the larger issue is that if Russia doesn't adopt rule of law and market – market-oriented economy, if they continue to steal money that goes into their country, that is a sign of a country that is in collapse.

DONALDSON: Governor Bush, my time is up.

This Week, ABC, 23 January 2000

If anyone was being obtuse in that exchange, it wasn't Bush, whose answers were quite clear: Russia is the Enemy, whether Communist or not. Donaldson just could not take that in, since he wasn't really listening, but merely looking for another chance to make rude noises.

Likewise, the mainstream press was strangely deaf to Bush's most anomalous propaganda riffs, even though they contradicted everything that Reagan/Bush had stood for. At the second debate, Bush rebutted Gore's contention that the US must 'be the leader' in the world:

'I just don't think it's the role of the United States to walk into a country and say, "We do it this way, so should you" . . . I think one way for us to end up being viewed as "the ugly American" is for us to go around the world saying, "We do it this way, so should you". Now, we trust freedom. We know freedom is a powerful, powerful, powerful force, much bigger than the United States of America, as we saw recently in the Balkans. But, maybe I misunderstand where you're coming from, Mr Vice President, but I think the United States must be humble and must be proud and confident of our values, but humble in how we treat nations that are figuring out how to chart their own course.'

Presidential debate, 11 October 2000

So Ghandian a credo sounded pretty funny on the lips of that fanatically devoted son, whose Dad's long fealty to the CIA, vice presidential doings in Nicaragua, kidnapping of Manuel Noriega and jihad against Saddam Hussein did not suggest a 'humble' diplomatic style. Jim Lehrer failed to ask the Governor about the contradiction (as did Gore), and all the post-show commentators likewise overlooked it. The failure was unfortunate, since Bush/Cheney's foreign policy – as all the world now knows – is dangerously unilateralist.

BA-DA-BOOM!

As usual, Bush eventually defused the issue of his global ignorance by playing it for self-effacing laughs.

'[W]e just had some really good news out of Yugoslavia. I'm especially pleased that Mr Milosevic has stepped down. That's one less Polyslavic name for me to remember.'

Al Smith Memorial Dinner, New York, 19 October 2000

AT THE HELM

'It's about past seven in the evening here, so we're actually in different time lines.'

New York Times, 30 January 2001

President Bush, in Washington, was speaking on the telephone to Gloria Macapagal Arroyos, the new President of the Philippines, in her office in Manila.

At his joint press conference with British Prime Minister Tony Blair:

Q: A question for both of you: There's been a lot said about how different you are as people. Have you already in your talks found something maybe that you – some personal interests that you have in common, maybe in religion or sport or music?

BUSH: We both use Colgate toothpaste.

Associated Press Online, 22 February 2001

A few weeks later, the President met with South Korean President Kim Dae Jung, who had lately won the Nobel Peace Prize for his efforts to stabilize relations with his northern neighbor. Bush dealt Kim's hopes a heavy blow by making clear that he did not intend to maintain the Clinton policy of missile talks with North Korea. The patent flimsiness of his excuse was further evidence that he and his cabal prefer that North Korea be 'our' enemy, so as to justify more big spending on missile defense and other costly chunks of pie-in-the-sky.

Today Mr Bush made it clear that he had little intention of

following Mr Clinton's path, at least not now. In a brief exchange with reporters after meeting Mr Kim in the Oval Office, Mr Bush said: 'We're not certain as to whether or not they're keeping all terms of all agreements.'

But the United States has only one agreement with North Korea – the 1994 accord that froze North Korea's plutonium processing at a suspected nuclear weapons plant. And at a briefing this afternoon two senior administration officials, asked about the president's statement, said there was no evidence that North Korea is violating its terms.

Later, a White House spokesman said that Mr Bush was referring to his concern about whether the North would comply with future accords, even though he did not use the future tense. 'That's how the president speaks', the official said.

New York Times, 8 March 2001

There are two ways to start a new job. You can size up the situation, listen to your colleagues, calmly evaluate the competition and then decide the proper course. Or you can pound the table, offend your colleagues, affront your opponents and wait for a reaction that is unlikely to be very friendly.

George W. Bush, who has just started his new job, picked the second strategy. This choice is especially unfortunate, since Bush is President of the United States, and therefore has a lot of power. Bush might remember from his schooldays that the strongest boy in class should not beat up his weaker classmates. The weak will avoid him, and could well join up against him. George W. Bush has flouted this very rule: in less than two weeks he offended several important allies in Europe (greenhouse gases and policies in the Balkans), took sides against the Arabs in the Mideast, overreacted against Russia with the expulsion of 54 embassy employees allegedly inclined to espionage, and told China that he means to keep on sending weapons to Taiwan.

In the past, it has been quite healthy for the world's weak and unpredictable nations to get a clear signal from Washington setting limits to their underhandedness. This is especially true of China, with its aggressive glances at Taiwan. But it is part of the wisdom of the strong not to humiliate the weak, and to point out the way to understanding. So far, Bush has not achieved this wisdom.

'Bully Bush' (editorial), *Süddeutsche Zeitung*, 24 March 2001

COMMANDER-IN-CHIEF

Ellington AFB, Tex., March 24, 1970 – George Walker Bush is one member of the younger generation who doesn't get his kicks from pot or hashish or speed. Oh, he gets high all right, but not from narcotics . . .

Lt. Bush, who is 23, is due to complete his pilot training June 23. He will then be released from active duty and assume reserve status in the Air National Guard. He plans to fly as much as possible with the Air Guard and work in his father's campaign. Beyond that, he hasn't any plans.

As far as kicks are concerned, Lt. Bush gets his from the roaring afterburner of the F-102.

'Flying, the whole thing, is kicks,' he said. 'But afterburner is the real kick.'

Press release, Office of Information, Texas Air National Guard;
quoted in Minutaglio, First Son, pp. 130–31

In 1968, Bush was slipped into the Texas Air National Guard, joining the 147th Fighter Wing – 'the Champagne Unit', as it was later known, because of all the wealthy young Houstonians whom it kept Stateside during the war in Vietnam. Promoted, in just a few months, to second lieutenant (an extraordinary rise), Bush went on to have a lot of fun, first in training at Moody Air Force Base in Georgia, then at Ellington Air Force Base near Houston. His buddies liked him ('He was a real outgoing guy,' remembers one),[62] and the system pampered him, prizing his A-1 connections to the top. He had the glamor of a VIP, and was allowed to go on leave for many a political assignment – helping out the GOP's congressional campaigns in Florida and Alabama, and dating Tricia Nixon at her dad's request. (That happened only once.)

However, Bush's military service offered more than space for partying and time for politicking. Our future leader learned to be an able pilot, mastering the F-102 Interceptor that the Guard used for training purposes (and which was being phased out of use in Vietnam). This was no mean feat, as Bush himself would later on remind the voters, or try to. 'I'm not suggesting I was any great war hero, but I want you to know that flying F-102 fighters, putting the thing in afterburner at the end of a runway, was something other than not being a part of the military,' he said at one point, in what may be the most anticlimactic statement in the history of military reminiscence.[63]

While Bush did learn to fly, however, his military service evidently taught him little about strategic thinking *off* the campaign trail. Although trained as a potential officer, Bush came away unable to articulate the simplest doctrine – such as, for example, the concept of deterrence that he tried repeatedly to propagate throughout the presidential race.

The concept is a valid and important one, and Bush did, now and then, put it with the necessary clarity:

> 'I'm worried about the fact that our mission is not clear. It ought to be to have a military that's properly trained and equipped

to be able to fight and win war, and, therefore, prevent war from happening in the first place.'

Campaign speech in Michigan; Federal News Service, 3 November 2000

The crucial phrase there is 'be able to fight' – the military's blatant readiness and might themselves inhibiting attack, as the mere presence of well-muscled bouncers will discourage brawls in nightclubs. For the most part, Bush just could not get it straight, but in his garbled comments kept on casting the *ability* to fight – the key component of the whole equation – as *secondary*. This had him saying, repeatedly, that you deter war best by fighting it – a proposition that he made in several slightly different ways.

For example, the military's proper mission is to fight wars, *and* be capable of winning them, which will deter them:

'The mission of the military is to fight and be able to win war, and therefore prevent war from happening in the first place.'

GOP debate, 15 February 2000

Or maybe it's the military's double job to fight-and-win wars, and *also* to be able (somehow) to prevent them from occurring:

'The purpose of the military is to fight and win war. And to be able to deter war.'

New Hampshire GOP debate, 6 January 2000

On the other hand, it could be the purpose of our military to deter wars by reversing the old-fashioned formula of fight-and-win:

'We ought to have a commander in chief who understands how to earn the respect of the military, by setting a clear mission, which is to win and fight war, and therefore deter war.'

This Week, ABC, 23 January 2000

Since the basic point of all such statements was to underscore the need for a 'clear mission', Bush's muddy utterances were not too promising. In any case, the doctrine as he mostly put it – deterring war by fighting it – is logically absurd (and morally untenable), a mere restatement of the slogan 'Kill for Peace', which the Fugs once sang, satirically.

And yet all this quibbling is irrelevant; for the candidate's point was not to offer a coherent military policy, but simply 'to earn the respect of the military', as that last entry puts it. In short, his purpose was, as usual, political – to win the soldiers' votes, and to reassure the Pentagon and weapons manufacturers that he meant business (literally). As his early presidential actions have made obvious, Bush's military vision is based wholly on the drive by those great interests to commit the nation to the costliest, and looniest, of weapons systems: a 'missile shield', and, later, other giant space-based novelties. Defense Secretary Donald Rumsfeld has long championed that Reagan-era program – which will make lots of money for such corporate giants as General Electric, owner of NBC; Lockheed Martin, which has a striking number of ex-employees and erstwhile board members working for this Bush administration; and the Carlyle Group, a huge 'private equity' firm that is the world's eleventh-largest defense contractor – and which now has George H. W. Bush expensively at work on its behalf, lobbying the monarchs of the Middle East to make the Carlyle Group (and so, eventually, George W. Bush) still richer.

Bush's statements on the military 'theme' betrayed no knowledge of or interest in the pertinent issues, despite the tutelage of Condoleezza Rice. His only aims appeared to be the demonstration of his deference to the Pentagon, and the frequent venting of alarmist rhetoric of the sort that helps to grow the military budget. (For his part, Al Gore spoke more expertly, but just as deferentially, straining to out-hawk the jut-jawed W, arguing that he would raise the military budget even higher, and retrospectively saluting the preposterous invasions of Grenada and Panama.) On other matters, Bush showed his usual disengagement:

BUSH: I am for don't ask, don't tell. This is a policy that Colin Powell thoughtfully put in place—

ROWLAND EVANS: That's the Clinton policy.

BUSH: Well, if that's the Clinton policy, I support that.

CNN, 14 August 1999

KOSOVO

'Uh, I support winning. And, uh, the strategy must – America must be slow to engage militarily, but once we engage, we must do so to win.'

Inside Politics, CNN, 7 April 1999

'That's dependent upon the military advisers that would be advising me.'

On whether he would have deployed troops in Kosovo;

Associated Press Online, 28 May 1999

NUCLEAR WEAPONS

'That's going to depend upon generals helping me make that decision, Tim.'

On the acceptable level of nuclear weapons for both the US and Russia;
Meet the Press, NBC, 21 November 1999

'That depends upon my advisors and the people who know a heck of a lot more about the subject than I do.'

Ibid; on whether, in the START II talks,
he would decrease the number of nuclear warheads to 1,000

'My point is, is that I want America to lead the nation – lead the world – toward a more safe world when it comes to nuclear weaponry.'

New York Times, 27 January 2001

'A WORLD OF MADMEN'

'This is still a dangerous world. It's a world of madmen and uncertainty and potential mential losses [*sic*].'

Financial Times, 14 January 2000

That assertion, made at a well-attended oyster roast in South Carolina, evidently mystified all hands: 'Bush's spokespeople could not immediately explain what a mential loss was, but it seemed only distantly related to missile launches,' the *Financial Times* reporter wrote.

'When I was coming up, it was a dangerous world, and you knew exactly who they were,' he said. 'It was us vs. them, and it was clear who them was. Today, we are not so sure who they are, but we know they're there.'

Iowa Western Community College, 21 January 2000; Slate

'This is a world that is much more uncertain than the past. In the past we were certain, we were certain it was us versus the Russians in the past. We were certain, and therefore we had huge nuclear arsenals aimed at each other to keep the peace. That's what we were certain of . . . You see, even though it's an uncertain world, we're certain of some things. We're certain that even though the "evil empire" may have passed, evil still remains. We're certain there are people that can't stand what America stands for . . . We're certain there are madmen in this world, and there's terror, and there's missiles and I'm certain of this, too: I'm certain to maintain the peace, we better have a military of high morale, and I'm certain that under this administration, morale in the military is dangerously low.'

Albuquerque, New Mexico; Washington Post, 31 May 2000

'We cannot let terrorists and rogue nations hold this nation hostile or hold our allies hostile.'

Iowa, 21 August 2000; Slate

'I don't want nations feeling like that they can bully ourselves and our allies. I want to have a ballistic defense system so that we can make the world more peaceful, and at the same time I want to reduce our own nuclear capacities to the level commiserate with keeping the peace.'

Des Moines, Iowa, 23 October 2000; Slate

CHARLIE ROSE: Okay. What if you thought Saddam Hussein, using the absence of inspectors, was close to acquiring a nuclear weapon?

BUSH: He'd pay a price.

ROSE: What's the price?

BUSH: The price is force, the full force and fury of a reaction.

ROSE: Bombs away?

BUSH: You can just figure that out after it happens.

Reader's Digest Online, August 2000

TOM BROKAW: Governor Bush, you have said that you supported the idea of rejecting the test ban treaty, and you want to build a missile defense system. If you were the President – if you were President Jiang Zemin in China, or you were President Boris Yeltsin in Russia, wouldn't you be saying to your military personnel, and to your scientists, 'They want to start it up again. We've got to do everything that we can to go on a hair trigger. And we've got to expand our own nuclear arsenal'?

BUSH: No, they'd be hearing a different message. They'd be hearing a message that the United States is a peaceful nation – that we intend to keep the peace. But we're not going to sit by and allow rogue nations to hold any of our friends hostage. That we're not going to allow for accidental launches. And we've got the technology necessary to keep the peace.

Mr Yeltsin will hear from President Bush that 'I intend to give you a chance to join us in the development of theater-based, and national anti-ballistic missile systems. But after a short period of time, if you choose not to, we'll withdraw from the treaty.' Because we're a peaceful nation.

But we're not going to miss an opportunity, Tom, if I'm

the President, to say to our friends and allies, 'We're going to provide a shield so you won't be blackmailed.' We're going to say to our friends, the Israelis, 'We'll provide you a shield and work with you, so you won't become blackmailed by Iranians or Iraqis.'

No, our country must not retreat. We must not worry about what the Russians and Chinese think. What we need to do is lead the world to peace. And that's exactly the kind of president I intend to be.

GOP debate, Des Moines, Iowa, 13 December 1999

MEANWHILE, BACK ON PLANET EARTH . . .

'That's Washington. That's the place where you find people getting ready to jump out of the foxholes before the first shot is fired.'

Westland, Michigan, 8 September 2000; *Slate*

As an airman, Lieutenant Bush had no need to be taught that nervous ground troops don't jump out of foxholes just before the shooting starts, unless they've lost their minds.

AT THE HELM

On the joint US/British air-strike against Iraqi air defense positions outside Baghdad:

'It is a mission about which I was informed, and I authorized.'

News conference, CNN, 16 February 2001

IT'S THE ECONOMY,
YOUR EXCELLENCY

'I don't care what the polls say [about economics]. I don't. I'm doing what I think what's wrong.'

New York Times, 15 March 2000

'[E]ntrepreneurship equals freedom.'

National Journal, 7 August 1999

'It's clearly a budget. It's got a lot of numbers in it.'

Reuters, 5 May 2000

'The best way to relieve families from time is to let them keep some of their own money.'

Westminster, California, 13 September 2000; *Slate*

'It's your money. You paid for it.'

LaCrosse, Wisconsin, 18 October 2000; *Slate*

In the event of a global financial crisis:

'I would have my Secretary of Treasury be in touch with the financial centers not only here but at home.'

Presidential debate, Boston, 3 October 2000

BRING ME YOUR TIRED, YOUR RICH

On the subject of economics, Bush's choicest gaffes were evidence not of stupidity but of a rich kid's utter insincerity. Repeatedly, in trying to communicate how much he *cared* about the poor and middle-class, he would mangle the attempt as surely as his father did before him. This Bush, however, did not use inappropriate upscale locutions like 'a splash of coffee', but simply burst into illiterate howlers that betrayed the awful truth.

'I know how hard it is for you to put food on your family.'

Greater Nashua, New Hampshire, 27 January 2000

(It was also in the downscale setting of New Hampshire that Bush Sr had announced, 'Message: I care.')

'I understand small business growth. I was one.'

New York Daily News, 19 February 2000

'This campaign not only hears the voices of the entrepreneurs and the farmers and the entrepreneurs, we hear the voices of those struggling to get ahead.'

Des Moines, 21 August 2000; *Slate*

'One of the features in my plan, John, says to the single mom with two children making $40,000 a year, you get a 53 percent

tax cut. For single moms with children who make less than
$40,000 a year get – get bigger tax cuts. My question to you is,
in reviewing of your plan, that single mom with children – two
children, making $40,000 – get no tax cut. And I'm wondering
why.'

GOP debate, Des Moines, 13 December 1999

In this question to John McCain, the Governor – as usual – had
trouble credibly envisioning a family in straitened circumstances. Either those 'two kids' have excellent part-time jobs, or
they get quite a nice allowance from their 'single mom'. In any
case, the Governor made clear, those children ought to get a tax
cut.

Bush's inability to take a walk in someone else's modest shoes
was once again apparent in the third presidential debate, when
a woman named Lisa Key asked him about his tax plan:

KEY: How will your tax proposals affect me as a middle-class,
         24-year-old single person with no dependents?

BUSH: . . . You're going to get tax relief under my plan. You're
         not going to be targeted in or targeted out. Everybody
         who pays taxes is going to get tax relief. If you take care
         of an elderly in your home, you're going to get the
         personal exemption increased.

         I think also what you need to think about is not the
         immediate but what about Medicare? You get a plan that
         will include prescription drugs, a plan that will give you
         options. Now, I hope people understand that Medicare
         today is important, but it doesn't keep up with the new
         medicines. If you're a Medicare person, on Medicare you
         don't get the new procedures. You're stuck in a time warp

in many ways. So it'll be a modern Medicare system that trusts you to make a variety of options for you.

You're going to live in a peaceful world. It'll be a world of peace because we're going to have a clearer, clear-sighted foreign policy based upon a strong military and a mission that stands by our friends, a mission that doesn't try to be all things to all people, a judicious use of the military which'll help keep the peace.

You'll be in a world hopefully that's more educated, so it's less likely you'll be harmed in your neighborhood, seeing an educated child [sic] is one much more likely to be hopeful and optimistic.

You'll be in a world in which fits into my philosophy [sic]: you know, the harder work – the harder you work, the more you can keep. That's the American way. Government shouldn't be a heavy hand. That's what the federal government does to you. It should be a helping hand. And tax relief in the proposals I just described should be a good helping hand.

Presidential debate, 17 October 2000

SOCIAL SECURITY

On the coming crisis:

'There's not going to be enough people in the system to take advantage of people like me.'

Wilton, Connecticut, 9 June 2000; *Slate*

This gaffe was another inadvertent truth from Bush's 'heart', since it betrayed the plutocratic view that social security is just a socialistic burden on the rich – the many 'people in the system' being allowed by Washington 'to take advantage of people like me', i.e., multimillionaires.

On whether social-security recipients would, under his plan, receive the same benefits as they did under the present system:

> 'Maybe, maybe not.'
>
> *Washington Post,* 1 November 2000

> Bush said he has 'ruled out no new Social Security taxes'.
>
> *Washington Post,* 1 October 2000

Bush meant to say that he had ruled out new social security taxes. (This gaffe was apparently an unconscious echo of his father's fateful vow of 'no new taxes'.)

> 'They want the federal government controlling Social Security like it's some kind of federal program.'
>
> *USA Today,* 3 November 2000

TAXATION

> 'I think we need not only to eliminate the tollbooth to the middle class, I think we should knock down the tollbooth.'
>
> Nashua, New Hampshire, *New York Times* (Gail Collins), 1 February 2000

> 'It is not Reaganesque to support a tax plan that is Clinton in nature.'
>
> Los Angeles, 23 February 2000; *Slate*

'A tax cut is really one of the anecdotes to coming out of an economic illness.'

The Edge With Paula Zahn, CBS, 18 September 2000

KING: [Gore] said: If you lopped off the top 1 percent that you are giving tax relief . . . you could pay for the cost of every other program.

BUSH: Oh, I don't – you know, I hadn't – I'm not so sure. I'm not quick in my mind at math, but I don't believe in trying to pick and choose winners when it comes to tax relief.

Larry King Live, CNN, 26 September 2000

'It's going to require numerous IRA agents.'

Houston Chronicle, 15 October 2000

The Governor was referring to Gore's tax plan, and the huge new bureaucracy it would create, somewhere in Dublin.

'Mr Vice President, in all due respect, it is – I'm not sure 80 percent of the people get the death tax. I know this: 100 percent will get it if I'm the President.'

Presidential debate, 17 October 2000

BUT SERIOUSLY, FOLKS . . .

'[M]y opponent keeps saying I give too much tax relief to the top 1 percent, but he hadn't heard my latest proposal. The bottom 99 percent will do well when they get to split Dick Cheney's stock options.'

(Laughter)

Al Smith Memorial Dinner in New York, 19 October 2000

At one point, Bush thundered that Mr Gore believes that the federal surplus 'is the people's money'. He meant to say that Mr Gore considers the surplus the 'government's money'. But he took his mix-up in stride and paraphrased Ronald Reagan to laugh at himself. 'Excuse me,' he said. 'There I go again,' and the crowd lapped it up.

New York Times, 31 October 2000

AT THE HELM

A lobbying campaign led by credit card companies and banks that gave millions of dollars in political donations to members of Congress and contributed generously to President Bush's 2000 campaign is close to its long sought goal of overhauling the nation's bankruptcy system.

Legislation that would make it harder for people to wipe out their debts could be passed by the Senate as early as this week. The bill has already been approved by the House, and Mr Bush has pledged to sign it.

Sponsors of the bill acknowledge that lawyers and lobbyists for the banks and credit card companies were involved in drafting it.* The bill gives those industries most of what they have wanted since they began lobbying in earnest in the late

---

* Among the biggest beneficiaries of the measure would be the MBNA Corporation of Delaware, which describes itself as the world's biggest independent credit card company. Ranked by employee donations, MBNA was the largest corporate

1990s, when the number of personal bankruptcies rose to record levels.

Consumer groups describe the bill as a gift to credit card companies and banks in exchange for their political largess, and they complain that the bill does nothing to stop abuses by creditors who flood the mail with solicitations for high-interest credit cards and loans, which in turn help drive many vulnerable people into bankruptcy.

'This bill is the credit card industry's wish list', said Elizabeth Warren, a Harvard law professor who is a bankruptcy specialist. 'They've hired every lobbying firm in Washington. They've decided that it's time to lock the doors to the bankruptcy courthouse.'

New York Times, 13 March 2001

---

contributor to the Bush campaign, according to a study by the Center for Responsive Politics, an election research group. MBNA's employees and their families contributed about $240,000 to Mr Bush, and the chairman of the company's bank unit, Charles M. Cawley, was a significant fundraiser for Mr Bush and gave a $1,000-a-plate dinner in his honor, the center said. After Mr Bush's election, MBNA pledged $100,000 to help pay for inaugural festivities.

THE NATION'S HEALTH

'For those that are uninsured, many of the uninsured are able-bodied capable people capable of buying insurance choose not to do so.'

Interview in Manchester, New Hampshire, with WMUR, 10 November 1999

Tim Russert asked Bush if he would support a person's right to sue his or her HMO (Health Maintenance Organization). Bush's 'yes' turned out to be a 'no', but seeing this required your careful concentration.

BUSH: Yes.

RUSSERT: Republicans in Congress don't like that. They voted three-to-one against it.

BUSH: I think it's important for people to have access to the courts of law if, in fact, there is a – if, in fact, once they have had an opportunity to have their claims heard, and if the findings of the arbitration panel, called an 'independent review organization', are ignored, there ought be a cause of action. People ought to have some kind of access to express their concerns, both in an arbitration panel, and, ultimately, in the courts.

Listen, I'm a tort reformer. I've fought for tort reform in the state of Texas. I signed seven pieces of major tort legislation because our civil justice system was unfair.

Meet the Press, NBC, 21 November 1999

'I'm sorry. I wish I could wave a wand.'

New York Times, 18 February 2000

Such was the Governor's compassionate response to a mother who had asked him how he planned to deal with cases like her own: a son with a chronic, life-threatening illness, and a medical insurance plan that would not cover the expenses of his care. Although she had asked the candidate to talk about his policy on health insurance, he replied as if she'd asked him for a handout.

'I don't know the statistics he's using, but I do know that there's a lot of women who are covered.'

60 Minutes II, CBS, 7 March 2000

The Governor had just been asked if Al Gore was correct in saying that Texas ranked forty-ninth among the fifty states for the number of its female residents with health-care coverage.

DAN RATHER: Al Gore has said that in Texas, where you're Governor, that, among women with health care, Texas ranks number forty-nine, children with health insurance ranks number fifty. Is that true, and what does this tell us about your governorship?

BUSH: Well, I think you can kind – find all kinds of statistics to make all kinds of cases. I rest my – I rest most of my case on the fact that people in Texas like the job I have done.

Ibid.

'Well, there'll be a health care debate, and there'll be a health care issue that I'm going to, I mean, a health care speech and policy that I lay out. I talk about health care all the time at these one-on-ones when asked. It's on people's minds.'

CNN interview, 8 March 2000

'We will promote individual choice. We will rely on private insurance.'

Fox News Report, 11 April 2000

'I don't think we need to be subliminable about the differences between our views on prescription drugs.'

Orlando, Florida, 12 September 2000; *Slate*

'FUZZY MATH'

AL GORE: Some people who say the word 'reform' actually mean 'cuts'. Under the Governor's plan, if you kept the same fee for service that you have now under Medicare, your premiums would go up by between 18 and 47 percent – and that's the study of the Congressional plan that he's modeled his proposal on, [the study] by the Medicare actuaries.

Let me just give you one quick example. There's a man here tonight named George McKinney from Milwaukee. He's seventy years old. He has high blood pressure. His wife has heart trouble. They have income of twenty-five thousand dollars a year. They cannot pay for their prescription drugs. And so they're some of the ones that go to Canada regularly in order to get their prescription drugs.

Under my plan, half of their costs would be paid right away. Under Governor Bush's plan, they would get not one penny for four to five years, and then they would be forced to go into an HMO or to an insurance company and ask them for coverage. But there'd be no limit on the premiums or the deductibles or any of the terms and conditions.

BUSH: I cannot let this go by – the old-style Washington politics of, 'We're going to scare you in the voting booth.' Under my plan, the man gets immediate help with prescription drugs. It's called 'immediate helping hand'. Instead of squabbling and finger-pointing, he gets immediate help. Let me say something. Now I understand—

JIM LEHRER: Excuse me, Governor.

GORE: Jim, can I—

LEHRER: All right, three and a half minutes is up. But we'll—

GORE: Could I make one other point?

BUSH: Wait a minute.

GORE: They get twenty-five thousand dollars a year income. That makes them ineligible.

BUSH: Look, this is a man, he's got great numbers. He talks about numbers. I'm beginning to think not only did he invent the Internet, but he invented the calculator. It's fuzzy math. It's a scaring – trying to scare people in the voting booth. Under my tax plan, that he continues to criticize, I set a third – the federal government should take no more than a third of anybody's check. But I also drop the bottom rate from 15 percent to 10 percent because by far the vast majority of the help goes to the people at the bottom end of the economic ladder. If you're a family of four in Massachusetts making fifty thousand dollars you get a 50 percent cut in the federal income taxes you pay. It's from four thousand to about two thousand.

Now, the difference in our plans is, I want that two thousand to go to you, and the Vice President would like to be spending the two thousand on your behalf.

Presidential debate, 3 October 2000

Bush's rhetoric was fuzzier by far than Al Gore's math. Rather than rebut Gore's claims, or even deny them, Bush simply changed the subject from his Medicare proposal to his tax plan, which he then defended by relying on a riff he knew by heart.

'Drug therapies are replacing a lot of medicines as we use to know it.'

Presidential debate, 17 october 2000

'It's one thing about insurance, that's a Washington term.'

Ibid.

'If I'm the President, we're going to have emergency room care, we're going to have gag orders, women will have direct access to OB-GYN.'

Ibid.

'And, folks, it's important we get this right, because we're a compassionate nation. We're a nation that says, when some-body cannot help themselves, we will as a government. We're a nation that says, anytime anybody has to choose between food and medicine: "That's not right. That's not our vision of America. That's not what America's all about as far as we're concerned."

(Applause)

'So one of our priorities is to say to Congress, both Republicans and Democrats, "Let's solve this problem. Let's make sure prescription drugs are a part of the Medicare plan for every senior. Let's help the poorest of seniors be able to afford the medicines of the future. Let's give people options in the Medicare program. Let's trust seniors to be able to make decisions about what's best for them."

'Now, I know there's a lot of talk about Medicare, and you've heard the debates about spending this money here and that money there, and this plan here and that plan there. It's got to be kind of confusing to some, and I understand that.

'But one thing they can't run and hide from is this fact: In 1992, they crossed our country – "they" being my opponent and his friend, our President. They crossed our country and they said: "Oh, just give us a chance. We'll do something on Medicare." And you may remember, in 1996, they had to say it again. And here we are now, eight years after the initial promise was made, and they're still saying it!

'And the message of this campaign is, "We're tired." [sic] The Vice President says, "You ain't seen nothing yet." Well, he's right. We haven't seen anything yet!

(Applause)

'This campaign is sending a clear message. It's a clear message. Leadership is going to bring people together to solve this important problem. That's what a leader does, is solve problems:

'*We*'re not going to use Medicare as a political issue! It's time to put that kind of thinking aside!'

Kalamazoo, Michigan, 27 October 2000; FCDH Political Transcripts

AT THE HELM

As part of his budget, President Bush intends next month to propose cuts in programs to provide child care, to prevent child abuse and to train doctors at children's hospitals, administration officials said today.

State officials contend that stable child care for low-income families has been a major ingredient of successful programs to move people from welfare to work. Congress provided $2 billion last year for the Child Care and Development Block Grant. That included an increase of $817 million, or 69 percent, so that states could provide day care to 241,000 additional children.

Budget documents from the Department of Health and Human Services show that Mr Bush plans to cut child care grants by $200 million, to $1.8 billion, as part of the budget he will send Congress early next month. The documents also show that spending for programs dealing with child abuse would be reduced by $15.7 million, or 18 percent. That would leave $71.8 million for federal grants to the states to prevent and investigate child abuse and neglect.

About 900,000 children are victims of abuse or neglect each year, federal data show, based on reports of cases investigated and confirmed by the states . . . The budget documents show that Mr Bush is planning to eliminate all the money, $20 million, that Congress provided for an 'early learning fund' to improve the quality of child care and education for children younger than 5 . . . In December, Congress also provided $235 million for a new program to train pediatricians and other doctors at children's hospitals across the country. Bush administration officials said the White House Office of Management and Budget had made a preliminary decision to seek large cuts in this program . . . Representative Jennifer Dunn, Republican of Washington, expressed concern about the possibility of a cut. 'We really need the money for training of physicians who deal directly with children', Ms Dunn said.

New York Times, 23 March 2001

THE COLOR LINE

Herein lie buried many things which if read with patience may show the strange meaning of being black here in the dawning of the Twentieth Century. This meaning is not without interest to you, Gentle Reader; for the problem of the Twentieth Century is the problem of the color-line.

W.E.B. DuBois, *The Souls of Black Folk* (1903)

'The color-line' observed by the exact DuBois is surely just as grave a problem as it was a century ago. It is, however, also harder to perceive than it was then – in part because of the disarming 'color line' deployed today by politicians of the right. By putting on big multicolored shows of 'tolerance', the GOP misrepresents itself, the party of Strom Thurmond, Trent Lott, Bob Barr, Rush Limbaugh, William Rehnquist, David Duke and Bob Jones University thereby appearing as if somehow dedicated to the same ideal of racial justice that they all have worked against for years. Thus they hand Americans, and black folk in particular, a 'color line' the way a deft seducer will assure some foxy feminist that he believes in women's rights and always has.

At such salesmanship our President works hard – as he has had to do, since, in the realm of race relations, he has so much to hide, not only in the GOP but in his own background. His 'victory' in Florida – an upset based directly on the systematic racial profiling of that state's voters – was but the climax of a personal history replete with hints of (let us call it) Southern comfort. The Skull and Bones connection, for example, doesn't augur well for Bush's sensitivity on race. In his day, Bonesman Prescott Bush, our President's grandfather, reportedly dug up Geronimo's grave and snatched the warrior's skull, which is, they say, still hidden in the club's dark monolithic quarters on Yale's campus, along with other Indian remains. (The story was reported by Ron Rosenbaum.) According to the *Greenwich Village Gazette*, moreover, the ghastly treasures kept inside the Skull and Bones retreat reportedly include a set of Hitler's silverware, which the initiates are said to dine with once a year – a fixed tradition by the time George W. Bush became a member back in 1964.[64]

Although such tales cannot be verified beyond a shadow of a doubt (although no Bonesman will deny them outright), there is abundant further evidence of Bush's lifelong blindness toward racism. Although not as lurid, the evidence is just as unencouraging as those Gothic rumors. First of all, there is Bush's absolute obliviousness to the fact of racial segregation in the Midland of his childhood, which is thus idyllically described in his campaign autobiography:

'Midland was a small town, with small-town values. We learned to respect our elders, to do what they said, and to be good neighbors. We went to church. Families spent time together, outside, the grown-ups talking with neighbors while the kids played ball or with marbles and yo-yos. Our homework and schoolwork were important. The town's leading citizens worked hard to attract the best teachers to our schools. No one locked their doors, because you could trust your friends and neighbors. It was a happy childhood. I was surrounded by love and friends and sports.'

(*A Charge to Keep*, p. 18)

That glimpse of paradise does not reveal (except between the lines) that Midland was a wealthy compound for whites only. The city's affluence is ably hidden by those Norman Rockwell touches: 'small-town values', 'marbles' and 'yo-yos' do not quite square with 'country club', although the privileged kids there all belonged to one. Likewise, the passage's hypnotic emphasis on 'neighbors' leads us to forget, or not to think, that Midland was a little Eden strictly segregated. The few black people there were menials. 'The blacks couldn't wear dress clothes going downtown, only overalls or a uniform,' recalls Otha Taylor, the Bushes' black maid, who minded little George, Jeb, Neil and Marvin from 1958.[65] There is no known instance of the eldest Bush boy ever mentioning that he grew up in a *de facto* state of apartheid – a lifelong silence which suggests that the arrangement didn't bother him, assuming that he even noticed it.

As Governor of Texas, Bush demonstrated that his comfort zone with white supremacy is just about as big as all outdoors. For instance, in November 1999 – when he was in full gallop toward the White House – Bush made Charles Williams, police chief in the town of Marshall, chairman of the Texas Commission on Law Enforcement Standards and Education. It was a curious choice for such a post, especially in light of Bush's own embrace of 'education' as his main concern. A year before his elevation, Williams testified, in a discrimination lawsuit, that the epithets 'porch monkey' and 'black bastard' are not offensive. 'If it's a general statement, no, I don't consider it a racial slur,' he said, in deposition. He has not modified that view. 'You just have to show me where it's a racial slur. It just depends on how it's used and who it's used toward,' he told the Associated Press in April 2000. Bush showed the same peculiar tolerance of racist ideology when he appointed Dr William 'Reyn' Archer (son of Representative Bill Archer, GOP power-house) as a state health commissioner. In 1998, Dr Archer gave a speech in which he claimed that blacks value loyalty far more than honesty (unlike Republicans), and that they 'don't buy' civilized arrangements such as marriage. Dr Archer later made more waves when he suggested that the state's high rates of teenage pregnancy reflect a powerful Hispanic yen for having babies. By nature, the commissioner suggested, Texas's Chicano citizens are disinclined to feel that 'getting pregnant is a bad thing', and so they just keep reproducing, wed or not.[66]

Bush's friends insist that there is not a biased bone in his whole body, just as he himself has often advertised his 'heart' as innocent of all such nastiness. If true, it is beside the point. Far more damaging than his promotions of unreconstructed white supremacists, or his refusal to condemn the use of the Confederate flag in South Carolina, or his mating dance with Pat Buchanan, was his extraordinary stewardship of the Texas criminal justice system – the busiest outpost of a larger national system that vastly over-concentrates on African-Americans.

The statistics are astonishing. As Governor, Bush came to oversee, in Molly Ivins' words, 'the largest prison system on the planet Earth'. According to a study published in August 2000 by the Justice Policy Institute in Washington, DC, Texas – pop. 20 million – has over 163,000 of its citizens in jail, with well over 700,000 under some form of juridical control. With one out of every twenty of the state's adults in prison, on parole, or on probation, Texas can account for one-fifth of all the people jailed throughout the nation in the nineties. For every 100,000 of its citizens, Texas has 700 behind bars – 248 more than the national average. If Texas were a separate country, the JPI concluded, 'it would have a higher incarceration rate than Russia, China, the United States and the rest of the industrialized and non-industrialized world.'

Such are the results, in Texas, of the nation's 'drug war' – which is in fact a race war waged by legal means. Although 72 percent of all illicit drug users are white, and only 15 percent black, African-Americans account for 36.8 percent of those arrested on drug charges, constituting 42 percent of those held in federal prisons for narcotics, and nearly 60 percent of those held in state jails. In the nineties, the number of black inmates busted for narcotics increased by 60 percent, while that of whites increased by 46 percent. In state courts, white drug users are less likely to do time than blacks, with 32 percent of all convicted white defendants going to jail, while 46 percent of blacks end up imprisoned.

It is this racist trend – and not, as Bush believes, the hippies' influence – that has played hell with 'family values' in poor black communities. 'Crime control policies,' note two scholars in *American Psychologist*, 'are a major contributor to the disruption of the family, the prevalence of single parent families, and children raised without a father in the ghetto,' and have contributed as well to unemployment rates among the poor. The move to lock them up has also had disastrous civic consequences. By 1997, 1.46 million black men – out of a total voting population of 10.4 million – had lost the right to vote because of felony convictions. According to Human Rights Watch: 'Thirteen percent of all adult black men – 1.4 million – are disenfranchised, representing one-third of the total of disenfranchised population and reflecting a rate of disenfranchisement that is seven times the national average.'[67]*

As Governor of Texas, Bush was by far the nation's proudest and most diligent enforcer of this racist trend – and reaped a large electoral benefit from doing so, his tough stance winning the approval of a clear majority of Texans. It is therefore no surprise that very few blacks voted for him in the last election; and, considering his cynicism, also no surprise that he would keep on trying to win them over, with many earnest words and tolerant gestures.

'In terms of being a president that says there's no place in racism [*sic*], it starts with saying there's no place for racism in America . . . And that's what leadership needs to do. Leadership needs to stand up and say, and condemn racism and condemn prejudice and hold people accountable as an individual, not as a group.'

Michigan GOP debate, 10 January 2000

'This month in particular, we remember the stories of those who have helped to build our nation and advance the cause of freedom and civil rights. We remember the bravery of the soldiers of the 54th Massachusetts Infantry Regiment and the sailors of the USS *Mason* in service to our country. We

---

* Such civic deprivation helped the Bush team to suppress the Democratic vote in Florida. As Gregory Palast reported in the *Observer* and *Salon*, the Bush administration in that state retained a private company called DataBase Technologies (now known as ChoicePoint DBT) to purge the names of all ineligible voters from the rolls. An outfit whose board is dominated by Republicans, ChoicePoint DBT went to town, incorrectly – albeit no doubt deliberately – purifying the names of over sixty-four thousand voters, most of them black Democrats. See Gregory Palast, 'Florida's Flawed "Voter Cleansing Program".' *Salon*, 12 December 2000.

remember those who marched on Washington, sat at whites-only lunch counters, and walked rather than use segregated buses. And we remember those, known only to each of us, who helped to build our families, places of worship, and communities.'

'National African American History Month, 2001:

A Proclamation by the President of the United States', 1 February 2001

'I don't remember any kind of heaviness ruining my time at Yale.'

Minutaglio, *First Son*, p. 117

Bush was here referring to the civil rights movement of the sixties, among other struggles of that time.

As a presidential candidate, Bush discussed his racial target-marketing with the same frank cynicism that marked all his campaign self-assessments:

As he traveled through East Texas last week, Bush acknowledged that his campaign has a specific Hispanic strategy but no specific Hispanic message.

'I think the message is the same. I've never been one to tailor my message to one group of people versus another group of people,' he said. 'In the case of Hispanic voters, it is a combination of developing a theme that says to the Hispanic community, "This guy understands . . . and he can speak the language somewhat."'

Bush, in words and ads, believes Hispanic issues are the issues of everyone: opportunity, education and the like. He is airing two Spanish radio ads, one stressing education, the other heavy on personal responsibility.

Luis Garcia of KJS, the San Antonio advertising firm handling the Hispanic campaign for Bush, said it's the effort, as much as the message, that makes it work.

'This is a campaign that recognizes the importance of Hispanics and does it in a way that shows what Governor Bush represents, which is exactly what's important to the Hispanic community,' Garcia said.

Things get a little trickier in seeking black voters, something Bush also hopes to be able to do in record numbers for a Texas Republican.

'Same thing,' he said, explaining that, as with Hispanics, there will be no special message for blacks. 'But obviously, the Spanish component is not there. But it is the same type of idea. It's how you make sure the message is heard.'

Austin-American Statesman, 23 August 1998

BUSH: First of all, Cinco de Mayo is not the independence day. That's diecisèis de septiembre, and—

MATTHEWS: What's that in English?

BUSH: Fifteenth of September.

Hardball, MSNBC, 31 May 2000

Diecisèis de septiembre means 16 September.

On Native-American rights:

'My view is that state law reigns supreme when it comes to the Indians, whether it be gambling or any other issue.'

Associated Press, 4 November 1999

Although Texas has a large Native-American population, Governor Bush was evidently unaware that the US government's treaties with the Indians take precedence over state laws.

'No one wants racial profiling to take place in any state. The Governor of this state doesn't, the Governor of my state doesn't. I'm interested in fair justice. I think we ought to hold people accountable if they break the law regardless of the color of their skin.'

Ibid.

'I mean, there needs to be a wholesale effort against racial profiling, which is illiterate children.'

Presidential debate, 11 October 2000

'People shouldn't read into venue locations into someone's heart.'

Associated Press, 12 January 2000

Bush was responding to complaints about his having given a speech at a former slave plantation in Lexington, South Carolina.

'What I am against is quotas. I am against hard quotas, quotas they basically delineate based upon whatever. However they delineate, quotas, I think vulcanize society. So I don't know how that fits into what everybody else is saying, their relative positions, but that's my position.'

San Francisco Chronicle (Molly Ivins), 21 January 2000

At the third presidential debate, a woman named Norma Kirby asked the Governor a pertinent question:

KIRBY: How will your administration address diversity, inclusiveness, and what role will affirmative action play in your overall plan?

BUSH: I've had a record of bringing people from all walks of life into my administration and my administration is better off for it in Texas. I'm going to find people that want to serve their country. But I want a diverse administration, I think it's important.

I've worked hard in the state of Texas to make sure our institutions reflect the state, with good smart policy, policy that rejects quotas. I don't like quotas. Quotas tend to pit one group of people against another. Quotas are bad for America. It's not the way America is all about. But policies that give people a helping hand so they can help themselves. For example, in our state of Texas, I worked with the legislature, both Republicans and Democrats, to pass a law that said if you come in the top 10 percent of your high school class, you're automatically admitted to one of our, one of our higher institutions, higher institutions of learning, college. And as a result, our universities are now more diverse. It was a smart thing to do, I called it, I labeled it affirmative access.

I think the contracting business in government can help, not with quotas, but help meet a goal of ownership of small businesses, for example. The contracts need to be smaller, the agencies need to be, you know – need to recruit and to work hard to find people to bid on the state contracts. I think we can do that in a way that represents what America's all about, which is equal opportunity and opportunity for people to realize their potential, so to answer your question, I support, I guess the way to put it is affirmative *access*. And I'll have an administration that'll make you proud.

LEHRER: Vice President Gore?

GORE: . . . I don't know what 'affirmative access' means. I do know what affirmative *action* means . . .

. . . Now, I just believe that what we have to do is enforce the civil rights laws. I'm against quotas. This is – with all due respect, Governor, that's a red herring. Affirmative action isn't quotas. I'm against quotas. They're illegal. They're against the American way. Affirmative action means that you take extra steps to acknowledge the history of discrimination and injustice and prejudice and bring all people into the American dream because it helps everybody, not just those who are directly benefiting.

LEHRER: Governor, what is your – are you opposed to affirmative action?

BUSH: No, if affirmative action means quotas, I'm against it. If affirmative action means what I just described, what I'm for, then I'm for it. You heard what I was for. Vice President keeps saying I'm against things. You heard what I was for and that's what I support.

LEHRER: What about – Mr Vice President, you heard what he said.

GORE: He said if affirmative action means quotas, he's against it. Affirmative action doesn't mean –

BUSH: Good.

GORE: – quotas. Are you for it *without* quotas?

BUSH: Well, I may not be for your version, Mr Vice President, but I am for what I just described to the lady. She heard my answer.

GORE: Are you for what the Supreme Court says is a constitutional way of having affirmative action?

Bush turned to Lehrer, to get him to change the subject.

BUSH: Jim!

LEHRER: Let's go on to another – another—

GORE: I think that speaks for itself.

LEHRER: It's a question—

BUSH: No, it doesn't speak for itself, Mr Vice President. It speaks
for the fact that there are certain rules in this that we all
agreed to. But evidently rules don't mean anything.

Presidential debate, 17 October 2000

OOPS

'Unfairly but truthfully [*sic*], our party has been tagged as being
against things. Anti-immigrant, for example. And we're not a
party of anti-immigrants. Quite the opposite. We're a party that
welcomes people.'

Cleveland, 1 July 2000; *Slate*

THE UNBORN

On the white-hot subject of abortion, Bush became extraordinarily vague – even by his special standard – whenever he was forced to range beyond his usual soundbites about 'life'.

'Part of ushering in the responsibility era, which I talk a lot about, is for folks to understand the preciousness of life. It's not only life for the unborn, it is life for the elderly, it is life of the young, it is life of the living.'

Meet the Press, NBC, 21 November 1999

'I'm going to lead the country to understanding the value of life – the preciousness of life. Life for the living and life for the unborn.'

This Week, ABC, 23 January 2000

'There's a larger issue than just abortion, and it's valuing life, a culture of life. It's not just life of the child or the unborn; it's life of the living.'

Larry King Live, CNN, 20 July 2000

'I don't know. Probably down.'

Talk, September 1999

This was Bush's answer to the question as to whether the number of abortions had gone up or down in Texas since he had been elected Governor. On hearing this, top campaign aide Karen Hughes was quick to set the record straight: 'We've doubled the number of adoptions in Texas. You've done a lot to cut abortions.' 'That's right,' agreed Hughes' colleague David Sibley: 'The crisis pregnancy centers.' 'We don't fund crisis pregnancy centers,' the Governor replied.

> 'I think it's important for those of us in a position of responsibility to be firm in sharing our experiences, to understand that the babies out of wedlock is a very difficult chore for mom and baby alike . . . I believe we ought to say there is a different alternative than the culture that is proposed by people like Miss [Naomi] Wolf in society . . . And, you know, hopefully, condoms will work, but it hasn't worked.'
>
> *Meet the Press*, NBC, 21 November 1999

> 'States should have the right to enact reasonable laws and restrictions particularly to end the inhumane practice of ending a life that otherwise could live.'
>
> Cleveland, 29 June 2000; *Slate*

JACK FORD: Governor, you have talked a great deal over this past week about your position on the issue of abortion. Assume for a minute, if indeed you were the President; if, indeed, Roe vs. Wade was overturned; if indeed there was a constitutional amendment banning abortions – what would you think would be the right thing to happen for a doctor who performed an abortion? Should that doctor be criminally prosecuted?

BUSH: You mean, if abortions were illegal?

FORD: Yes.

BUSH: Yeah, I mean that's a huge 'if'.

FORD: Right.

BUSH: This country needs a president who can lead us to understanding of life. There's a lot of people who disagree with what you just said, and there is good people on both sides of this issue. [It was unclear what the Governor meant by 'what you just said'.] The real fundamental question is can our party and our nation have a president who leads us to respect life?

FORD: But if we got to—

BUSH: But I mean, eventually – well, eventually if the law is broken, of course there needs to be some kind of prosecution.

FORD: Would we also then find ourselves in a situation where if a woman had an abortion, that she would also be criminally prosecuted?

BUSH: No, I don't think that would be the case.

Good Morning America, ABC, 25 January 2000

CHRIS MATTHEWS: Abortion – is it going to be an issue in this campaign? Should it be?

BUSH: I think – I think the – the life issue is an issue. And I – I – one of my jobs is to set an ideal for America that says we'll protect life, life of the elderly.

MATTHEWS: Yeah.

BUSH: I think one of the issues that faces Amer– that America

294

faces – I know you oftentimes worry out loud, what should America be like is one of your concerns.

MATTHEWS: Yeah, what kind of a country you want to live in?

BUSH: What kind of country you live in. When—

MATTHEWS: Let me ask you—

BUSH: Let me – let me – let me answer that, because –

MATTHEWS: Sure.

BUSH: – I – I'm pretty good about asking myself the own question [*sic*], then answering it, see?

MATTHEWS: OK.

BUSH: I – well, the country I want to live in is a country that respects life, and – and – and respects life of the unborn and the living, respects life of people living in tough neighborhoods and good neighborhoods, and respects the elderly. That's the ideal world and that's what I intend to lead towards. I understand not everybody agrees with me, but that's not going to deter me from trying to set the right tone for America.

MATTHEWS: President Clinton promised when he ran – he made a number of promises the – for people – people who work hard and play by the rules.

BUSH: Yeah.

MATTHEWS: He also said he was going to make abortion safe, legal and rare, which I think helped him with Roman Catholic voters that last one.

BUSH: It's a pretty interesting line.

MATTHEWS: Do you buy it? Do you think he's made it rare?

BUSH: Do I buy that – no, otherwise, he would not have vetoed a ban on partial birth abortion.

MATTHEWS: Right.

BUSH: I think there's a lot of things we can do to work together to reduce abortions. I think there's a lot of things we can do to increase adoptions.

MATTHEWS: Do you think abor– banning abortion would work? Step aside from the morality for a second. If you outlawed it, if you banned it in the states, the states all separately banned it after Roe v. Wade –

BUSH: Yeah.

MATTHEWS: – was overruled, or whatever, wouldn't we go back to the 1950s we grew up with? The movie stars all went to Denmark, people – you can go to – you can go to –

BUSH: There's going to be abo– if—

MATTHEWS: – walk to Windsor, Canada, and have an abortion.

BUSH: Yeah.

MATTHEWS: You can take a bus ride or a car ride to Vancouver. How can you stop people from getting an abortion if they want one?

BUSH: You can't. You can't. I – I—

MATTHEWS: So why ban it?

BUSH: Well, I – I don't – I – I don't – I think the key is, is to change the culture first and foremost. I don't think anybody is

BUSH: under – I don't believe people believe it can be banned. I believe we can do everything we can to make it, as the President said, more rare.

MATTHEWS: Yeah.

BUSH: I believe we can ban partial-birth abortion. That's clearly an issue that people on both sides of the political –

MATTHEWS: Right.

BUSH: – fence should be able to come and agree on. And—

MATTHEWS: What about a woman who's forty-eight years old and she's listening to the biological clock and she knows all the arguments morally and she's been raised by her par– her parishioner – she's – by a priest who say not to have an abortion, but she decides she wants one. Whose decision is that under – under God? Whose decision is that?

BUSH: Well, here's – here's – here – here's the thing. I mean, you can bring up every hypothetical –

MATTHEWS: All right.

BUSH: – situation on this issue and what I—

MATTHEWS: Well, we'll – we'll come right back. We'll be right back with Governor Bush –

BUSH: Wait a minute.

MATTHEWS: – for his answer. It's not hypothetical. It's every woman you talk to.

(Commercials)

BUSH (on videotape): My job will be to lift the spirits of America, to set our sights higher. My job will be to usher in the Responsibility Era – a culture that will stand in stark contrast to the last few decades, which has clearly said to America: 'If it feels good, do it. And if you've got a problem, blame somebody else.'

MATTHEWS: We're back with Governor Bush. Thank you, Governor. Sorry for interrupting. You want to – you said it was a hypothetical case. I want to give you a chance to expand on that. When it really comes down to it, after all the advice a woman gets, all the state laws are passed, federal laws are *not* passed or whatever, whose final decision is it whether you have an abortion or not? Who has the final call?

BUSH: You know, I would hope that the person would make the decision, for example, to put the child up for adoption. I'm gonna talk about the ideal world, Chris. I've read – I understand reality. If you're asking me as the President, would I understand reality, I do.

MATTHEWS: OK.

BUSH: I do. The – but the role of the President is to set a tone and a – and a – and a – and a – and to appreciate life. I've said a lot in the campaign, I want the goal for America to be that born and unborn children be protected in law and welcomed to life. That's the goal. That's – that's the ideal world and that's exactly where I intend to lead.

Hardball, MSNBC, 31 May 2000

DEATH ROW

The offender never pardons.

George Herbert, *Outlandish Proverbs* (1640)

BUSH: You should head down to Sixth Street.

REPORTER: Why, what's there?

BUSH: Bars. Lots of 'em.

REPORTER: Should I mention your name?

BUSH (laughing): Well, if you do, and end up in jail, you ain't never
                   gonna get out!

The Times, 15 February 1999

'I like the law the way it is right now.'

Fort Worth Star-Telegram, 3 April 1999

Governor Bush said this in opposition to a legislative effort to
exempt the mentally retarded from the Texas execution law.

On Karla Fay Tucker:

KING: All you could have done was give her thirty days, right?

BUSH: That's right.

KING: Why didn't you give it to her, the thirty days?

BUSH: Because my job is to uphold the law of the land. My job is to ask the question, innocence or guilt. My job is not to judge hearts. That's not the job of the Governor.   '

Larry King Live, CNN 16 December 1999

On the execution of Gary Graham, whose impending punishment had been the cause of widespread protests:

'This case has had full analyzation and has been looked at a lot. I understand the emotionality of death penalty cases.'

Seattle Post-Intelligencer, 23 June 2000

'The only thing that I can tell you is that every case I have reviewed I have been comfortable with the innocence or guilt of the person that I've looked at. I do not believe we've put a guilty – I mean, innocent person to death in the state of Texas.'

All Things Considered, NPR, 16 June 2000

On the murderers of James Byrd:

GORE: . . . I think [hate] crimes are different. I think they're different because they're based on prejudice and hatred, which gives rise to crimes that have not just a single victim but they're intended to stigmatize and dehumanize a whole group of people.

LEHRER: You have a different view of that.

BUSH: No, I don't, really.

LEHRER: On hate-crimes laws?

BUSH: No. We've got one in Texas and guess what. The three men who murdered James Byrd. Guess what's going to happen to them? They're going to be put to death. A jury found them guilty and – it's going to be hard to punish them any worse after they get put to death. And it's the right cause so it's the right decision.

Presidential debate, 11 October 2000

BUSH: I want to repeat, if you have a state that fully supports the law, like we do in Texas, we're going to go after all crime, and we're going to make sure people get punished for the crime. And in this case, we can't enhance the penalty any more than putting those three thugs to death, and that's what's going to happen in the state of Texas.

Ibid.

The mere transcript cannot convey the look of pleasure that lit up George Bush's face as he foretold the fate of James Byrd's murderers. The look struck one viewer in particular – a black man named Leo Anderson, who, at the next debate, implored the Governor to say it wasn't so.

ANDERSON: In one of the last debates held, the subject of capital punishment came up. And in your response to the question you seemed to overly enjoy – as a matter of fact, [be] proud that Texas led the nation in execution of prisoners. Sir, did I misread your response, and are you really, really proud of the fact that Texas is number one in executions?

BUSH: No, I'm not proud of that. The death penalty's very serious business, Leo. It's an issue that good people obviously disagree on. I take my job seriously. And if you think I was proud of it, I think you misread me. I do.

I was sworn to uphold the laws of my state. During the course of the campaign in 1994, I was asked, 'Do you support the death penalty?' I said I did, if administered fairly and justly. Because I believe it saves lives, Leo, I do. I think if it's administered swiftly, justly and fairly, it saves lives.

One of the things that happens when you're a governor, often times you have to make tough decisions. And you can't let public persuasion sway you because the job's to enforce the law. And that's what I did, sir. There've been some tough cases come across my desk. Some of the hardest moments since I've been the governor of the state of Texas is to deal with those cases.

But my job is to ask two questions, sir. Is the person guilty of the crime? And did the person have full access to the courts of law? And I can tell you looking at you right now, in all cases those answers were affirmative.

I'm not proud of any record. I'm proud of the fact that violent crime is down in the state of Texas. I'm proud of the fact that we hold people accountable. But I'm not proud of any record, sir. No.

Presidential debate, 17 October 2000

That reply was noteworthy, first of all, for the skill with which Bush charmed his questioner, not only with that deferential 'sir', but, after the debate had ended, by making a bee-line for Anderson and giving him the whole full-body treatment. The Governor's mendacity is also worth remarking. As Texas's

Chief Executive, he was never known to spend a minute more – at most – than half an hour on *any* business, death penalty appeals included. Moreover, the claim that 'violent crime is down in the state of Texas' was disingenuous. 'Crime has dropped in Texas,' the *Toronto Globe and Mail* had reported some weeks earlier, 'but at a significantly slower rate than in the rest of the country, and well behind states of similar size, such as New York.' ('Texas Tops All States in Prison Population', *Toronto Globe and Mail*, 29 August 2000.)

MESSAGE: I'M REAL

'I don't feel like I've got all that much too important to say on the kind of big national issues.'

20/20, ABC, 15 September 2000

'The important question is, How many hands have I shaked?'

New York Times, 23 October 1999

The primitive grammatical mistake in that much-quoted gaffe is far less troubling than the point that Bush was trying to make: that 'the important question' in his case was not exactly where he stood on 'the kind of big national issues', and not (of course) his suitability for higher office, but only the extent and vigorousness of his *campaigning*. In part, Bush's over-emphasis on minor matters like hand-shaking was a way to keep on under-emphasizing complicated or contentious issues, which might cost him votes if he were forced to talk about them.

And yet his constant focus on his own campaigning was not only an evasive measure. First of all, such talk betrayed the Governor's assumption that his arduous campaigning was *itself* enough to justify his being elected. 'How many hands have I shaked?' The note of self-congratulation – and self-pity – in that question gave away his view that he should be rewarded not for his deserts, but for so stoutly going through the long ordeal of running.

> 'I don't want to win? If that were the case, why the heck am I on the bus sixteen hours a day, shaking thousands of hands, giving hundreds of speeches, getting pillared [*sic*] in the press and cartoons and still staying on message to win?'
>
> *Newsweek*, 28 February 2000

A politician, one would think, must take all that abuse in stride – the long days 'on the bus', the speechifying, the criticism in the press – and stay 'on message' in the face of it; and yet Bush seemed to think that he deserved a medal for it. Beyond his laziness, however, the candidate's incessant yammering about his job performance as a candidate bespoke a general uninterest in all other subjects. With his campaign (his governance included), what finally mattered was not good and bad, or right and wrong. Despite the heavy Christian props, on Bush's stage the *only* thing that played was 'theme' and 'message'.

Bush would sometimes sound as if he might be talking about something deeper:

> 'There's nothing like the humbling experience of getting whipped pretty bad in New Hampshire to cause a man to re-evaluate.'

Despite that hint of introspection, the Governor wound up that non-confession right back on the surface:

'And I re-evaluated my message and I re-evaluated how I was conducting myself as a candidate.'

New York Times Online, 15 March 2000

At best, such relentless self-reflection – the messenger repeatedly delivering the message that he'd done a really great job as a messenger repeatedly delivering a message – was merely comic in its flagrant emptiness.

'I've changed my style somewhat, as you know. I'm less – I pontificate less, although it may be hard to tell it from this show. And I'm more interacting with people.'

Meet the Press, NBC, 13 February 2000

'People make suggestions on what to say all the time. I'll give you an example; I don't read what's handed to me. People say, "Here, here's your speech, or here's an idea for a speech." They're changed. Trust me.'

New York Times, 15 March 2000

CARL CAMERON: What premium price [*sic*] do you put on a harmonious convention, and why?

BUSH: Well, this is an event, and a big event in the course of a long campaign. You and I have been through several of them. The kickoff of the campaign was a big event. The primaries, of course, were big. And since – had I not won, I wouldn't be sitting here. The period between the primaries and the convention has been an important period. And, of course, the convention – and the convention is important because it gives a sense of who I am, and I think if we do our job right, to lead our party and lead the country, I think what you are going to find is that this is going to be a convention that spells out what we're for.

Fox Special Report with Brit Hume, 19 July 2000

At its worst, the endless dwelling on mere 'message' evidenced the sort of moral bankruptcy that finally did in Richard Nixon:

'I readily concede I missed an opportunity at Bob Jones; I'd have been a hero. If I had gone down there and said, "We're all God's children; we can receive redemption in all different kinds of ways; the Catholic religion is a great religion, Judaism is a great religion." It's all I would have needed to have said. One sentence.'

New York Times Online, 15 March 2000

'LET ME PULL THE MOTE OUT OF THINE EYE'

Despite – or as an expression of – his own unremitting calculation (see also 'Profile in Courage'), Bush was always quick to wonder righteously at the unremitting calculation of the Democrats.

'If somebody's so calculating that they spend their whole life calculating the path to the Presidency, when they become President, they'll be calculating. I mean, calculation is a part of their being.'

Reader's Digest Online, 30 August 2000

'I've been, frankly, amazed at the amount of polling that goes on to determine the behavior in the White House. Starting with, for example, where to take a summer vacation. I was floored.'

Meet the Press, NBC, 21 November 1999

Even Bush's very protestations that *he* wasn't calculating were themselves apparent calculations, clearly memorized (including, in this case, his stubborn use of 'resignate' for 'resonate'):

'They said, "You know, this issue doesn't seem to resignate with the people." And I said, you know something? Whether it resignates or not doesn't matter to me, because I stand for doing what's the right thing, and what the right thing is hearing the voices of people who work [*sic*].'

Portland, Oregon, 31 October 2000; *Slate*

'There are a lot of nice pundits. And other kind of pundits. They say, they say, you know this issue doesn't seem to resignate. And I said, you know something, whether it resignates or not, that doesn't matter to me, because I stand for doing what's the right thing.'

St Petersburg Times, 2 November 2000

In short, it matters not that Bush spoke as a malapropist, but that such statements were so hypocritical. The same is true of his reply to a question as to whether he was using the Elian Gonzalez case for mere political advantage:

'You subscribe politics to it. I subscribe freedom to it.'

Associated Press, 6 April 2000

HE CAN DISH IT OUT . . .

> 'Other Republican candidates may retort to personal attacks
> and negative ads [*sic*].'
>
> From a Bush/Cheney fund-raising letter, *Washington Post*, 24 March 2000

Although his own political attacks were blatant, Bush seemed not merely to be feigning outrage at others' counter-moves against himself. As thin-skinned as his father (and his father's mentor), he was always quick to charge his adversaries with doing the sort of thing to him that he had done – and was still doing – to them. This is a venerable propaganda trick (although it's not entirely tactical, but also symptomatic of a paranoid approach to combat, whether martial or electoral).

> 'The senator [McCain] has got to understand if he's going to
> have – he can't have it both ways. He can't take the high horse
> and then claim the low road.'
>
> Florence, South Carolina, 17 February 2000; *Slate*

In fact, McCain's attack on Bush was nothing in comparison with Bush's on McCain – a massive smear job that entailed push-polling (telephonic rumor-mongering disguised as polling), racist innuendo (by subtly using pictures of McCain's adopted Asian daughter), frank impugnment of the Senator's record as a champion of veterans' rights (notwithstanding his war-hero status), and accusations of religious prejudice (because the Senator had rashly criticized the Christian right).

Then, having thoroughly trashed McCain in South Carolina, Bush abruptly craved the Senator's forgiveness, and endorsement – although he himself could never have forgiven such a libel, if he had been its target (as he never was).

> 'I think we agree, the past is over.'
>
> *Dallas Morning News*, 10 May 2000

In the presidential contest, Bush was always quick to cry that he was getting hit below the belt – although the Democratic campaign propaganda was remarkably impersonal, considering the Governor's many failings (and the GOP's astounding record of *ad hominem* assaults on Clinton/Gore). Indeed, Bush always used the loud complaint about his adversaries' 'negative campaigning' as a way to shut down all discussion of his dismal record as the Governor of Texas.

> 'Well, that's going to be up to the pundits and the people to make up their mind. I'll tell you what is a president for him, for example, talking about my record in the state of Texas [*sic*]. I mean, he's willing to say anything in order to convince people that I haven't had a good record in Texas.'
>
> MSNBC, 20 September 2000

Meanwhile, Bush always represented *his* attacks as mere defenses – even when his team struck first. Thus he justified one of his anti-Gore commercials:

> 'The point is, this is a way to help inoculate me about what has come and is coming.'
>
> *New York Times*, 2 September 2000

In Bush's view, Gore/Lieberman's chicanery knew no bounds. He even thought that Gore had stooped to plagiarizing Bush's own material – an accusation based on his belief that the cliché 'a fresh start' was an invention by his own campaign, and that the Democrats had stolen it.

> Bush poked fun at Gore's suggestion, in an interview with *USA Today*, that a Gore administration would be a 'fresh start', noting that the phrase had been an early slogan of his own. Aides passed around a copy of Bush's 1999 collection of speeches entitled *A Fresh Start for America*.
>
> 'Unbelievable, isn't it?' Bush said.
>
> Associated Press, 11 August 2000

PLAYING POLITICS WITH PEOPLE'S LIVES

During the 1992 Republican convention, Larry King interviewed George W. and Jeb Bush. At one point the subject turned to a *New York Times* article suggesting that the President had been politically motivated in mounting Operation Desert Storm.

KING: What do you make of the *New York Times* piece today and your father's angry reaction to it?

BUSH: I think it's lousy journalism. I think for the *New York Times* to say that George Bush would commit US lives to Iraq for political purpose stinks [*sic*]. And American people ought to be outraged at that kind of journalism. That's what we call impact journalism. And it seems like to me that, on the verge of this convention, they're trying to impact my good dad's chances of sending out a positive message to the American people.

Larry King Live, CNN, 16 August 1992

According to two *Time* reporters, the younger Bush's jubilation after Desert Storm was gleefully, aggressively political:

'Despite [President] Bush's deliberately leaked exhortation that his aides should avoid inserting partisan politics into foreign policy, the President's intensely partisan eldest son, George W. Bush, universally known as "Junior", couldn't help but exult on *Air Force One* during the flight back to Maine: "Do they think the American people are going to turn to a *Democrat* now?"'

Michael Duffy & Dan Goodgame, Marching in Place:
The Status Quo Presidency of George Bush (1992), p. 200

'Desert Storm was one of the great achievements of the twentieth century. And it had a shelf life of about a month.'

Texas Monthly, November 2000

OOPS

And yet, for all his own chicanery, the Governor, at times, could not help almost blurting out the truth:

'If you're sick and tired of the politics of cynicism and polls and principles, come and join this campaign.'

Hilton Head, South Carolina, 16 February 2000; Slate

'The fact that [Gore] relies on facts – says things that are not factual – are going to undermine his campaign.'

New York Times, 4 March 2000

THE MAKING OF THE PRESIDENT 2000

Anyway, after we go out and work our hearts out,
after you go out and help us turn out the vote,
after we've convinced the good Americans to vote – and while
    they're at it, pull that old George W. lever, if I'm the one –
when I put my hand on the Bible,
when I put my hand on the Bible, that day when they swear us in,
when I put my hand on the Bible,
I will swear to not – to uphold the laws of the land.

George W. Bush, Toledo, Ohio, 27 October 2000

BUSH: We're pleased to welcome the Cheneys and Andy Card
        here, and we're just going to continue our discussions
        about the future. And as I said yesterday, I think it's
        responsible that Dick and I and others contemplate a
        potential administration.

        First Lady Bush will be arriving here soon.

Bush campaign press briefing, 11 November 2000

Like Brother Jeb's election-night conviction that Bush/Cheney had won Florida, the candidate's certainty, just four days later, that his wife already was 'First Lady Bush' suggests extraordinary confidence.

REPORTER: Governor, why did you decide to go forward and seek the injunction in Florida?

BUSH: I think you ought to call Jim Baker and let him – he made the explanation today, and I thought it was a very sound and reasoned explanation. And if you've got any further comment – questions about that, just call him. Call his office. He'll be the person in charge of explaining our position as to why we don't think there needs to be three elections.

Ibid.

REPORTER: Governor, do you plan to appeal the Florida Supreme Court decision?

BUSH: We will refer you to my lawyers in Florida. Jim Baker is doing a good job.

REPORTER: What options are you considering?

BUSH: I refer you to our folks in Florida. They are – Jim Baker is in charge of the team in Florida, and he's doing a really good job down there.

22 November 2000

BUSH: Well, I'm – we're both being kept abreast of the options and opportunities. I decided that it was best to take our case to the Supreme Court of the United States, which will be heard tomorrow. All options are on the

table. But one of our strategies is to get this election rati-
fied. And the sooner the better for the good of the
country.

REPORTER: Governor, how do you respond to the criticism that
in fact your legal team, through your decisions, are in
essence delaying – not delaying, but sort of running out
the clock to prevent the additional ballots, disputed
ballots, from being counted?

BUSH: As I recall, the facts are these: On election night we won.
And then there was a recount, and we won. And there
was a selected recount as a result of different legal
maneuverings, and we won that. And I believe one of
these days, that all this is going to stop, and Dick Cheney
and I will be the President and the Vice President.

Bush campaign press conference, 30 November 2000

'As far as the legal hassling and wrangling and posturing in
Florida, I would suggest you talk to our good team in Florida
led by Jim Baker.'

Ibid.

REPORTER: Governor, now that the Supreme Court has had its
hearing, how do you feel your prospects stand right now?

BUSH: Well, I – we'll wait and see what they say [at] the
Supreme Court, and all these different courts. Dick and I
felt like we won the first three elections. The first election
three times. And we're confident that when it's all said
and done, that – that he and I will be honored to be the
President and the Vice President. That's why we're
having these meetings. That's why we're in the process

of preparing to assume the offices to which we feel like we've been elected.

2 December 2000

BUSH: I felt like the Supreme Court of the United States made a very positive statement on our behalf. And I think that the important – what I – the sentiment I want to convey is this: that I am comforted by the fact that the highest court of our land heard our case and will make sure this election is fair. I think that's – I think that's very important for our citizenry to hear. And as far as what the legislature does in Florida, that's going to be up to the leadership in the legislature.

4 December 2000

BUSH: I felt like [the Florida Supreme Court's] decision was not a fair decision at the time, and I felt like they had rewritten a law and – you know, so therefore.

REPORTER: But are you saying you will abide by the rulings of any law-courts in this matter?

BUSH: Well, I think the court system is very important in the country. But I felt like in the case of the Florida Supreme Court, like I said in my statement, and like Secretary Baker said in his statement, that they changed the rules. And the Supreme Court reviewed that. And now remember, many of the – many of the experts were saying, 'Well, the Bush team has no chance to get their case heard by the Supreme Court.' Not only was the case heard, but the Supreme Court acted in a way that I think is a positive – positive for our campaign.

4 December 2000

'The great thing about America is everybody should vote.'

Austin, Texas, 8 December 2000

AT THE HELM

'See, I believe in the power of the people. I truly do. I do.'

New York Times, 6 March 2001

AFTERWORD

The fetters imposed on liberty at home have ever been forged out of the weapons provided for defense against real, pretended, or imaginary dangers from abroad.

James Madison, 23 February 1799

Our system suffers from a grave disorder at the top – both in the nation's capitol, where a callow and illiterate President sits unelected, gamely fronting for a far-right oligarchy; and throughout the mainstream media, whose personnel will not perceive the evidence before their very eyes. As we have seen, that dual disorder is suggestive of dyslexia, which blocks perception of the written word; and it is even more suggestive of *amnesia*. Indeed, the President's peculiar language is the language of forgetfulness – which is also the language of TV, the medium, despite its ever-swelling archive of taped moments, tending always to transfix the audience in an eternal *now*.

The oblivious effect of Bush's speech is as complex as his illiteracy. On the one hand, the President's forgetfulness is tactical: a *willed* amnesia, meant to be contagious. Like the father's, the son's talk is intended largely to induce us to forget whatever ugly thing we may suspect or know about his life or record. Through mere lying, and/or by blitzing questioners with claims half-true or intimidating or distractingly emotional, both Bushes, despite their intellectual dimness, have always been astute enough to change the subject when confronted with embarrassing reminders of the past – HW's criminal participation in Iran/contra; W's non-political trans-gressions, whether felonies or midemeanors, and his dirty doings as Governor of Texas. More important, both men have always been as ready to deny the dark parts of the nation's past as they have been to sanitize their own. Although not as skilled at such nostalgic improv as Ronald Reagan (who, with his archaic haircut and pre-televisual quips, was himself a walking fiction of 'the way things used to be'), neither Bush was ever a mean hand at whiting out America's past – as when the father vowed, before that gathering of ex-fascists, that 'I will never apologize for the United States of America – I don't care what the facts are'; or as when Bush the Younger summed up the Cold War 'lessons' – 'that our nation's greatest export to the world has been, is, and always will be the incred-ible freedoms we understand in the great land called America'.

Of course, all politicians try to talk away their priors, and all rightists prettify the national past. In his forgetfulness, how-ever, this Bush has no peer; for his speech does not just cause forgetfulness in others, but is *itself* essentially oblivious – its very sound and sense determined by amnesia. At his clearest, Bush tends to speak in serial declaratives, very short and simple, and linked together, quasi-Biblically, with 'and'.

'As I recall, the facts are these: On election night we won. And then there was a recount, and we won.

> And there was a selected recount as a result of different legal maneuverings, and we won that.
>
> And I believe one of these days, that all this is going to stop, and Dick Cheney and I will be the President and the Vice President.'

The statement is amnesiac, then, not only in its meaning – 'the facts' that Bush claimed to 'recall' all being fabrications. He and President Cheney had *not* 'won' on 'election night', nor had there ever been a *manual* recount, which was the only kind of 'recount' that the Democrats were calling for. Thus his statement was to some extent *deliberately* oblivious, like his evasive answers to the question of his past drug use.

While such forgetfulness was surely tactical, Bush's statement, typically, was also structured by *his own* amnesia – its bite-sized syntactic units being the only kind that he can handle. When he tries for a grammatical arrangement more complex than see-Dick-run, Bush often breaks down in mid-effort, having just . . . forgotten how he'd started out, and where he ought to go.

> 'I felt like their decision was not a fair decision at the time, and I felt like they had rewritten a law and – you know, so therefore.'

As it dictates the endless parataxis of his sentences, so does the President's amnesia often have him flailing in supreme rhetorical confusion, blurting out disjointed bits of prose until some propaganda tag-line pops into his head, which then gives him something clear to say, repeatedly. It is because of such forgetfulness – and not stupidity per se – that Bush has always been averse to speaking off-the-cuff, and tries to keep all such appearances as rare and imperceptible as possible.*

Whether it's a handicap that he was born with, or a consequence of youthful boozing and/or drug abuse, our President is not alone in his forgetfulness: TV too is thoroughly amnesiac – an entity with little memory, and one that also urges its forgetfulness on those who watch.[68] It is therefore not surprising that TV was quick to reconfirm the President-select's forgetful take on what had taken place in Florida, and, since the inauguration, eager to keep on forgetting, and to have us keep forgetting, what had really happened. To understand what's going on today, then, we must resist TV's oblivious influence, and first of all remember what went down after Election Day. And yet to understand what really happened, we must also look much further back; for that coup was the climax of a history far richer, darker and more complicated than TV, as we now know it, could ever convey. We must therefore look way back – back to the very dawn of time, as far as TV is concerned – so that we might begin to understand how, for the House of Bush, it all finally came together in the year 2000 – every anti-democratic force in the United States converging to suppress the will of the majority. Only such a longer view can help us to start understanding how the Bush team 'won', and everybody lost.

---

* Running for re-election in 1998, Governor Bush took every step to minimize the audience for his sole debate against opponent Garry Mauro – holding it in remote El Paso, and scheduling the face-off for a Friday night during Texas's high school football season. Similarly, President Bush held no official press conference for over a month after his inauguration – then quickly called one on 23 February, right in the wake of the big news that Hugh Rodham, Hillary Clinton's brother, had taken several hundred thousand dollars as a lobbyist for certain felons seeking presidential pardons. Thus Bush held his first press conference on the same day that Senator Clinton also answered questions from reporters – a stroke of timing whereby his performance was protectively upstaged by the latest chapter of his predecessor's very long ordeal.

*　　　*　　　*

Although it has its partial precedents in US history, the Rehnquist Putsch was something new. First of all, it was effected by a GOP that is not only dominated by the super-rich (who also own much of the Democratic Party), but managed by a host of vengeful ultra-rightists whose alliance is peculiar to this time and place: Nixon men still seething over Watergate; military men still smoldering over Vietnam; Southerners still livid over the desegregation of the schools, the end of lynch law, the extension of the franchise and the burning of Atlanta; Christian Fundamentalists still steaming over rock'n'roll, the Scopes trial and modernity in general; Catholics fuming over Roe v. Wade. The whole enterprise is funded, and its larger moves dictated, by the corporate network of big oil and petro-chemicals, 'defense', tobacco, pharmaceuticals, insurance, pesticides and automotives, among other industries, their top brass and top shareholders all still smarting at the heavy hand of 'regulation', as if there were a lot of that in the United States.

Each of these factions is forced forward by a toxic memory, or illusion, of defeat. What has now made them all especially dangerous, however, is a victory: the fall of Soviet Communism. We cannot afford to underestimate the trauma – or ignore the consequences – of that disappearance. On the one hand, the whole huge bureaucracy of national security is still in place, but lacks a global enemy to justify its appetite. That system needs a state of war – just like its Soviet counterpart (which was finally ruined by the cost of that requirement). And yet the need is not only material, but psychological. For as long as Stalin's empire shared the planet with us, the wildest of our citizens, and not just grass-roots kooks, but many high and mighty maniacs, were suitably preoccupied by that external threat. Although they did great harm to the Republic in pursuit of their apparent mission ('McCarthyism', the war in Vietnam, the Watergate conspiracies and Iran/contra being only the most infamous examples), the patriots never went so far as to subvert our democratic institutions openly – the way that rightists did in other countries, with ample CIA support. Fixated on the dictatorial Other, American extremists, by and large, respected the legality and peacefulness in our elections, ritually proclaiming them as blessed examples to the wider world.

But all that changed with the collapse of Communism. In general, wars often tend to leave a certain stubborn rage among the soldiers and the masses – an emotional holdover that is easily manipulated by domestic interests that have scores to settle, or that want to strengthen their position. Our Cold War was no exception. Fifty years of mass mobilization left this country with a boiling residue of paranoid anxiety that, now lacking any foreign object, had to find some other focus. That need was more than answered by the born-again Republicans, who swiftly trained the sights of all their propaganda guns on Washington itself, the Democrats, 'the liberals' – Nixon's enemies, but now assailed with an unprecedented violence and sophistication, far surpassing even the right-wing crusade against the Roosevelts.

Thus has our system been profoundly damaged by a subtle form of blowback, the savage forces roused against the Soviets now wreaking havoc here in the United States. That dynamic had atrocious consequences nationwide, when, in the hospitable climate of 'the Gingrich Revolution', with Rush Limbaugh, among others, calling openly for gunplay, far-right activists started committing racist murders, taking shots at Jewish children, assassinating doctors who performed abortions, and, most shockingly, blowing up a federal office building in Oklahoma City – the worst act of domestic terrorism in American history. (Although quick to credit the old fantasy that 'Commie propaganda' was a fatal snare, Limbaugh waxed indignant at the charge that his incitements might have had some consequence.)

It was, of course, the White House that lay directly in the sights of all those propaganda guns (and at least one real gun*) – a consequence not of the President's behavior, but of that aggravated need for some new enemy. There is no other explanation for the rightist animus against Bill Clinton who, in calmer times, would surely stand out as a great Republican, what with his winning economic policies, tolerance of Reagan-style deregulation, tough approach to crime and (yet) FDR-like popularity among the nation's have-nots. That he has been cast as a *leftist* has to do exclusively with cultural and generational mythology, as exploited by the GOP.** Especially in the South, Bill Clinton seemed to carry all the sins of the detested sixties counterculture. His youthful disapproval of the war in Vietnam, and clear avoidance of the draft, whipped American

---

* On the afternoon of 29 October, 1994, a man named Francisco Martin Duran, 26, armed with a Chinese-made SKS semi-automatic assault rifle, fired up to thirty rounds at the front of the White House, hitting the mansion with at least eight bullets. To carry out that mission, Duran had driven all the way to Washington from Colorado Springs, Colorado, where he worked as an upholsterer. (According to his neighbors, he always dressed in camouflage – a habit that he picked up in the army, where he had served from 1987 to 1991.) There were bumper stickers on the gunman's pick-up truck: 'Fire Butch Reno' (referring to Janet Reno, Clinton's stolid Attorney General) and 'Those who beat their guns into plows will plow for those who don't'.
** Such cultural mythifying was squarely based, however, on the pathological hatreds of a few of Clinton's far-right enemies in Arkansas – in particular, the bloody-mouthed arch-segregationist 'Justice Jim' Johnson, who had loathed Clinton ever since his own failed run against Senator William Fulbright in the state's 1968 Democratic primary. (Clinton, who had once berated Johnson to his face, worked for Fulbright in that contest.) See Joe Conason and Gene Lyons, *The Hunting of the President: The Ten-Year Campaign to Destroy Bill and Hillary Clinton* (New York, 2000), pp. 67–82 *et passim*.

revanchists into a seditious frenzy. (Meanwhile, such patriots ignored the military records of those rightists who, while hawkish on that war, found ways to keep from fighting in it: Limbaugh, Gingrich, Quayle and Cheney, among other war supporters who had dodged the draft for sound careerist reasons.) The peacenik Clinton also was a figure of demonic hippie hedonism, smoking pot (although denying it) and, as everybody knows, getting it on with as many chicks as Charlie Manson. While linking him to the Aquarian ideal of sex and drugs and rock'n'roll (his White House staff was 'Berkeley, California, with an Appalachian twist,' one vilifier wrote),[69] the fiction also played on ancient racist fears of Negro sexuality. 'Our first black President', as friend and foe alike soon deemed him, Clinton bore the mark of Ham because of his unusual rapport with African-Americans, whose fondness for him was, in rightist eyes, just one more strike against him. (The myth of Clinton's negritude is something of a miracle, considering how many African-Americans were sent to prison while the brother was in office.*) And, of course, the negative effect of all those anti-countercultural clichés – draft-dodger, pothead,

---

* According to a study by the Justice Policy Institute, released in February 2001, under Clinton the number of Americans jailed increased by 673,000 – as opposed to an increase of 478,000 under Reagan. Throughout the Clinton years, the prison population overall jumped from 1.4 million to over 2 million; and the racial dispro-portion only worsened in that time. Under Reagan/Bush, the rate of African-Americans imprisoned rose from 1,156 per 100,000 black men to about 2,800. Under Clinton, that rate grew to 3,620 per 100,000 black men. Justice Policy Institute, 'Too Little Too Late: President Clinton's Prison Legacy', www.cjcj.org/clinton/

Of course, Clinton was not himself responsible for such acceleration, which was built into the system that the state in general created. Nor did Clinton loudly cham-pion such mass imprisonment, as did, for example, Governor Bush. Rather, he colluded in that evil passively, by not making any fuss about it, for political reasons – or perhaps, because he always had a gun pointed at his head.

hippie swinger, nigger-lover – was amplified immeasurably by Clinton's marriage to the polarizing Hillary, whose lawyerly demeanor, unapologetic liberal activism, ever-changing hair and blunt disdain for cookie-baking quickly set her up for rightist diabolization as the Anti-Mom, America's Worst Lady – a terrifying spectre of the sixties' 'women's lib'.

The Clintons' actual flaws and/or misdeeds bore no relation to that crackpot vision of pure evil. Likewise (to compare small things to great), the Soviets' true record and intentions were irrelevant to the Cold War's wildest agitators – who were also the most effective of the champions of that crusade. While there were surely anti-Communists of principle, many of them socialists, who did their best to tell the world what Leninism really meant, the crucial animus in Cold War anti-Communism came not from them, but from the fierce emotion of a certain lunatic plurality, roused and guided on behalf of powerful interests in both parties, and in the world of what they used to call 'big business'. That mighty undertow – which flowed through Nixon's mind, and J. Edgar Hoover's, and James Forrestal's, and James Angleton's, and all throughout the CIA and US military, as well as through the Joe McCarthy cult and the John Birch Society – is a factor that revisionist historians forget, or downplay, in their efforts to re-glamorize the great US propaganda drive against the reds. And that same war-like sentiment, peddled in the grass roots by the propagandists of the right, dominated US politics throughout the nineties, and finally helped the House of Bush to put their boy in office. While Clinton had the genius to survive the long attack against him, Al Gore lacked the crucial smoothness. Therefore, among the reasons for that Democrat's defeat we must include the winning GOP campaign to replace the Soviets with Clinton/Rodham Clinton/Gore in US far-right demonology. Although it failed to finish Clinton, the slander stuck to Gore sufficiently to drive up Bush's numbers in the heartland, so that the Republican endgame in Florida became decisive.

US interference with democracy is nothing new. Indeed, it was the very hallmark of US Cold War foreign policy. As the world learned in the seventies, the CIA had long routinely meddled in the politics of other lands – from Italy to Ecuador, from Iran, Guatemala and the Philippines to Vietnam, Cambodia and Chile, using violence and every other kind of dirty trick to jar electorates into voting for 'our' choices, not their own. The same sort of subversive operation was exposed by Watergate, which chillingly revealed that it *could* happen here – and did in 1972, George McGovern's very candidacy having been arranged through covert means by Nixon's team.* Iran/contra was another major crime against democracy, the zealots in the White House and the CIA conspiring to ignore Congressional constraints on their worldwide *jihad* against the reds. 'We're too timid. The attitude is "Don't stick your neck out. Play it safe." This kind of crap is smothering us,' CIA Director William Casey grumbled at one agency conclave.[70] And so the Reagan/Bush team forged an international arms-trading network answerable only to themselves, so as to fund the contras by selling arms covertly to Iran's extremist

---

* Under orders from Charles Colson, Nixon's henchmen worked the eminently beatable McGovern into place primarily by wrecking the campaign of front runner Ed Muskie. Through an impressive range of dirty tricks, including forgery and fabricated libel, the Nixon team sowed many anxious doubts about the candidate's trustworthiness and sanity. At length their efforts paid off handsomely when, on 26 February 1972, Muskie, campaigning in New Hampshire, threw a tearful fit outside the offices of the Manchester *Union Leader*. Its far-right publisher, William Loeb, had run a piece insulting Muskie's wife, and then a letter charging that the candidate had laughed at a pejorative description of the state's French Canadians ('Canucks'). The letter had been drafted by a Nixon operative.

government, in violation of the law, and of official US policy.*
Aside from the hefty profits realized by certain of the principals,
for the true believers in 'the Enterprise' its main attraction lay
in their apparent role as deputies of God, as Ollie North and
his lieutenants all made clear.

The belief that they were acting in the name of Freedom kept
such patriots on the job, from the founding of the CIA until the
fall of Soviet Communism. Certainly there were a lot of cynics
in that company, hard-boiled players who were only in it for
the savage fun. Such adventurism was, however, always tacitly
legitimized by the official view that the clandestine struggle was
a necessary evil in the face of worldwide Communist subversion
– and there were agents who did not just pay lip service to that
view, but held it fervently. But whether they were opportunists
or fanatics, or both at once, *all* the Cold War's activists could
justify their anti-democratic coups, both foreign and domestic,
as moves essential to the rescue of democracy.

That position was absurd and self-destructive – just like
the Leninist defense of vast repression in the name of vast
emancipation. And yet, although irrational, the anti-democratic
argument of either side *was* justified, to some extent, by

---

* There is still abundant evidence – which a subsequent Congressional investigation
scrupulously overlooked – that the Reagan/Bush team had come to power in the first
place through an earlier covert arrangement with Iran. As Gary Sick first suggested,
and as subsequent research has reconfirmed, in 1980 the Reagan campaign, under
William Casey's management, may well have persuaded the lieutenants of the
Ayatollah Khomenei not to free the US hostages they had taken in the coup of 1979,
but to wait at least until Election Day. That delay would keep the incumbent Jimmy
Carter from negotiating an 'October surprise' – a sudden, joyous liberation of the
men and women who had been imprisoned in Teheran for months – and associate
such liberation with the new US regime. As it happened, the timing of the hostages'
release could not have been more flattering to Reagan/Bush, with that emancipation
coming *at the very moment* that the Gipper was sworn in. TV's split-screen spectacle of those two simultaneous events was an exhilarating propaganda coup.

the Other Side's mere presence on the planet. That self-perpetuating face-off, which lasted until 1989, was already evident by the end of 1946, as Martin Walker has observed. 'The more each side became convinced of its image of the other, the more they were locked into hostility.'[71] Thus, for all their crimes against democracy, the busy agents of the CIA – as well as Nixon, Kissinger, Haldeman and Ehrlichman, Reagan, Bush, Weinberger, North and Casey – always had a pretty good excuse (as did their Soviet counterparts).

There is no excuse for President George W. Bush. The coup that raised him was a first in US history. This time, the plotters offered no dire warnings of an imminent take-over by the foreign Other – the crucial touch in every US rightist insurrection from the federalist crackdown of 1798 (in which the enemy of choice was France) to the federal move against dissent during World War I (the enemy then being Germany), up through the anti-Soviet campaign whose consequences we are living with today. The Bush campaign's unprecedented silence on the foreign threat was, first of all, necessitated by the simple fact that there *was* no such threat, and had not been for quite some time. Despite much strenuous effort to concoct a foreign stand-in for the Soviets – 'narco-terrorists', Islamic fundamentalists, China and/or one or all of the 'rogue states' – no recent surrogate has had the staying power of the mammoth tyranny that quickly fell apart on Bush the Elder's watch (much to his obvious chagrin).

In any case, Bush/Cheney had no need for the old xenophobic rationale, because the GOP had long since managed to convince the mad plurality of voters that the Democrats were now the most sophisticated enemies of the United States. Thus did the propagandists of the US right accomplish, finally, what the tiny US ultra-left had tried to do back in the latter days of

Students for a Democratic Society, 'bring the war home'. Long persuaded that the neo-liberal Democrats were Communists, if not Satanists, the GOP's fringe-dwelling fellow travellers were aroused almost to violence by the innuendo coming from the party's operatives in Miami, Palm Beach, Washington and Austin. As soon as Karl Rove, James Baker, Limbaugh, Novak, Bennett and the rest had started hinting darkly that the Democrats were up to some generic 'mischief' (a charge accompanied by not a shred of evidence), there were grass-roots paranoids converging on South Florida – some common citizens showing up with guns, to help prevent *Al Gore* stealing the election – while the campaign's somewhat cooler players ran the show.

And yet there was also a deeper reason why Bush/Cheney did not justify their moves by pointing scarily abroad. They offered no excuse because they didn't really see the need for one, the interruption of democracy not being such a bad thing in their eyes. Of course, if such a coup had taken place in Russia – a ballot recount halted, say, by a judicial bloc of five ex-Stalinists, so that the likely loser of a presidential contest was proclaimed the winner – the very players who made it happen here would be expressing steely outrage, and blaming it on Clinton, and calling for more spending on 'defense'. But it did happen here – and with exactly the same ruthless cynicism and subversive cunning that the right has always claimed to find appalling in *the Communists*. To anyone who ever heard the standard diatribe against the Soviets' global strategy of terror, the tactics used to put this President in office had to seem uncannily familiar. 'Terrorism attempts to erode the legitimacy of democratic institutions,' wrote one patriot in Ronald Reagan's time. 'Its real and lasting effects cannot be measured in body counts or property damage but by its long-term psychological impact and the subsequent political results. The terrorists' cry is: Don't trust your government, your democratic institutions, your principles of law. None of these pillars of an open society can help you. Give in to our demands.'

When Vice President Bush spoke those words in January 1987, he was, of course, referring to the governments of Libya, Nicaragua and Cuba, El Salvador's FMLN, Colombia's M-19, and all related 'murderous outfits.'[72] (His purpose was to counteract the general 'perception', as he put it, 'that this Administration traded arms for hostages' in terrorist Iran.) As a reflection on the true intentions of those states and movements, it was a statement typically dishonest and sensational. As a prophetic self-description, on the other hand, it was as right as rain. 'Don't trust your government, your democratic institutions, your principles of law.' Thus did the Bush revanchists tell America throughout their post-electoral propaganda drive to smear the ballot and the courts – but only insofar as those great institutions threatened to assist the Democrats. The rightists would support our system, and assert its health, but only if it did their bidding. If it did not, they would proclaim it hopelessly corrupt, and get their goons and others to dismantle it. In short: 'Give in to our demands.' It is indeed a strategy as un-American as Bush and all his cohorts liked to claim it was. The fact that they have used it to enthrone his son against our wishes now makes one thing, finally, clear – that it was always *they themselves* who posed the greatest danger to democracy, and not whatever alien subversive movement they might rail against to keep themselves in power.

The spectacle of all those rightist factions working in overt collusion – religious maniacs and corporate lobbyists, radical free-marketeers and diehard segregationists, GOP opportunists and impatient military men – is quite a lurid picture. It is also incomplete, because it leaves out what is surely the most influential of the interests that have ravaged our democracy. Crucially, the mainstream media, and TV in particular (although not just TV), has helped the rightists out at every turn, as we have seen – throughout the race, by always giving their preposterous candidate a passing grade, despite the daily evidence of our own senses, and largely snickering at his adversary for his loud sighs and makeup; and then, throughout the slo-mo post-electoral coup, by glossing over all the right's immense self-contradictions, and always tactfully refraining from investigation of the copious and graphic evidence of major 'mischief' by the GOP; and by authoritatively demanding, early on, that Al Gore pack it in, and do it graciously – as if it had been stipulated in our Constitution that the media, and not America's electorate, decides who should be president; and then, as soon as Bush had finished reading his inauguration speech, by instantly and totally forgetting everything that had just happened, and hailing the new President for his aplomb (which was apparent to no viewer), while always noting solemnly the 'slender margin' of his 'victory', and otherwise repressing the stark fact that he was *not elected*. The GOP helped make it just a little easier to manage that denial, first by neutralizing Jesse Jackson – the foremost champion of our learning how the vote had really gone in Florida – by leaking word of his love child to the *National Enquirer*; and then by orchestrating a whole new post-presidential re-impeachment drive against the Clintons, for their having taken certain items from the White House, and for the pardon of Marc Rich. However questionable those deeds might have been, they were nothing in comparison with stealing an election; but the watchdogs of the media all went along with it enthusiastically – as if they all felt grateful for the opportunity to turn their eyes, and ours, away from the subversion of democracy.

It is unlikely that the media will keep up this particular distraction. The anti-Clinton craze – a frenzy never broadly popular to start with – is certain shortly to become old news, however many more slight crimes or errors may be left to bring to light. (It may be old news by the time you read this.) On the other hand, the President's own closet is well known to be packed tight with skeletons, any one of which might do the trick should some élite decide that he must go. The tales are mostly rumors; and yet rumors, as the Clinton era has reminded us, are certainly enough to paralyze a president, or do him in. For instance, the media may report, as if it were a fact, that Bush still drinks, or that he was arrested more than once for driving drunk, or that he got his girlfriend an abortion back in 1970, or that he *was* arrested for possession of cocaine in 1972, or – still more fantastic – that, when newly married to his Laura, he fathered a love-child on the family's Chicana maid, and that his parents paid the woman off to go and raise the child in Mexico. The media may even find occasion to report, as if it were the truth, that Laura, in her youth, committed murder, or manslaughter, with her car – running down her boyfriend in the heat of passion (they had had a fight). Such rumors are no wilder – and certainly no better founded – than all the Gothic tales of treachery and depravity that swirled for years around the Clintons. Some or all of them may therefore end up in the news all day and night, for weeks and months on end, regardless of their truthfulness, if our President should ever anger the wrong people, or make some other serious mistakes.

Such payback will gratify a lot of Democrats, just as Nixon's people have for years been tickled pink by Clinton's woes. To those of us concerned about democracy, however, that next wave of scandals, if and when it comes, cannot provide the slightest consolation, even if it finishes the House of Bush. For such revelations, even at their gamiest, are simply not important. Indeed, it is encouraging that most Americans could, finally, not care less about those epoch-making blowjobs in the Oval Office, or even about Clinton's disappointing 'cover-up' – a squalid lie about a private episode. Such matters were irrelevant when Jefferson used them to slander Hamilton, and when Jefferson's own enemies used them to slander him – and they are still irrelevant, despite the frequent plaints about 'the death of outrage' vented by the likes of William Bennett, Robert Bork, and other big-time founts of natural gas. As the custodians of a government empowered to represent their interests, the citizens of a democracy must face the world as adults, not like children sitting in a Sunday school, or watching some big patriotic movie. What *should* stir public outrage – and what *does*, despite TV – is the subversion of democracy; and when that crime does not work anybody up, and only then, it will be time to call it quits.

The petty morals charges are not just beside the point. Such titillating fare is yet more evidence of how our media system actually regards us: as nasty-minded dimwits, able to grasp nothing but the dumbest arguments, incapable of thinking past the next Big Mac, and interested only in the dirty parts of any story. Thus the media gave us almost no real news throughout the long electoral campaign. The coverage stuck to trivialities, in large part by adhering strictly to the tried-and-true Coke/Pepsi paradigm of Democrats/Republicans, *neither* of whose candidates made any waves on 'free trade', military spending, foreign policy, 'the drug war', the death penalty, campaign finance reform – or media deregulation. With Nader noted only as a spoiler, so as to intensify the thrill-a-minute horse-race aspect of the narrative, there was no way to broaden 'the debate' beyond the usual foot-wide consensus. (When that inconvenient candidate was threatened with *arrest* unless he left the premises of the first debate – an anti-democratic stroke as shocking as the mob effort to disrupt the Miami recount – the media ignored the crime, as did the Democrats.) Such deliberate narrowness of focus was, at best, paternalistic, the media's employees protecting us from all complexity for their, and our, own good.

And yet their motivation was really not that simple; for if those employees were mainly driven to protect the interests of their parent companies, the anchors and reporters might just as easily have been pro-Gore, both men being near-impossible to tell apart on media-related issues, and Gore being, by a nose, the people's choice. Rather, what finally seemed to drive the anti-Democrat consensus at the top end of the mediocracy, among the likes of Brian Williams, Chris Matthews, Tim Russert, Cokie Roberts and Sam Donaldson, was their wish to make it clear to all that *they* are in control. While certainly no flaming democrat, Gore did at least make sense, and knew his stuff, and otherwise evinced a certain civic expectation of the audience – that they would listen carefully to what he had to say, and make their judgments based on reason. His references to Dingell/Norwood made this clear – too clear for the tribunes of the media, who seemed resentful of such efforts to engage the viewers in terms a little more complex than those of advertising, TV news, and other forms of super-simple propaganda. And so they finally sneered at Gore – as they had done at Clinton – for knowing much of anything, and for replying with long sentences. On the other hand, the ill-prepared and in-coherent Bush was, literally, more their style. Repeating his catch-phrases endlessly, and making errors that got easy laughs, he spoke no language but the language of TV – which, in their eyes, made him fit for office, whether he was voted in or not.

Thus we Americans have been tricked out of our democracy

by a vast and very smart conspiracy of stupid talkers – people deftly talking *down* to us, so as to sell us shoddy goods of slightly different kinds. Throughout the GOP, there are the rustic-seeming demagogues, kickin' back 'n' talkin' folksy to the TV audience – as if they were not fronting for the multi-nationals, and/or working for theocracy to benefit the Christian ultra-right. And that oppressive spectacle is moderated, and its darker hints ignored or laughed away, by telejournalists who talk the talk of advertising – constantly assuring us that they know what we'll buy, and what it takes to sell it to us.

On either side of the equation, the political and the commercial, the populist pretense can barely hide the absolute contempt that all those talkers really feel for us, the people – whose show this is supposed to be. Nor, of course, is that contempt apparent only in this latest, most egregious of electoral thefts. The gradual suppression of democracy has taken place on many fronts, by varied means: through the GOP's refusal to update the methods of the national census, a tactic that has disenfranchised some three million voters, mostly black; through the 'drug war', which has likewise had disastrous civic consequences, by sidelining a few million more minority voters, among others, in the system's federal and for-profit jails; through sophisticated union-busting methods, which have helped to keep America's workers isolated, anxious and compliant; through 'tort reform' and other steps to limit the prerogative of juries. At the top, all such moves are variously certified by a Supreme Court whose far-right majority – the dearest legacy of Reagan/Bush – invariably finds against the people on behalf of state, industrial and/or commercial *power*, whether its representatives are prison guards or corporate lobbyists, TV station owners or insurance companies, media barons or right-wing presidential candidates. It is that overriding interest, and not 'states' rights' or 'strict constructionism', that guides the legal thinking of the Rehnquist bloc – whose champions, meanwhile, keep on sounding off against 'judicial activism'.

And, day by day, the media cartel facilitates this huge infringement of democracy, primarily by failing to report it. That cartel's aim is not to serve us, but to serve us up to advertisers; and so, increasingly, its 'journalism' is all murder stories, sports and weather, show biz items, corporate ads disguised as news, and lurid scandals that amount to nothing. Thus we are deprived of that routine illumination on which all democracy depends – a general blackout that has lately disenfranchised all of us, regardless of class, creed or color. It was precisely to prevent just such a national catastrophe that Jefferson and others pushed the First Amendment, ensuring freedom of the press. It is a sign of just how hostile to democracy 'the press' itself has now become that its own managers invoke the First Amendment to *deny* the public any worthwhile news – arguing, perversely, that it would violate *their* free speech rights if they were forced to serve 'the public interest', and to justify their massive exploitation of the public airways, by giving us a little non-commercial fare. (Rehnquist et al. buy that argument.)*

A media system thus deregulated does not benefit its audience with more robust protection from the state: on the contrary. The mightier and less accountable that system, the *closer* its relations with the state's top dogs. Its journalists cannot afford to be too enterprising – as we have lately seen.

---

* For example: 'In a majority victory for large cable television companies, a U.S. appeals court on Friday set aside federal rules that limit the number of customers one cable company can serve.

'The unanimous decision by a three-judge panel of the appeals court in Washington DC, could ultimately clear the way for AT&T Corps. and AOL Time Warner Inc., the nation's largest cable companies, to strengthen the grasp they already have on the U.S. cable market.

One anecdote should make the point. A few days before Election Day, British journalist Greg Palast broke the story of how Governor Bush's minions had illegally purged the names of over 64,000 voters, mostly Democrats, from the rolls in Florida. That revelation having received major play in Britain, as well as in *Salon*, Palast heard from a CBS news producer interested in doing a version of the story. Palast provided her with all his information on that scandal – and then gave her the makings of what would have been another hot exclusive:

> 'I also freely offered up to CBS this information: The office of the Governor of Florida, brother of the Republican presidential candidate, had illegally ordered the removal of the names of felons from voter rolls – real felons, but with the right to vote under Florida law. As a result, thousands of these legal voters, almost all Democrats, would not be allowed to vote.
>
> 'One problem: I had not quite completed my own investigation on this matter. Therefore CBS *would have to do some actual work*, reviewing documents and law, and obtaining statements. The next day I received a call from the producer, who said, "I'm sorry, but your story didn't hold up." Well, how did the multibillion-dollar CBS network determine this? Why, "we called Jeb Bush's office". And that was it.'

'AT&T . . . and AOL Time Warner challenged the FCC's rules that say one company can serve no more than 30 percent of the US cable market. The companies also challenged the agency's rule preventing companies from putting channels in which they hold a financial interest on more than 40 percent of a system's offerings.

'The companies argued the rules violate constitutional free speech rights and are arbitrary and capricious. The court ruled the FCC never justified the basis for its limits, and sent the rules back to the FCC to be reworked . . .

'A spokeswoman for AOL Time Warner said it is "a good day for cable operators' 1st Amendment rights."' 'Court Sets Aside Limits to the Number of Customers One Cable Firm Can Serve', *Chicago Tribune*, 3 March 2001.

While it appalled him, that lame response did not surprise him, Palast writes, since it is now 'standard operating procedure for the little lambs of American journalism. One good, slick explanation from a politician or corporate chieftain and it's case closed, investigation over'.[73] So much for the democratic ardor of 'the liberal media' – an institution every bit as docile and reactionary, in its own ironic way, as the Fourth Estate in Baghdad or Havana.

The whole show, in a word, has got out of hand. To take it back, and finally master that production, we will have to pay some close attention to the boring stuff that made the TV people laugh throughout the last, abortive presidential race: campaign finance reform, thorough media reform, electoral reform. Only then will we be able even to discuss, much less effect, those larger changes that are also now required – in economics, criminal justice, education, national healthcare, foreign policy, environmental regulation, and all the other areas that our new unelected President so dimly understands.

And yet, before we talk about reforms, there is something everyone now disenfranchised can and must do right away. We need to realize that the United States has been transformed – before our very eyes – into an outright plutocracy. The likes of Jefferson and Madison would never recognize this land of ours, whose major media serve only multinational corporations, and where the will of the majority no longer matters. It is a grim and painful situation; and yet we cannot rectify it until we've looked at it unflinchingly – just as Jefferson and Madison would do, and as the talking heads today will not. In short, before we can recover any democratic possibility, we must first face the fact that we don't live in a democracy – and that we still deserve it, and can manage it.

RECOMMENDED READING

GEORGE H. W. BUSH

Blumenthal, Sidney, *Pledging Allegiance: The Last Campaign of the Cold War* (New York: HarperCollins, 1991).

Cramer, Richard Ben, *What It Takes: The Way to the White House* (New York: Random House, 1992).

Duffy, Michael and Dan Goodgame, *Marching in Place: The Status Quo Presidency of George Bush* (New York: Simon & Schuster, 1992).

Parmet, Herbert S., *George Bush: The Life of a Lone Star Yankee* (New York: Scribner, 1997).

Tarpley, Webster G. and Anton Chaitkin, *George Bush: The Unauthorized Biography* (www.tarpley.net/bush2.htm).

Walsh, Lawrence E., *Firewall: The Iran-Contra Conspiracy and Cover-Up* (New York: W. W. Norton, 1997).

GEORGE W. BUSH

Abraham, Rick, *The Dirty Truth: The Oil & Chemical Dependency of George W. Bush* (Houston: Mainstream Publishers, 2000).

Begala, Paul, *'Is Our Children Learning?':The Case Against George W. Bush* (New York: Simon & Schuster, 2000).

Carlson, Tucker, 'Devil May Care', *Talk*, September 1999, pp. 103–10.

RECOMMENDED READING

Didion, Joan, 'God's Country', The New York Review of Books, November 2, 2000, www.nybooks.com/nyrev/WWWarchdisplay.cgi?20001102068F.

Hatfield, J. H., *Fortunate Son: George Bush and the Making of an American President* (New York: Soft Skull Press, 2000).

Ivins, Molly and Lou Dubose, *Shrub: The Short But Happy Political Life of George W. Bush* (New York: Vintage Books, 2000).

Lemann, Nicholas, 'The Redemption', *The New Yorker*, 31 January 2000, pp. 48–63.

Minutaglio, Bill, *First Son: George W. Bush and the Bush Family Dynasty* (New York: Times Books, 1999).

Mitchell, Elizabeth, *W: Revenge of the Bush Dynasty* (New York: Hyperion, 2000).

Sheehy, Gail, 'The Accidental Candidate', *Vanity Fair*, October 2000, pp. 164–95.

POLITICAL BACKGROUND

Bellant, Russ, *Old Nazis, the New Right, and the Republican Party* (Boston: South End Press, 1991).

Conason, Joe and Gene Lyons, *The Hunting of the President: The Ten-Year Campaign to Destroy Bill and Hillary Clinton* (New York: St Martin's, 2000).

Engelhardt, Tom, *The End of Victory Culture: Cold War America and the Disillusioning of a Generation* (New York: BasicBooks, 1995).

Gibson, James William, *Warrior Dreams: Violence and Manhood in Post-Vietnam America* (New York: Hill & Wang, 1994).

Gitlin, Todd, 'The Renaissance of Anti-Intellectualism', *The Chronicle Review*, B7, in the *Chronicle of Higher Education*, 12 August 2000.

Irons, Peter H., *A People's History of the Supreme Court* (New York: Penguin, 2000).

Lazarus, Edward, *Closed Chambers: The Rise, Fall and Future of the Modern Supreme Court* (New York: Penguin, 1999).

Rosenfeld, Richard N., *American Aurora: A Democratic Republican Returns* (New York: St Martin's, 1997).

Simpson, Christopher, *Blowback: America's Recruitment of Nazis and Its Effects on the Cold War* (London: Weidenfeld & Nicolson, 1988).

Toobin, Jeffrey, *A Vast Conspiracy: The Real Story of the Sex Scandal That Nearly Brought Down a President* (New York: Touchstone, 1999).

ON MEDIA

Hertsgaard, Mark, *On Bended Knee: The Press and the Reagan Presidency* (New York: Farrar, Straus & Giroux, 1988).

McChesney, Robert W., *Rich Media, Poor Democracy: Communication Politics in Dubious Times* (New York: New Press, 2000).

Palast, Gregory, 'Silence of the Lambs: The Failure of US Journalism', available at www.gregpalast.com/columns.cfm.

Schechter, Danny, *The More You Watch, The Less You Know: News Wars/Submerged Hopes/Media Adventures* (New York: Seven Stories, 1998).

Scheuer, Jeffrey, *The Sound Bite Society: Television and the American Mind* (New York: Four Walls Eight Windows, 1999).

ELECTION 2000

Bugliosi, Vincent, 'None Dare Call It Treason', *The Nation*, 5 February 2001, *http://www.thenation.com/docPrint.mhtml?i=2001 0205&s=bugliosi*

Crowley, Michael, 'Media Hounds', *The New Republic*, 12 March 2001, pp. 18–20.

Danielson, Catherine, 'Vote Fraud in Tennessee: Worse Than Florida?' Alternet, 13 March 2001, www.alternet.org/story. html?storyID=10589.

Grann, David, 'Quiet Riot', *The New Republic*, 25 December 2000, pp. 16–17.

McCormack, Win, 'Deconstructing the Election', *The Nation*, 24 March 2001.

Palast, Gregory, 'What Really Happened in Florida?' 'Newsnight', BBC News, 16 February 2001. This transcript of Palast's BBC appearance – along with his invaluable newspaper columns on Bush/Cheney's vast electoral mischief – is available at www.gregpalast.com.

Schell, Jonathan, 'A Force to Reckon With', *The Nation*, 1 January 2001, pp. 4–5.

ONLINE RESOURCES

Alternet, www.alternet.org

Bushwatch, www.bushwatch.com

Center for Public Integrity, www.publicintegrity.org

Center for Responsive Politics, www.opensecrets.org

Fairness and Accuracy in Reporting (FAIR), www.fair.org

The Media Channel, www.mediachannel.org

The Project on Media Ownership (PROMO), www.promo.org

TomPaine.common sense ('A Journal of Opinion'), www.tompaine. com

NOTES

[1] 'discharge the complicated', 'who cannot spell': John William Ward, *Andrew Jackson: Symbol for an Age* (London, 1955), p. 64; 'A barbarian who': John T. Morse, Jr, *John Quincy Adams* (Boston, 1891), p. 242, quoted in William A. DeGregorio, *The Complete Book of U.S. Presidents* (New York, 1996), p. 118.

[2] 'everyday businesslike sanity': Bernard Bailyn, *The Ideological Origins of the American Revolution* (Cambridge, Mass., 1967), p. 19; Attorney General Crittenden on Fillmore's sensible speech: Robert J. Rayback, *Millard Fillmore: Biography of a President* (Buffalo, 1959), p. 335.

[3] 'If we wish': Alyn Brodsky, *Grover Cleveland: A Study in Character* (New York, 2000), p. 39; Eisenhower's editorial acumen: Emmet John Hughes, *The Ordeal of Power: A Political Memoir of the Eisenhower Years* (New York, 1963), pp. 24–25; 'His mental cassettes': Lou Cannon, *President Reagan: The Role of a Lifetime* (New York, 1991), p. 293.

[4] 'It's no exaggeration': Campaign rally in Troy, Ohio, 21 October 1988; 'You cannot be': Campaigning in Dover, New Hampshire, 15 January 1992: both gaffes are included in *Bushisms: President George Herbert Walker Bush in His Own Words*, a volume compiled by the editors of *The New Republic* (New York, 1992); 'inarticulate as though': 'Campaign Trail', *New York Times*, 4 November 1988; 'cramped down on': 'Bush Works on Image, but Says He Must "Be Me"', *New York Times*, 8 August 1988; 'We have made mistakes': *Financial Times*, 9 May 1988. (What the Vice President had meant to say, apparently, was 'setbacks'.) 'The most important': *San Antonio Express News*, 30 January 2000. (Bush was trying to say that the duties of parenting should come before the obligations of one's job.)

[5] 'like a 16-year-old': 'Bush Works on Image', *New York Times*, 8 August 1988; 'This election is': 'Quayle, in South, Accuses Dukakis of Lacking Issues', *New York Times*, 3 September 1988; 'We understand the importance': 'Two Campaigns Have Same Emphasis and Tone; Quayle Borrows

Bush Props, Malaprops', *Los Angeles Times*, 16 September 1988; 'There is nothing': 'Quayle Discards His Script on Military Issues and Raises Eyebrows', *New York Times*, 9 September 1988. ('The audience was left wondering whether the Senator favored offensive or defensive weapons', noted the reporter, Lisa Belkin.)

[6] 'Looking back': Maureen Dowd, 'The Education of Dan Quayle', *New York Times Magazine*, 25 June 1989, p. 20; 'really is the studious sort': 'Quayle's No. 1 Colleague Hits the Campaign Trail', *New York Times*, 11 September 1988.

[7] George H. W. Bush's reading: 'For Bush, Culture Can Be a Sometime Thing', *New York Times*, 27 September 1988; 'Bush's Tastes Down Home to Less So', *New York Times*, 1 May 1990; 'He jogged and drove his boat': Dan Quayle, *Standing Firm: A Vice-Presidential Memoir* (New York, 1994), pp. 252–53.

[8] Baseball cards: Gail Sheehy, 'The Accidental Candidate', *Vanity Fair*, October 2000, p. 168.

[9] 'A guy who's been': 'Shades of Gray Matter; The Question Dogs George W. Bush: Is He Smart Enough? There's No Simple Answer', *Washington Post*, 19 January 2000.

[10] 'Behold, then': George Bancroft on Andrew Jackson, quoted in Richard Hofstadter, *Anti-Intellectualism in American Life* (New York, 1963), p. 159.

[11] 'calculated bluntness': Kenneth Cmiel, *Democratic Eloquence: The Fight over Popular Speech in Nineteenth-Century America* (New York, 1990), p. 63; 'the rich richer': quoted in DeGregorio, p. 119. For a detailed study of how cautiously the franchise was, in fact, extended during the heyday of 'Jacksonian democracy', see Alexander Keyssar, *The Right to Vote: the Contested History of Democracy in the United States* (New York, 2000), pp. 53–76.

[12] 'I'll answer some questions': 'Presidency Takes Shape With No Fuss, No Sweat', *New York Times*, 10 February 2001.

[13] 'TV is still', 'vaudeville': Michael R. Beschloss, *Taking Charge: The Johnson White House Tapes, 1963–1964* (New York, 1997), p. 253, n. 3.

[14] 'I'm not a bit': Memo to H. R. Haldeman, 9 May 1971, in Bruce Oudes, ed., *From: The President: Richard Nixon's Secret Files* (New York, 1989), p. 251.

[15] 'I don't think': Robert Odle Jr, quoted in Gerald S. Strober and Deborah Hart Strober, *Nixon: An Oral History of His Presidency* (New York, 1994), p. 49.

[16] 'One weakness in': Oudes, *From: The President*, pp. 203–4.

[17] 'Need now to establish': Entry for 21 July 1969, in H. R. Haldeman, *The Haldeman Diaries: Inside the Nixon White House* (New York, 1994), pp. 73–74.

[18] Nixon's readings in philosophy: Monica Crowley, *Nixon in Winter* (New York, 1998), p. 344 ('When I walked', "No wonder the Greeks"), p. 347 ('"Boy, there's the truth!"'), p. 353 ('"It's so complex"'); Nixon on 'little Negro bastards', homosexuals, etc.: From an Oval Office conversation taped on 13 May 1971, transcribed by James Warren – Nixon on Tape Expounds on Welfare and Homosexuality, *Chicago Tribune*, 7 November 1999 – and reprinted as 'All the Philosopher King's Men' in *Harper's*, February 2000, 22–24.

[19] Barbara Bush on Geraldine Ferraro: *New York Times*, 4–5 October 1984; *Houston Chronicle*, 6 October 1984; 'bozos', 'Ozone Man': 'Bush, Clinton Begin Finish Line Sprint; Upbeat President, Charged by Polls, Steps Up Rhetoric', *Washington Post*, 30 October 1992; 'asshole': Minutaglio, *First Son*, p. 223; 'He had on': Barbara Bush, *Barbara Bush: A Memoir* (New York, 1994), p. 37.

[20] 'It's not that he': Monica Crowley, *Nixon Off the Record* (New York, 1996), p. 46; 'Oh, yes': Bush made this remark to historian Barbara Tuchman, quoted in an Associated Press story, 13 August 1988; 'A lot of people': Associated Press, 19 October 1987.

[21] Bush's pitch: Richard Ben Cramer, *What It Takes: The Way to the White House* (New York, 1992), pp. 26–29. (Throughout, Cramer's book offers an incisive view of Bush's background and temperament.) The supermarket scanner flap: 'Bush Encounters the Supermarket, Amazed', *New York Times*, 5 February 1992; 'That Amazing Scanner', *Washington Post*, 12 February 1992; Howard Kurtz, 'The Story That Just Won't Check Out', *Washington Post*, 19 February 1992; 'Bush wrongly ridiculed about grocery scanner', *Houston Chronicle*, 25 February 1992.

[22] Charles Colson to Pat O'Donnell, 24 July 1971: 'We should always consider using George Bush more often as a good speaking resource. He is very good on his feet, he generally can get media attention, he does have Cabinet rank and he takes our line beautifully. I would make more of an effort to get him into things as you find good forums than we have done in the past': Oudes, *From: The President*, p. 302; 'I am convinced': letter of 23 July 1974, in George Bush, *All the Best: My Life in Letters and Other Writings* (New York, 1999), pp. 181–82; 'a political jackpot': Kevin Buckley, *Panama: The Whole Story* (New York, 1991), p. 254.

[23] 'He connects with': Bush media advisor Lionel Sosa, quoted in the *Pittsburgh Post-Gazette*, 29 October 1998.

[24] This judgment was confirmed by the Brookings Institution, which, on 13 November 2000, released a useful overview: *How the Television Networks Covered the 2000 Presidential Campaign*. (Parts of the report are available online, at http://www.brookings.edu/comm/transcripts/20001113.htm.)

[25] 'I remember what': Governor Bush on 'Larry King Live', CNN, 29 September 2000; 'twice mopped the floor': Dennis Byrne, 'Even great intellects have dumb days', *Chicago Sun-Times*, 1 November 2000; 'The intelligentsia said': George Will, 'Demeanor Does Matter: It Can Denote Political Sentiment', *Sun-Sentinel* (Fort Lauderdale, Florida), 29 October 2000; 'The country can afford': Michael Kelly, 'Dumb vs. Dishonest', *Washington Post*, 27 September 2000; 'A Gore administration': George Will, 'The Case for Bush', *Washington Post*, 5 November 2000.

[26] 'grammatical English': Rush Limbaugh, *The Way Things Ought To Be* (New York, 1993), p. 206.

[27] 'Bush's ambling on the': George Will, 'Demeanor Does Matter: It Can Denote Political Sentiment', *Sun-Sentinel* (Fort Lauderdale, Florida), 29 October 2000.

[28] 'Because he is black': George Will, 'The Way the Media Treat Jackson', *Washington Post*, 28 January 1988. For more background on the episode, see 'Jackson Faults Media Minority Portrayals: Says Press "Poisons Minds" in Speech at Sacramento Fund Raiser', *New York Times*, 20 January 1988.

[29] 'You don't have to be': 'Fellow Governor Touts Texan With a Double-Edged Anecdote', *Washington Post*, 1 June 2000.

[30] 'political campaign terrorist': Mary Matalin quoted in Minutaglio, *First Son*, p. 260; 'soul of an alley cat': Rusher quoted in Strober and Strober, *Nixon: An Oral History*, p. 50; 'He'll do positive things': Nixon to Charles Colson, Oval Office conversation, 2 January 1973, in Stanley Kutler, *Abuse of Power: The New Nixon Tapes* (New York, 1997), p. 193. Bush's contribution to his father's presidential drive in 1988 has been noted by all his biographers, but it is J. H. Hatfield whose account is most detailed. See 'Home Run' in *Fortunate Son*, pp. 75–96.

[31] 'If you're not': 'Behind Bush Juggernaut, an Aide's Labor of Loyalty', *New York Times*, 11 January 2000.

[32] 'went up the walls': Harlow quoted in Greg Mitchell, *Tricky Dick and the Pink Lady: Richard Nixon vs. Helen Gahagan Douglas—Sexual Politics and the Red Scare, 1950* (New York, 1998), p. 40; 'A total Nixon man': Elizabeth Mitchell, *W: Revenge of the Bush Dynasty* (New York, 2000), p. 116.

[33] 'Just wait will': *Ibid.*, p. 63; 'While Kennedy was running': Fitzhugh Green, *George Bush: An Intimate Portrait* (New York, 1989), p. 64; 'I may not be eloquent': from Bush's acceptance speech at the 1988 Republican National Convention; 'in love with the Kennedys': Peggy Noonan, *What I Saw at the Revolution: A Political Life in the Reagan Era* (New York, 1990), pp. 6, 9.

[34] Georgetown dinner party: Barbara Bush, *Barbara Bush: A Memoir*, p. 67.

[35] 'The country – we turned': Oval Office conversation between President Nixon and Alexander Haig, 16 May 1973, in Kutler, *Abuse of Power*, p. 506.

[36] 'The Beatles went through': Minutaglio, *First Son*, p. 110; 'There is an arrogance': George Bush, *All the Best*, p. 182.

[37] 'I don't remember': Minutaglio, *First Son*, p. 117; 'we in Texas': Parmet, *George Bush: The Life of a Lone Star Yankee*, p. 130.

[38] 'I'm a warrior': Bush on 'Larry King Live', CNN, 16 August 1992; 'WHAT HAS HE': Minutaglio, *First Son*, p. 286.

[39] Andover classmate Bob Marshall, quoted in Minutaglio, *First Son*, p. 66.

[40] 'It was gruesome': Mitchell, *W: Revenge of the Bush Dynasty*, pp. 35–36; 'only a cigarette burn': 'Branding Rite Laid to Fraternity', *New York Times*, 8 November 1967.

[41] The Telecommunications Act of 1996 – a bill essentially dictated by the media industries themselves, and stealthily approved by Congress – proclaimed the outright giveaway of the digital TV spectrum to the same great corporate players that already dominate the media, both 'new' and 'old'. As a sop to those who took exception to that massive theft of public property, President Clinton asked Al Gore to chair a commission whose ostensible purpose was to come up with a (voluntary) code of public service obligations for the broadcasters, who might thereby 'give something back' for being given such a handsome oligopoly. The commission included media activists as well as corporate heavy hitters – a group that could arrive at no agreement without some moral leadership, which Gore did not provide. Of all the public service obligations that the group might have discussed at length (educational programming, non-commercial local shows, a limit on ads aimed at children, etc.), the only one that the commission entertained was a minimal requirement of free broadcast time for the top contenders during campaign seasons. The group's corporate types rejected even that, and so the 'Gore Commission' finally came up empty. See Robert W. McChesney, *Rich Media, Poor Democracy* (New York, 2000) pp. 70–76, 146–59.

[42] 'ABC and CBS': Colson to Haldeman, 17 November 1970, in Oudes, *From: The President*, p. 171.

[43] The poll by Fairness and Accuracy in Reporting (FAIR) is available online at http://www.fair.org/reports/journalist-survey.html.

[44] 'He has made': 'Bush's Selections Signal a Widening of Cabinet's Role', *New York Times*, 31 December 2000; 'What happens in': William Safire, 'Bush's Two Pumpkins', *New York Times*, 1 January 2001.

[45] 'Only the most': Hughes, *The Ordeal of Power*, p. 319; 'I can't be': 'Bush Works on Image, but Says He Must "Be Me"', *New York Times*, 8 August 1988; 'Bush is always': Meg Greenfield, 'The Broccoli Breakthrough', *Newsweek*, 2 April 1990; 'What these tics': Michael Kinskey, 'Introduction', *Bushisms*, p. 2.

[46] 'The receptivity of': Adolf Hitler, *Mein Kampf*, trans. Ralph Manheim (Boston, Massachusetts, 1943), p. 180.

[47] Prescott Bush's financial involvement with the Nazis is a story that has long been tactfully ignored, for obvious reasons. The bare facts are these: On 20 October 1942 – almost a year after Pearl Harbor – the US government impounded the Union Banking Corporation under the Trading with the Enemy Act. All Union Banking's stock shares were seized by the US Alien Property Custodian. The shares were held by Prescott Bush, managing partner of Brown Brothers Harriman, and six other men: three Bush associates, including E. Roland 'Bunny' Harriman, and three Nazi executives, who were instruments of the mighty pro-Nazi industrialist Fritz Thyssen.

On 28 October, the government seized two more Nazi entities run by Union Banking: the Holland-American Trading Corporation, and the Seamless Steel Equipment Corporation. On 17 November – as US troops were fighting in North Africa – the US government seized the Nazi interests in the Silesian-American Corporation, which Prescott Bush had co-managed with his father-in-law George Herbert Walker. (The government did not impound their shares.)

In its volumes for the thirties and forties, the *New York City Directory of Directors* has Bush listed as a director of Union Banking Corporation from 1934 through 1943. See: John Loftus and Mark Aarons, *The Secret War Against the Jews: How Western Espionage Betrayed the Jewish People* (New York, 1994); Wesley G. Tarpley and Anton Chaitkin, *George Bush: The Unauthorized Biography* (available at www.tarpley.net/bushb.htm).

[48] On the Republican party's employment of ex-Nazis and ex-fascists, see Christopher Simpson, *Blowback: America's Recruitment of Nazis and Its*

Effects on the Cold War (London, 1988), and Russ Bellant, *Old Nazis, the New Right and the Republican Party* (Boston, Massachusetts, 1991).

[49] On the *Lawrence Eagle-Tribune*'s treatment of the Horton case, see Steve Burkholder, 'The *Lawrence Eagle-Tribune* and the Willie Horton Story', *Washington Journalism Review*, July–August 1989. On the Bush/Quayle campaign's use of the Horton episode, see Sidney Blumenthal, *Pledging Allegiance: The Last Campaign of the Cold War* (New York, 1990), pp. 295–96, and Jack W. Germond and Jules Witcover, *Whose Broad Stripes and Bright Stars?: The Trivial Pursuit of the Presidency, 1988* (New York, 1989), pp. 262–64.

[50] The atrocity tales about Saddam Hussein's invasion were, necessarily, purveyed through every medium. However, the best-known and most comprehensive source of such inventions was Jean P. Sasson, *The Rape of Kuwait* (New York, 1991), a quickie paperback that suddenly appeared in several thousand US bookstores, drugstores and supermarkets – and, in bulk, on every US military base in Saudi Arabia – about a week before Desert Storm began, heavily advertised (on a six-figure budget) with the commanding tag-line, 'Read it, and you'll know why we're there.' According to the publisher's chief executive, the book was circulated among US troops 'with the help of the Saudis'. 'Book Notes', *New York Times*, 9 January 1991. On Nayirah al-Sabah, see John R. MacArthur, *Second Front: Censorship and Propaganda in the Gulf War* (New York, 1992), pp. 57–60. In general, my assertions about the propaganda side of Desert Storm are based on my own research on that episode, which I intend to analyze at length in a forthcoming study.

[51] Myron Magnet, *The Dream and the Nightmare: The Sixties' Legacy to the Underclass* (San Francisco, California, 1993), p. 35.

[52] Aaron Latham, 'How George W. Found God', *George*, September 2000.

[53] J. H. Hatfield, *Fortunate Son: George W. Bush and the Making of an American President* (New York, 2000), pp. 237–44.

[54] (The Bushes' keen awareness of Joe Kennedy's influence in West Virginia raises further questions *vis-à-vis* their influence in Florida). Minutaglio, *First Son*, pp. 300, 304.

[55] 'Shades of Gray Matter; The Question Dogs George W. Bush: Is He Smart Enough? There's No Simple Answer', *Washington Post*, 19 January 2000.

[56] It is instructive to compare Chace's book, which appeared in 1998, with Carolyn Eisenberg's *Drawing the Line: The American Decision to Divide Germany, 1944–1949*, which had come out two years earlier from Cambridge University Press – and which Chace fails even to include in his

bibliography, much less discuss, even though it contradicts certain of his claims about Dean Acheson. It is no less instructive to compare the copious mainstream praise for Chace's book with the near-total mainstream silence about Eisenberg's, despite the great newsworthiness of her discoveries, and the universal praise her book received from academic reviewers. See Mark Crispin Miller, 'When Good Books Vanish', *Free Inquiry*, fall 2000, 16–18.

[57] Peter Conrad, *Television: The Medium and Its Manners* (Boston and London, 1982), p. 48.

[58] Dr Ed Young, pastor at Houston's Second Baptist Church, is quoted in Latham, 'How George W. Found God', *George*, September 2000; Fawn Hall's crucial testimony at the Iran/contra hearings is quoted in William S. Cohen and George J. Mitchell, *Men of Zeal: A Candid Inside Story of the Iran/Contra Hearings* (New York, 1988), p. 130–36.

[59] The data are available on the website of the Center for Responsive Politics, at www.opensecrets.org.

[60] For background on the Boston Harbor ad, see Sidney Blumenthal, *Pledging Allegiance*, and Jack W. Germond and Jules Witcover, *Whose Broad Stripes and Bright Stars?*, as well as Kathleen Hall Jamieson, *Dirty Politics: Deception, Distraction and Democracy* (New York, 1992) pp. 105–6. For a visual analysis of the ad, see Mark Crispin Miller, 'The 1988 Campaign: Decoding the Hidden Messages', *Columbia Journalism Review*, January/February 1992, pp. 36–39.

[61] Associated Press Online, 28 May 1999.

[62] Col. Ralph Anderson, quoted in Hatfield, *Fortunate Son*, p. 45.

[63] *Ibid.*, p. 43.

[64] Rosenbaum's article is included in *The Secret Parts of Fortune: Three Decades of Intense Investigations and Edgy Enthusiasms* (New York, 2000, pp. 155–72. On the possibility that Skull and Bones keeps some of Hitler's silverware, see Toby Rogers, 'Sympathy for the Devil, Part 5', *Greenwich Village Gazette*, available online at http://www.gvny.com/columns/rogers/page5.html.

[65] Gail Sheehy, 'The Accidental Candidate', *Vanity Fair*, October 2000.

[66] Paul Begala, *Is Our Children Learning?: The Case Against George W. Bush* (New York, 2000), pp. 103–5.

[67] 'The largest prison system': Molly Ivins and Lou Dubose, *Shrub*, p. 141 (and see pp. 141–55); JPI study: 'Texas Tops All States in Prison Population', *Toronto Globe and Mail*, 29 August 2000; racial percentages on incarceration for drug charges: Substance Abuse and Mental Health Services Administration, *National Household Survey on Drug Abuse:*

Summary Report 1998 (Rockville, Maryland, 1999), p. 13; racial percentages on state court convictions: David J. Levin, Patrick A. Langan and Jodi M. Brown, US Department of Justice, *State Court Sentencing of Convicted Felons, 1996*, (Washington, DC, 2000), p. 8; 'Crime control policies': Craig Haney and Philip Zimbardo, 'The Past and Future of US Prison Policy: Twenty-five Years After the Stanford Prison Experiment', *American Psychologist*, vol. 53, no. 7 (July 1998), 716; disenfranchisement: 'Study Suggests Black Male Prison Rate Impinges on Political Process', *Washington Post*, 30 January 1997; Human Rights Watch: Jamie Fellner and Marc Mauer, 'Losing the Vote: The Impact of Felony Disenfranchisement Laws in the United States' (Washington, DC: Human Rights Watch and the Sentencing Project, 1998), p. 8. These and further pertinent data are available at http://www.drugwarfacts.org/racepris.htm.

[68] TV's inordinate focus on the *now* is but one aspect of the medium's inherent rightist bias, according to Jeffrey Scheuer, whose book *The Sound Bite Society: Television and the American Mind* (New York, 1999) offers an invaluable discussion of TV's impact on US politics.

[69] Gary Aldrich, *Unlimited Access* (Washington, DC, 1996), quoted in Jeffrey Toobin, *A Vast Conspiracy: The Real Story of the Sex Scandal That Nearly Brought Down a President* (New York, 1999), p. 96.

[70] Joseph Persico, *Casey: From the OSS to the CIA* (New York, Viking Penguin, 1990), p. 290.

[71] Martin Walker, *The Cold War: A History* (New York, 1993), p. 47.

[72] George Bush, 'Uniting Against Terrorism', a speech delivered to an international conference on terrorism sponsored by the magazine *Discover* on 20 January 1987; *Department of State Bulletin*, April 1987, 3–5.

[73] Greg Palast, 'Silence of the Lambs: The Election Story Never Told', posted on the Media Channel at http://www.mediachannel.org/views/whistleblower/palast.shtml